THE YEAR ROUND

THE YEAR ROUND

A BOOK OF THE OUT-OF-DOORS

ARRANGED ACCORDING

TO SEASON

By

CLARENCE J. HYLANDER, A.M., PH.D.

ILLUSTRATED BY THE AUTHOR

Living Library Press
Bristol, Virginia
2019

Original Copyright, 1932, By CLARENCE J. HYLANDER
and published by G. P. Putnam's Sons, New York

All rights reserved. This book, or parts thereof, must
not be reproduced in any form without permission.

TO

BOBBY AND BETTY

FOREWORD

Charlotte Mason said, "The real use of naturalists' books is to give the child delightful glimpses into the world of wonders he lives in, reveal the sorts of things to be seen by curious eyes, and fill him with desire to make discoveries for himself." The Year Round is one such naturalist's book.

C.J. Hylander wrote and illustrated this volume exploring typical and prominent characteristics of each season; from the lifecycle of frogs and toads and the earliest wildflowers of spring through the verdant profusion of summer into the fall reproduction of plants and preparations of animals for the coming winter to the leafless trees, ample information will inspire and inform the study of nature.

Living Library Press is delighted to bring this excellent book back into print. In its pages, readers will discover not only what it is they see around them but also the why and the how that will cause their curious eyes to probe the outdoor wonders more keenly.

PREFACE

FOR PARENTS AND TEACHERS

THE wild life of the out-of-doors is of perennial interest to our children and pupils, no matter what the season or where the place. For this reason a great share of juvenile reading deals with the lives and habits of the common plants and animals; such stories, vividly told by observant nature enthusiasts, appear in print in great numbers. Which is all as it should be.

But this book is not merely another such Nature Reader.

It has been the writer's experience both at camp and at school that boys and girls want to know what an animal is, as well as how it lives. They wish to be able to recognize animals and plants, to be able to call them by name when they see them. Such familiarity with the wild life which surrounds them is a boon to all children no matter what their age. Upon discovering a new flower or tree, or seeing an unfamiliar bird or turtle, the child is fortunate indeed if he has at his side a parent or a teacher who is able to answer his questions readily—and correctly.

But what about the situation where young Bobby, off on a summer vacation with his dad and mother, returns from a private foraging expedition and displays a few flowers, a slippery frog, some gray mossy stuff and a butterfly or two? He asks dad or mother, as the case may be, what they are. They look duly interested, go through all the motions of intense thinking, and then admit—rather ruefully—that they don't know. Perhaps father and mother know much less about the out-of-doors than young sonny; when they were young nature classes were not included in school curricula.

Or what about the situation where the teacher, at school or camp, either is not trained sufficiently in nature lore or has not the time to treat each pupil's questions individually? The teacher needs a handy reference book in which she can look it up herself, or ask the pupil to get the information by himself. The latter course is naturally the preferable one. But how, and where? There are numerous butterfly guides, bird guides, flower guides, etc. Usually what the pupil has discovered is a fern or a snake, not covered in the usual books. And the books available, even if they contain the answers to the child's questions, are too technical and thorough for young and untrained minds.

It is just to fill such needs that this book of the out-of-doors was written. Its aims may seem rather sweeping and pretentious; but it is offered as an attempt at something much needed and at present not available—a comprehensive and elementary nature guide, designed for a child's mind as well as for a teacher's or a parent's guidance in answering the child's questions.

In order to encompass the vast amount of information ordinarily found in the field books on various phases of plant and animal life, rigid selection of the material was necessary. It is hoped that all the common birds, butterflies, moths, reptiles, frogs and marine invertebrates that a young explorer will find in northeastern United States are included; as well as the common trees, flowers, ferns, mushrooms and seaweeds of the same area. Once the budding naturalist has become familiar with the forms of life here described, he will be well prepared to go on to the adult and specialized guide books (advised in the Appendix), where each book covers one special field of nature.

PREFACE

The arrangement of the chapters by seasons will be found helpful in eliminating forms of life not found at that particular time of year, making it easier to identify the object in hand. For example, in considering the blue flowers of woods in spring, all the asters and gentians can be omitted. This seasonal arrangement makes the book especially applicable as supplementary reading in part time nature work in grades three, four, five and six; assuring correlation between classroom reading and the securing of material in the field.

The ecological treatment of some of the chapters makes it easier for the child to remember what kinds of plants and animals are usually found together, in the same sort of environment.

The purpose of this book is frankly that of instruction. But the use of the narrative form, wherever possible, has eliminated the dry style of the technical field guide. If, as a result of using this little book, the youthful naturalist will be stimulated to go afield and find new friends, introduced in these pages but as yet undiscovered in the out-of-doors; then will the aim of the author be realized to the full.

C. J. HYLANDER

WHITE PLAINS, N.Y.,
April, 1932

CONTENTS

SPRING

CHAPTER PAGE

I. THE STORY OF THE TADPOLE 3

From eggs to frogs—and toads. The Tree Frog. The Wood Frog. The Spring Peeper. The Leopard Frog. The Pickerel Frog. The Green Frog. The Bullfrog.

II. WHEN TREES HAVE FLOWERS 17

Why do plants have flowers? The conspicuous flowers of Dogwood, Mountain Ash, Catalpa, Tulip, Shadbush, Horse Chestnut and Cherry. The modest flowers of Willows, Aspens and Maples. Catkin-flowers of Birches and Oaks.

III. THE BIRDS RETURN 28

Birds about towns and houses, such as the Woodpeckers, Blue Jay, Swallows, Phoebe and Chickadee. Birds of fields and orchards, such as Orioles, Bluebirds, Goldfinches, Sparrows, Bobolinks and Kingbirds. Birds of swamps and pond margins, such as Red-winged Blackbirds, Kingfishers and Sandpipers. Birds of roadside thickets, such as Catbirds, Redstarts, Maryland Yellowthroats and Thrashers. Birds of the deeper woods, such as the Thrushes, Oven Bird, Towhee, Pewee, Warblers and Vireos.

IV. PIONEERS AMONG THE FLOWERS 51

Likes and dislikes among flowers. Flowers of swamps—Skunk Cabbage, Jack in the Pulpit,

CONTENTS

CHAPTER   PAGE

Cowslip, Marsh Blue Violet, Blue Flag and Forget Me-Not. Flowers of mediumly moist woods—Bunchberry, Bellwort, Meadow Rue, Solomon's Seal, False Solomon's Seal, Canada Mayflower, Rue and Wood Anemones, Spring Beauty, Blood Root, Saxifrage, Violets, Hepatica, Lupine, Columbine, Trilliums, Adder's Tongue, Dutchman's Breeches and Wood Betony. Flowers of dry fields and roadsides—Wild Strawberry, Five-finger, Yellow Star Grass, Tansy, Blue-eyed Grass, Bluet, Daisy Fleabane and Heal All.

V. THE STORY OF THE CATERPILLAR 70

From eggs to caterpillars, and what happens to the caterpillar when he grows up. Swallowtail, Monarch, Vice-Roy, Banded Purple, Silverspot, Mourning Cloak, Wood Nymph and Sulphur Butterflies. Luna, Polyphemus, Cynthia, Sphinx, Underwing and Tiger Moths.

SUMMER

VI. DWELLERS IN THE DAMP AND SHADE 87

Some common mosses—Peat Moss, Mnium, Feather Moss, Tree Moss, White Moss and Hairy Cap Moss. Some common ferns—Brake, Cinnamon, Interrupted, Royal, Lady, New York, Polypody, Beech, Oak, Maidenhair. Some common mushrooms—Fly, Destroying Angel, Russula, Inky Cap, Coral, Puffballs. Lichens, strange half-and-half plants.

VII. ANIMALS CLAD IN ARMOR 110

Warm-blooded vs. cold-blooded animals. Some common turtles—Snapping, Musk, Mud, Painted, Spotted, Wood and Box. Some common snakes—Black, Grass, Garter, Ribbon, Ring-necked, Red-bellied, Water, Copperhad, and Rattlesnake.

CONTENTS xiii

CHAPTER PAGE

VIII. OUR FURRY FRIENDS 128
The mole and the Shrew. Bats. Raccoon. Weasel. Skunk. Foxes and Wolves. Wild Cats. The Gnawing Clan—Woodchucks, Chipmunk, Squirrel, Mice, Porcupine, Rabbits and Beaver. Deer.

IX. SOME TELL-TALE LEAVES 134
The reason plants need leaves. Different kinds of leaves. The simple leaves of Maple, Oaks, Birches, Beech, Chestnut, Dogwood and Sassafras. The compound leaves of Sumac, Hickories and Ashes.

X. EXPLORING AT THE SEASHORE 147
Why seaweeds are different looking from land plants. Some common seaweeds—green, red and brown. A sandy beach at low tide—animals with single shells such as Snails and Whelk; and with double shells, such as Clams, Mussels, Scallops and Cockles. Tidal pools in rocks, with Crabs, Lobsters, Limpet, Periwinkles and Sea Urchins. The underwater posts of wharves, with Sea Anemones, Starfish, Snails. Jellyfish.

AUTUMN

XI. THE REAR GUARD OF THE FLOWERS 173
Two large families—the Asters and the Golden Rods. Milkweeds and their relatives. Queen Anne's Lace. Yarrow. The Hawkweeds. The Roadside Mullein. Lilies of the Fields and Woods.

XII. WHEN PLANTS TRAVEL 186
On the wings of the winds—Maple, Ash, Catalpa, Dandelion, Milkweed and Clematis. By stealing rides—Beggar Ticks, Burrs and Stick Tights. By offering inviting fruits—Berries and Juicy Fruits. By sailing on the water, Cocoanut. By being shot out by springs—Touch Me Not.

CONTENTS

CHAPTER   PAGE

XIII. WHAT'S WHAT AMONG THE BERRIES 195
       Blueberries, such as Viburnum, Woodbine, Indian Cucumber Root, Solomon's Seal and Dogberry. Red berries, such as False Solomon's Seal, Bittersweet, Jack in the Pulpit, Bunchberry, Wintergreen, Partridge Berry and Baneberry.

XIV. HOW THE TREES PREPARE FOR WINTER . . . 200
       Why some trees are evergreen and some deciduous. Leaves as food-makers for the tree. Why leaves are green. The cause of autumn colors. Loss of leaves.

XV. HOW THE ANIMALS PREPARE FOR WINTER . . 205
       What the furry animals do. What the birds do. What the insects and other cold-blooded animals do.

WINTER

XVI. WHAT THE EARTH IS MADE OF 213
       Where soil comes from. Fire-born Rocks such as Lava and Granite. Water-born rocks such as Sandstone, Limestone and Shale. Transformed Rocks, such as Slate, Marble and Schist. Some common minerals and how to recognize them.

XVII. CHRISTMAS TREES 224
       The Pines. The Spruces. The Fir Balsam. The Hemlock. The Cedars and Arbor Vitae. Shrubby Evergreens. The Larch.

CONTENTS XV

CHAPTER
PAGE

XVIII. THE LEAFLESS TREES 233
With buds and leaf-scars as guides. Those with opposite leaf scars—Horse Chestnut, Catalpa, Dogwood, Maples and Ashes. Those with alternate leaf scars—Locusts, Hawthorn, Oaks, Birches, Nut Trees, Poplars, Cherry, Tulip, Sassafras, Sycamore and Ailanthus.

XIX. OUR WINTER BIRDS 251
Attracting Birds in winter. The Game Birds—Bob White, Grouse and Pheasant. The Birds of Prey—Owls, Hawks and Eagles. Water Birds—Ducks, Loons, Gulls and Terns. Our Permanent Residents—Starling, Crow, Chickadee, Blue Jay, Goldfinch and Creepers. Our visitors from the Northland—Junco, Snow Bunting, White-throated Sparrow and Shrike.

APPENDIX 263

INDEX 267

LIST OF ILLUSTRATIONS

Toads	*Frontispiece*
	PAGE
Frogs' Eggs and Toads' Eggs	4
Young Tadpoles	7
The Tadpoles Grow Hind Legs	8
The Tadpoles Grow Front Legs	9
The Tadpole Becomes a Frog	9
Some Common Frogs	13
Where the Flower Hides the Eggs	19
Pollen Makes Eggs Grow into Seeds	20
The Flowers of a Dogwood Tree	21
Flowers of Maple and Elm	25
Catkin-Flowers of Birch and Oak	26
Birds of Towns and Farms	31
Birds of Fields and Orchards	37
Birds of Roadside Thickets	41
Birds of the Deep Woods	43
Spring Flowers of Wet Woods and Swamps	55
Spring Flowers of Woods	59
More Spring Flowers of Woods	63
Spring Flowers of Fields and Roadsides	67
Moth Eggs and Butterfly Eggs	71
A Few Caterpillars	72
The Caterpillar Becomes a Chrysalis	73
Some Common Butterflies	77
Some Common Moths	81
Some Common Ferns	93
More Common Ferns	97
Some Fern Relatives	100
Some Common Mushrooms	103
Old Man's Beard; a Lichen	107
Reindeer Mosses Are Lichens	108
Some Other Lichens	108
Some Common Turtles	113
More Turtles	115
Some Common Snakes	119

LIST OF ILLUSTRATIONS

	PAGE
Some Common Snakes	119
More Snakes	123
Simple Alternate Leaves, without Teeth	37
Simple Alternate Leaves, with Teeth	139
Compound Alternate Leaves	142
Opposite Leaves	144
Some Green Seaweeds	149
Some Brown Seaweeds	151
Sea Urchins	155
Sea Cucumber	157
Barnacles	158
Some Marine Worms	159
Some Crabs and Their Relatives	161
Univalve Sea Shells	164
Bivalve Sea Shells	168
Autumn Flowers: the Asters	175
Autumn Flowers: the Goldenrods	178
Some Other Autumn Flowers	181
Seed Dispersal by Wind	189
Seed Dispersal by Animals	192
Berries That Are Blue	196
Berries That Are Red	198
The Workshop Inside of a Leaf	202
Some Common Evergreen Trees	226
Deciduous Trees with Opposite Leaf-scars	236
How to Recognize the Oaks by Their Acorns	241
Deciduous Trees with Alternate Leaf-scars	243
More Deciduous Trees with Alternate Leaf-scars	245
Birds of Prey	253
Some Winter Birds	257

SPRING

THE YEAR ROUND

CHAPTER 1

THE STORY OF THE TADPOLE

IT is not only the trees and flowers that wake up in the early days of spring. Certain animals begin stirring about in March and April—eager to lay their eggs so that their babies may get a good start in the world before the warm days of summer are all gone.

No sooner are the reddish-brown hoods of the Skunk Cabbage safely through the tangle of half-frozen brown grasses and mosses of the swamp, than the Leopard Frog and the Wood Frog stir from their long winter's sleep and tend to laying their eggs. It is still March, and the chill of winter lingers in the shaded portions of the swampy pond margin.

This does not discourage Mrs. Frog one bit. During the latter half of March her voice, with that of hundreds of other frogs, makes vibrant music around the shallow ponds. If we search carefully in the icy water we find jelly-like masses of eggs, several inches in diameter; they may be floating about or they may be attached to some stick or fern frond. Do not mistake any jelly-like mass you find for frog's eggs. There are some green plants of a very simple type which form jelly-like growths. If you are going frog egging be sure you bring back jelly with black specks scattered through it.

There is nothing one can find in the woods which equals the interesting development of frog's eggs. We will have the most success in finding them by exploring the swamps where there may be, in places, several feet of water. In deeper ponds and lakes, the chances are that you can find the eggs along the shallow coves where there is a grassy tangle and plenty of plant remains in the water. Once you have found a place where there are eggs, you can return to that same spot year after year and be sure of finding the eggs.

Do not be greedy and take home several hundred of them.

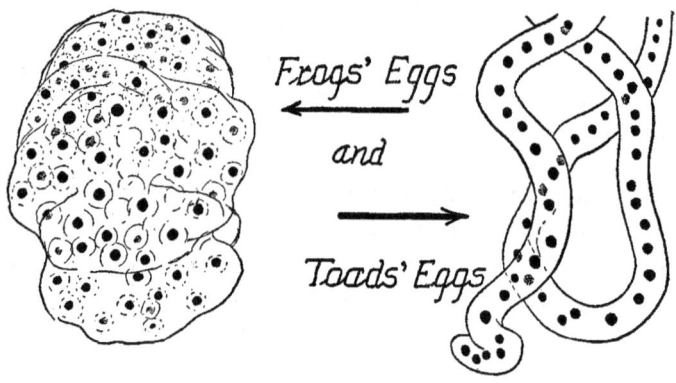

Frogs' Eggs and Toads' Eggs

Even though each frog mother does lay about five thousand eggs, and there will be plenty left if you do take five hundred, you will soon find out that the growing eggs need more space than you can furnish in a home aquarium. The average sized fish-bowl can accommodate only fifty baby tadpoles—at the very most.

Having put our jelly, with its imprisoned eggs, in cold clean water, we are now ready to watch the fascinating show. Keeping the aquarium out of the direct sunlight and providing a few water plants to keep the right amount of gases in the water, we watch closely day by day and discover—

THE STORY OF THE TADPOLE

WHAT FIRST HAPPENS TO THE EGGS

When first laid, the bottom half of each egg is light yellow while the upper half is black. The lower white part is food stored in the egg for the baby tadpole, who commences to grow in the upper dark half of the egg. This black color is very useful, because black absorbs much more heat from sunlight than a lighter color. Thus the eggs are kept warmer than the outside chilly water; and the transparent jelly which surrounds them keep this heat in, the same way a blanket would.

During the first few days we notice that the white portion of the egg gets smaller and smaller until the whole egg is black except for a tiny pin-point of white. These first few days the egg also becomes slightly larger. If we have a magnifying glass, and look at the egg during the first two days through the lens, we will see some most remarkable changes.

A few hours after the egg is laid, a groove forms at the top of the egg and grows downwards until it circles the egg and divides it into two parts. Then another groove grows around the egg from top to bottom, but cutting the first groove at right angles. This division of the egg results first in two parts, then in four. Each of these parts is called a cell. Then a third groove forms crosswise around the egg, making eight cells out of the four. From then on the divisions take place so rapidly that we soon see nothing but a tiny golf ball marked with divisions—that is, cells—which become smaller and smaller as they become more numerous. The second day after being laid the eggs are all black, except for the little white "plug" at the bottom.

In the meantime the egg—all but the stored food—has become divided into thousands of tiny cells. And some of these cells, beginning at the edge of the white dot which we can call the yolk plug, begin to form the stomach part of the tadpole. This plug marks the tail end of the future animal.

During the third day the egg lengthens a little, and a groove forms along the top. This groove is growing into the backbone and spinal cord of the tadpole. In another day the little yolk plug entirely disappears and the egg has lost its spherical shape. It is now much longer than broad, and commences to look like a chubby little fish. The groove on the back is edged by folds which broaden out at the head end to form the head and brain.

THE YOUNG TADPOLES

The tadpoles are still in the jelly, and have shown no signs of being alive except by their slowly changing shape while growing. By the end of the week the sleek black animals begin to take on a definite form. On the under side of the head is a pair of openings which act as suckers until the tadpole's mouth forms. On either side of the head three elevated ridges appear; these will later form the breathing organs known as gills. The tail becomes thinner and longer, with muscles arranged along it so that it looks like a fish's tail.

About the ninth day the tadpoles begin to wake up. Often they may be seen curving their heads and tails together; and then straightening out with a jerk. Each struggle and jerk seems to encourage them. Soon they are wriggling their way out of the jelly. And in our aquarium we now find a school of little black fish-like tadpoles. They are not very active at first. They seem satisfied to have escaped from their transparent egg cases. They hang by their suckers to the glass sides of the aquarium or to the green plants.

THE STORY OF THE TADPOLE

The tadpoles are now hatched. After a few days they start moving about by the aid of their delicate yet effective tails. A real mouth has formed; and on either side of the head have appeared feathery projections. These are the gills; and as the water flows past them the blood in the gills is able to take up enough air to keep the tadpole alive. Fishes also have gills; but their gills remain with them all their lives. As we shall see later, tadpoles have gills for only a part of their lives. As they

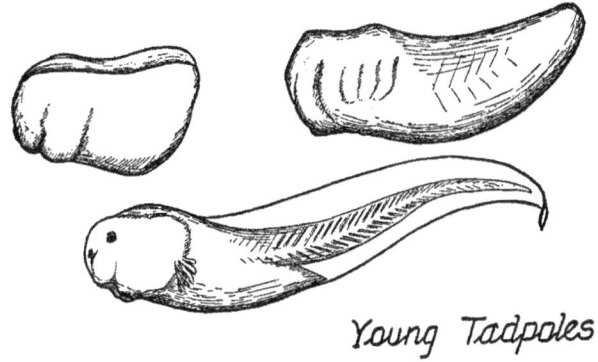

Young Tadpoles

grow older the gills are replaced by lungs much like those we have in our bodies.

From now on the tadpoles grow rapidly. We see the head increasing in size, until it seems out of all proportion to the rest of the body. About the twelfth day, much to our surprise, the feathery gills disappear. The animals still breathe by means of gills, but by ones which are inside instead of outside of the body. A few days after the disappearance of the external gills, the tadpoles become very active. Their mouths are open now, and it is not long before they are busily engaged in exploring for food. They go nibbling at the green plants, or anything else of vegetable nature they can find.

For the next few weeks they swim about, eat a lot, and

change from black to a brownish-spotted gray. And how they do increase in size!

THE FULL-GROWN TADPOLES

Out in the swamps and ponds the death rate among these tiny tadpoles is very high. Water-tigers, beetles and other water bugs eat thousands of them. Fish, turtles and even their own brothers and sisters are their enemies. But some of them live through all these dangers; so that by early June we find them

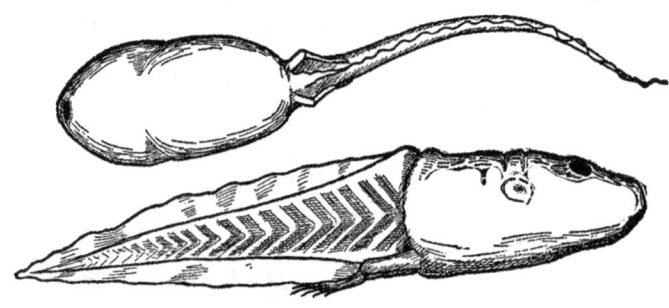

The Tadpoles Grow Hind Legs

several inches long (or, if they are Bullfrog tadpoles, much longer).

During the early summer months the tadpoles grow legs. First we see the hind legs appearing as tiny projections at the junction of the tail with the swollen body. These grow rapidly and soon look like ordinary frog's legs with webbed toes. In the meantime the front legs have commenced to develop, bursting through the skin of the head where the external gills were once located.

There is only one more change necessary before the tadpoles become frogs in appearance as well as in name. The long tail begins to shorten; gradually it is absorbed into the body of the changing tadpole. And in the last stages, many a young frog

The Tadpoles Grow Front Legs

bears for months traces of his tadpole existence, as a stumpy little tail.

The length of time of the tadpole stage of development varies with different kinds of frogs and with different living

The Tadpole Becomes a Frog

conditions. Some remain tadpoles but a few weeks; others for two or three years.

TOAD TADPOLES

In late April or in May the toads arrive at the pond margins to lay their eggs in the water. Toads' eggs are laid in long stringy rows, thus being different from the irregular masses of the frogs' eggs. The jelly very soon becomes a dirty brown, so that the eggs themselves are often invisible.

To collect some of these and watch their development, as we did that of the frog's eggs, will provide some astonishing sights. The changes take place much more quickly. In fact, four days after being laid, the little tadpoles are wriggling out of their jelly and attaching themselves to the water plants. They rapidly go through the same changes as the frog tadpoles. However, these tadpoles remain very small (less than an inch long) and keep their jet-black color. Have you ever seen the shallow water over some sandy beach just black with these darting tiny tadpoles?

In two weeks, many of the little tadpoles have become miniature toads; and this is another difference between frogs and toads. Frog tadpoles are almost the size of frogs when they grow their legs and lose their tails. But toad tadpoles stay small and change into small toads. So tiny are they that, as they jump about in the grass after leaving the ponds, we mistake them for crickets!

FULL-GROWN FROGS AND TOADS

Having passed their babyhood in the water, most of the grown-up frogs and toads prefer to spend their adult lives on land. Because of this double habit of living—in water when young and on land when grown up—they are called Amphibians.

THE STORY OF THE TADPOLE

Now let us get acquainted with a few of the common Amphibians. They are divided into two groups, depending upon whether they have a tail or not, when full grown.

Those with tails are the lizard-like little animals known as newts and salamanders. Some day while wandering about in the woods near a swamp or stream, lift up a few stones or roll over that half-buried log. If you are quick at catching slimy little animals who scurry speedily through mud and water, you will find in your fist a long slender animal with four short legs and a tapering tail. If quite small and brownish-red, with a row of spots along each side, it is a NEWT. If bigger and blacker, with wrinkles on its sides, it is a SALAMANDER. They can often be found hiding in springs and wells.

THE TOAD

The Amphibians without tails are the toads and frogs. The common TOAD hardly needs describing. It can readily be recognized by its yellow-brown back which is covered with big and little warts. At first sight it may seem ugly to you. Since it really cannot give you warts, as some people think, or harm you in the slightest way, pick one up sometime and look at it carefully. The eyes are very beautiful and have often been compared with jewels of black and gold. Notice the chubby four-fingered hand and the webbed five-fingered toes. A toad is not slimy, as popular stories would have you believe; though the body does feel cold, due to its being a cold-blooded animal.

Toads like to live in cool moist places because the only way they drink is by absorbing water through their skins. Therefore they hide under houses, in wells, under porches and stairways, and in the thick undergrowth of gardens. No animal does more good and less harm. In our gardens, each one eats some nine thousand insects each summer! Multiply this by the number of toads and you see what an ally they are in keeping the number of injurious bugs, beetles, cutworms and caterpillars from increasing.

SOME COMMON FROGS

There is the acrobatic TREE FROG which can be found in the orchards and near the house in early summer and through September. Early in autumn he hides away for his winter's sleep, and not until May when he goes to the ponds to lay the eggs do we see or hear him again. The Tree Frog is fairly small, never growing much more than two inches in length. He may be gray, or he may be green; sometimes he shades into brown. He has darker cross bands on his legs and a star-shaped mark on his back. His fat pudgy body and the queer disks at the ends of his toes make him easy of recognition. The disks on the toes help the Tree Frog to cling to smooth surfaces. Have you ever seen any of these frogs, seemingly glued to a bit of lichen-covered bark? They jump about more actively towards evening, when they are hunting for beetles and caterpillars.

The WOOD FROG is the spirit of the shaded and damp woods. He too is a small member of the family, rarely growing more than two inches long. A dark black streak behind each eye stands out clearly in contrast to the light brown or tan color of his body. The subdued coloring of this little dweller of the deep woods makes him a fit companion for the mosses and delicate ferns. The Wood Frogs are about the first to wake from their winter's sleep. Often they stir to life in March and head for the ponds where their eggs will be laid at the same time as those of the Leopard Frog.

SOME COMMON FROGS

The Tree Frogs and the Wood Frogs invite us to orchards and woodlands; all the other frogs dwell in the neighborhood of streams and ponds and swamps. The Spring Peepers, the Leopard Frogs and the Pickerel Frogs venture away from their streams and lakes, but not too far. The Green Frog is generally in or near the water, while the Bullfrog rarely leaves his native pond.

The smallest of all the frogs is the SPRING PEEPER. We all have heard the chorus of sleigh-bells ringing out from the swamp and pond. And we all are glad to hear them; for they are the earliest signs of spring. Late February is none too early for these hardy little frogs, who migrate to the moist places to lay their eggs. The Peeper chorus lasts until May, though most of the eggs are laid in April.

Everyone has heard the Spring Peeper. But how many have seen him? Try creeping cautiously up to the edge of a swamp, where the Pussy Willows are just opening their silky silver catkins and the Red Maples are bursting their swollen buds. Right at your feet you hear the clear bell-like trills; search closer and the voice stops. You find nothing. It takes a patient searcher to discern these tiny singers. Finally you spy a mite of a frog; for each Peeper is less than an inch long. His color varies from light tan to a reddish brown, with bars of dark brown across his legs and back. His head is more pointed and his body more slender than the chubby Tree Frog, his close cousin. These noisy little frogs sleep for only two months—December and January. Most of their lives are spenT in the woods, where one very rarely can find them.

The LEOPARD FROG is as familiar to every child who has explored a stream or pond as the robin or bluebird. Walking along the grassy margin of a tiny stream which is winding its way through the meadows, we are preceded by splash after splash as the Leopard Frogs leap from beneath our very feet. He is about three to four inches long, with a green body covered by rows of rounded black spots.

The PICKEREL FROG at first sight may be confused with the Leopard Frog. But he is usually some shade of bronze or brown, and the spots on his back are square instead of round. If we watch closely when he jumps out of the grass we will see a flash of orange between his hind legs. A Pickerel Frog which has been sunning himself is a most beautiful coppery green; his body glistens as if it were made of metal. He likes to live in the grass and feed on the insects and caterpillars he can find there.

The GREEN FROG can be found near the edges of ponds and streams. His body is a solid greenish-brown; we might mistake him for a small Bullfrog if we didn't look closely and see the two folds extending on each side of the back from the head. His voice surprises us by being a shrill shriek which is very different from the sounds made by the other frogs. The Green Frog is larger than any of the other frogs except the Bullfrog; in size he averages three to five inches in length.

The BULLFROG lives most of his life in the water of a large pond or lake; to catch a glimpse of him we must paddle or row quietly along the shore where the undergrowth comes down to the water as a protective screen. On the rocky bottom we see a huge greenish-black form, six inches or more in length, looking at us suspiciously with projecting eyes. He is the last of the frogs to wake up from the winter's sleep, often not appearing until May. In June we can hear his deep bass voice booming across the lake; perhaps answered by another solitary Bullfrog at the other end of the lake. The Bullfrog is a good swimmer, due to completely webbed feet. The eggs hatch into tadpoles which sometimes take three years before they change into frogs.

CHAPTER 2

WHEN THE TREES HAVE FLOWERS

AS the last snow banks are melting on the northern slopes of the hills, and as the sun begins to rise earlier every morning and set later every evening, we explore the out-of-doors expectantly, looking for the first signs of returning life. Most of us would search for flowers such as the Skunk Cabbage or the Hepatica; others would look for the early migrant birds. But I am sure few of you would think to look on the tops of the trees for the first signs of spring.

Yet the flowers of a great many trees are the first of Nature's children to awaken after the winter's sleep.

If I were to ask any of you what a flower was, you would all probably answer very quickly, "A flower is the brightly colored part of a plant."

That is why you have never thought of looking for flowers on trees—except perhaps in the case of the few trees with conspicuous blossoms, such as the cherry and apple trees or the horse chestnut and dogwood.

Yet trees do have flowers. And all flowers are not big yellow or white or red blooms waving at you from dense masses of foliage. Some flowers are green or brown, hardly noticeable at all.

Before we go much further on our search for the first spring flowers, let us find out just *why* plants have flowers.

It is a most interesting fact that every kind of plant or animal, no matter how tiny and useless it seems, has an inherited urge to leave other plants or animals like *themselves* after them. So that when they die, their particular kind of life will persist on earth. This is called reproduction. In all the more common plants it is the *flower* to which is entrusted the important duty of reproduction. Without flowers, trees would leave no seeds and would soon become extinct.

When you think of a flower, I am sure you are thinking only of the brightly-colored petals of the flower. These petals, however, are not really necessary for every flower. The color is to attract birds and insects. If a plant does not need to attract animals it may have a very inconspicuous and colorless flower.

Then why do certain plants wish to attract insects and birds to their flowers, while other plants do not? You have all seen bees flitting from flower to flower, or hummingbirds darting their long beaks into the heart of some brilliant garden flower. I wonder how many of you have stopped to ask yourselves why they do this. You may guess that they are going for the honey; and your guess will be right. But what if I should ask you why the flowers provide the honey for the insects? It is a very kind thing for flowers to do—but have they any reason for doing it?

Every flower has two very important little parts tucked away inside the petals. Some flowers have both of them, while others have only one, with some other flower having the other one. In the center of the petals is a post or stalk which may be very sticky on top. Take a knife and cut this stalk open lengthwise, right down through the bottom of the flower; and at the bottom of it you will find a number of little white *eggs*!

Around this central egg-bearing pistil, as it is called, are several other stalks, each with a rounded swelling at its tip.

WHEN THE TREES HAVE FLOWERS 19

Sometimes the outside of this swollen cap is covered with a yellowish powder, though usually the yellow particles are inside the cap, where they are formed. These tiny bits of yellow dust are called pollen.

And this is the explanation of the whole mystery. No seed, with its baby plant inside, is ever formed except when some of this yellow powder is carried to the egg-bearing pistil. After the pollen has been brought to the egg, then the egg starts at

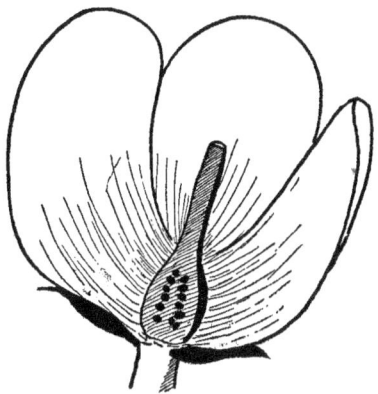

Where the Flower Hides the Eggs

once growing into a seed. But how to get the pollen to the egg?—that is a problem. And again the plants show their cleverness. They set a trap for unsuspecting bees and butterflies and hummingbirds. They surround the eggs and pollen with petals of many colors, which wave like bright flags in the wind. They tuck away sweet-smelling drops of honey deep down in the flower. And very soon insects come by the thousands; they explore flower after flower, and take the honey—but not before they have gathered some of the yellow dust on their hairy legs and bodies. As they hum from flower to flower, pollen is brushed off and shaken on to the tops of the pistils of the different flowers which they visit. Thus do the colored flowers solve the problem of getting the pollen dust to the tops of the pistils. And to this day, I am sure that the insects little suspect how they have been put to work for the plants.

But to get back to our trees in spring. If a plant is able to

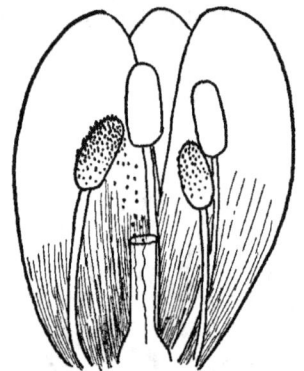

Pollen Makes Eggs Grow into Seeds

get the pollen dust to the egg-bearing pistil by the wind, then it becomes independent of the animals. No colored petals are necessary. Thus the flowers of most of the trees and the grasses are little greenish things which are never noticed by most of us. But they are flowers just the same; for they make pollen grains and eggs; and these eggs grow into baby plants and seeds.

TREES WITH COLORED FLOWERS

All the trees do not have small greenish-white flowers hidden away in their leafy boughs. Some have quite conspicuous blossoms.

The DOGWOOD, that little tree so common in the woods of

WHEN THE TREES HAVE FLOWERS

southern New England and New York, has big white flowers which appear in March, if spring comes early. From then until May, the Dogwood trees are solid masses of white amid the light green of the newly-leaved trees. Each flower consists of four yellowish or greenish white "petals" surrounding the

Dogwood trees have large white flowers

central egg-bearing and pollen-bearing parts. Nothing can compare with the sight of a Dogwood grove below one, as he stands on the higher slopes of a valley. The masses of white flowers are cupped upwards, looking like a cotton field ready for picking.

The MOUNTAIN ASH is a small tree with feather-like compound leaves. A compound leaf is one which has become subdivided into many smaller leaflets; in the case of the Mountain Ash these leaflets are arranged on two sides of the main stem. The individual flowers are small and creamy white, but they are clustered in showy spreading masses at the ends of the branches.

The CATALPA produces its flowers later than the other trees of this group. It is not until June (sometimes even July) that they appear. Each flower is large and white, with yellow stripes and purple dots. If you have never seen this attractive flower, with its frilled petals, you have missed one of the most beautiful of the tree-flowers.

The TULIP TREE is a relative of the Magnolia. And like the Magnolia, its flowers are unusually attractive. High up among the limbs of the straight-trunked tree, we can see the large erect yellow flowers at the ends of the smaller branches. After a windstorm these flowers may be scattered in great numbers over the ground. Each flower, which appears early in May, consists of six yellowish petals marked with orange near the center. Now we know why this is called the TULIP; the flower reminds us very much of the common garden flower of the same name, similar to it in its arrangement of the pollen-bearing stalks in a circle around the central pistil.

There is a small tree, about the size of the Mountain Ash, which you may have seen and mistaken for an overgrown shrub. It is the SHAD BUSH, Shad Blow or Service Berry; it goes by many names. In April, before its leaves have opened, the Shad Bush is covered with drooping clusters of white flowers. The narrow petals are set off by silky red leaf-like parts below each petal.

Is there any need of describing either the HORSE CHESTNUT or the WILD CHERRY? The former, with its huge upright Hyacinth-like clusters of showy flowers; and the latter, with the white blossoms so well known in the cultivated Cherry trees. The Horse Chestnut blossoms in April and the Cherry in May.

TREES WITH GREENISH AND INCONSPICUOUS FLOWERS

The time of flowering of the trees becomes a Nature calendar which varies but little from year to year. The brave scouts who

WHEN THE TREES HAVE FLOWERS 23

precede the main army are the Pussy Willows, whose silvery flowers break through their restraining bud scales while there is yet snow on the ground. Likewise in March we may find the Elms, Aspen Poplars and Silver Maples showing their varying types of flowers. An April there is a procession of Red Maples, Poplars, Norway Maples, Birches, Sugar Maples and some Oaks. By the time the warmer days of May have appeared, the Oaks and Nut trees have taken heart, and bring up the rear of the parade with their drooping catkin.

Most of these flowers hang as sensitive and delicate tassels and fringes which are easily shaken by the slightest breeze. In this way the light pollen grains are borne to the waiting eggs tucked away in the bottom of the pistils.

The PUSSY WILLOW often grows into a tree twenty to thirty feet high. Anywhere in wet ground this gladdening tree sets forth its reddish-brown shoots, covered with gleaming gray catkins or "pussies." Each catkin is a flower, with the colored petals lacking. The pollen and egg-making parts are safely surrounded by silky hairs, which give the young catkins their downy and soft appearance. The Pussy Willow flowers cover the twigs long before the leaf-buds open.

Soon after the Pussy Willows have appeared, we can see the swollen flower buds of the ELM bursting open as the March days warm them. From each bud comes forth a dense cluster of long-stemmed flowers, which soon assume a drooping attitude. The flowers take on a pink color as the reddish pollen-producing stalks project beyond the green flower-cup.

We have to leave the fields and roadsides if we wish to find the early flowering LARGE TOOTHED ASPEN. This Poplar prefers the woods; and it is there that we can find its loosely arranged catkins. All the Poplars (as well as all the common Willows) have catkins which are either pollen-producing or egg-bearing. One never finds a Poplar catkin with both pollen and egg-producing parts. The wind carries the pollen from the drooping catkins of one Poplar tree to the egg-producing catkins of another Poplar. The pollen-bearing catkins are longer and thicker than the egg-bearing ones; the tiny flowers attached to the stem of the catkin are nothing but scales covered with red pollen stalks. The egg-bearing catkin looks a little greener; but a close view shows slender red threads projecting from the scales.

The Maples have small flowers of varying shades, blossoming from March through May. First comes the SILVER MAPLE, a rare tree along the Atlantic coast states except under cultivation. The stemless clusters of greenish-yellow flowers often burst through their bud-scales early in March.

The RED MAPLE is true to its name—in autumn, when we see it gorgeously dressed in bright red; in winter, with its reddish twigs and dark red buds; and now in spring, decked in red flowers before most of the trees show any sign of green leaves. In the swamps and around the borders of streams and ponds, we can see the soft gray of the limbs and trunks made rosy by the clusters of small red flowers. Here again we find the pollen-bearing flowers on one tree and the egg-bearing ones on another. Each pollen-bearing flower is borne on a short stem, and consists of five yellowish outer leaf-like sections and five inner red petals. Even the tips of the pollen stalks are tinted with red. The egg-bearing flowers have a single red-tipped pistil projecting beyond the petals, and for this reason the trees covered with these flowers appear more brilliantly crimson.

Still later, in April, the NORWAY MAPLE becomes covered

with dense clusters of yellowish-green flowers which appear together with the satiny young leaves.

And last of all, the SUGAR MAPLE produces its greenish flowers. Those clusters of delicate flowers have longer stems and are not as closely packed together as the other Maples.

The Birches blossom forth some time in April. Like the

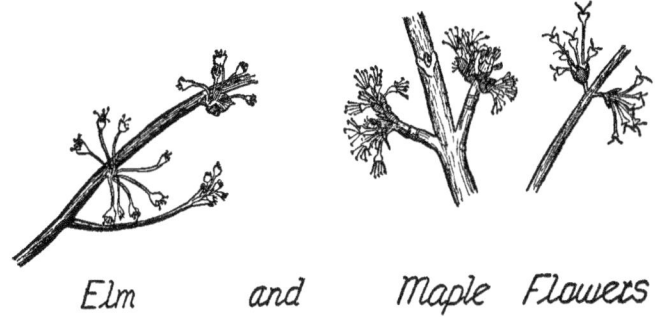

Elm and Maple Flowers

Poplars and Willows, their flowers are in the form of catkin. But the pollen-bearing catkins are drooping tassels, while the egg-bearing ones look like erect little cones. All winter long— if we have had observing eyes—we have noticed the drooping catkins, with the scales firmly locked together. Now in spring these hanging catkins lengthen, the scales separate, and the loosened flower-cluster shakes gracefully in the wind. With every movement, the pollen dust is carried from the catkin scales; and is born by the wind to the egg-bearing flowers.

The SILVER BIRCH, or Yellow Birch, has brownish yellow pollen-producing catkins and much smaller rosy egg-producing ones. These appear in April, before the leaves. The same is true of the RED BIRCH or River Birch. The last of the Birches to open the staminate catkins is the common GRAY BIRCH of our fields and open woodlands.

The Oaks, Hickories and other Nut trees have both kinds of flowers on the same tree. The pollen-producing flowers are grouped in clusters as drooping catkins, resembling those of the Birches and Poplars. The egg-producing flowers, which will form the nuts, are very small and complicated. Most of the Nut trees flower in May.

The RED OAK—and sometimes the SCARLET OAK—is among the first Oaks to display its tassels of flowers. They hang in

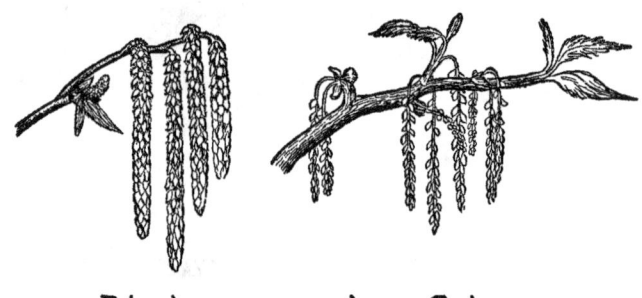

Birches and Oaks have catkins as their flowers

bunches of ten and twenty, each catkin being hairy and yellowish brown; the egg-bearing catkins are a greener shade, due to the long green egg-bearing stalks which project beyond the catkin.

The WHITE OAK has hairy catkins of a yellowish hue and a knotted appearance, due to the irregular spacing of the little flowers along the stem of the catkin.

The HICKORY has its large silky bud scales folded back in an appropriate setting for the downy little leaves and drooping green catkins. The long and pointed flower-scales are a contrast to the orange-colored pollen stalks which grow out beneath them.

These are just a few of the many kinds of flowers one can

WHEN THE TREES HAVE FLOWERS 27

find on the trees in spring and early summer. As the weeks progress from early March on, it is worth the trouble to watch for the appearance of these flowers since they give such distinct colors to the awakening landscape. Greens and yellows, whites and reds, they all contribute to the colorful and triumphant aspect of Spring;—Spring, the conqueror of the bare and lifeless woods and fields where Winter has held its sway for many months.

Keeping step with the blossoming trees, the smaller but better known flowering plants and the various forms of animals awaking to life increase in rapid succession as March gives way to April, and April passes on into sunny May.

CHAPTER 3

THE BIRDS RETURN

OF all the animals which we might discover in the out-of-doors, the birds are the best known and loved. There are many reasons for this. Some of us know what great service they render mankind by eating the thousands of bugs which damage crops and trees. Others have learned to treasure their cheerful songs and joyful behavior; for in all their work and play birds seem to be so cheery and optimistic. And all of us have found that birds are really not afraid of man and his home. There are dozens of birds that will come and live right in our back yards, if we only invite them.

But as a matter of fact very few people are on speaking terms with more than ten or twelve birds. Ask any of your friends to name some common birds, and he will boldly start with—Sparrow, Robin, Bluebird—and here he will hesitate. He may add Woodpecker, Oriole and perhaps a Swallow or a Thrush. When you tell him that there are about a hundred and fifty birds which one can find by observing only one bit of woods and meadow throughout the year, he will be greatly surprised.

The reason so few people are acquainted with more birds, is that it takes keen eyes to see a bird, as well as considerable knowledge of how to walk through the woods in order not to disturb them. Perhaps another good reason is that most of the birds are in action between four and six in the morning, so a bird walk takes one from a warm and comfortable bed. Bird lovers are never lazy people.

Since every bird has such a distinct personality, we cannot help but be interested in them, once we learn their names and habits. So let's be off for the bird trips.

Certain birds, like the flowers and trees, prefer to live in certain places. Some are found in special situations because their food is found there. Others like to stay near people and their homes, while their cousins move far away from man into the deep woods. And many birds are found in certain places because they like best to nest there.

Thus we can study the spring birds—which are also the summer birds—by taking four walks. First we will explore the places right near our homes and city streets, our farms, orchards and gardens. Then we will take a second walk out into the fields and meadows, where there are lots of grasses and plenty of sunshine, with perhaps a little stream winding here and there. On this walk we will skirt the edge of a swampy pond and find the birds living there. On our third trip we will wander along a country road which winds through thickets and open woodlands. And for a last walk we will get up early and hike through the shady and quiet aisles in the deep woods and forests.

BIRDS OF CITIES AND FARMS

Some birds have overcome their fear of man, and have become friendly neighbors to him. These familiar birds ought to be known by everyone, they add so much to the enjoyment of our lawns and gardens. Some of them have red or reddish brown markings on their bodies—such as the Downy Woodpecker, the Red-headed Woodpecker, The Flicker, the

Hummingbird, the Robin and the Barn Swallow. Some are noticeably blue—for example the Blue Jay and the Purple Martin. Grayish and black birds include the Chimney Swift, Phoebe, Chickadee, Red-eyed Vireo, Warbling Vireo and Nuthatches. Yellow can be seen on the Yellow Warbler, and a flash of orange on the Baltimore Oriole. The brownish colored birds include the Sparrows and the Wrens.

The three woodpeckers are inquisitive birds who remain with us the year 'round. The Downy and the Red-headed Woodpeckers spend most of their time on the trunks of trees; while the big speckled Flicker is often seen hopping along on the lawns in search of insects.

The ROBIN is such a well-known and favorite bird that we often take his virtues for granted. His homely, good-natured habits have made him a welcome companion for city and country homes alike. The Robin is a member of the Thrush family, and his arrival in March is one of the well-known signs of spring. The nests are built in any tree, no matter how near a house it may be; and when the greenish-blue eggs hatch in May we can watch the family life of the Robin without fear of scaring away either parents or children. At times we may see a Robin eating cherries or strawberries, but his main diet is earthworms, cutworms, caterpillars and wild berries.

The RUBY THROATED HUMMINGBIRD is a tiny visitor from the tropical regions, who flashes his metallic green and red coat in flower gardens and wild flower thickets. Hardly more than three inches long, this fearless little fighter uses his long beak to attack bumblebees and birds, as well as to get honey out of flowers. The Hummingbird has no song; he is usually silent, though at times he will utter several squeaky high-pitched notes. His nest is a dainty affair the size of a doll's teacup

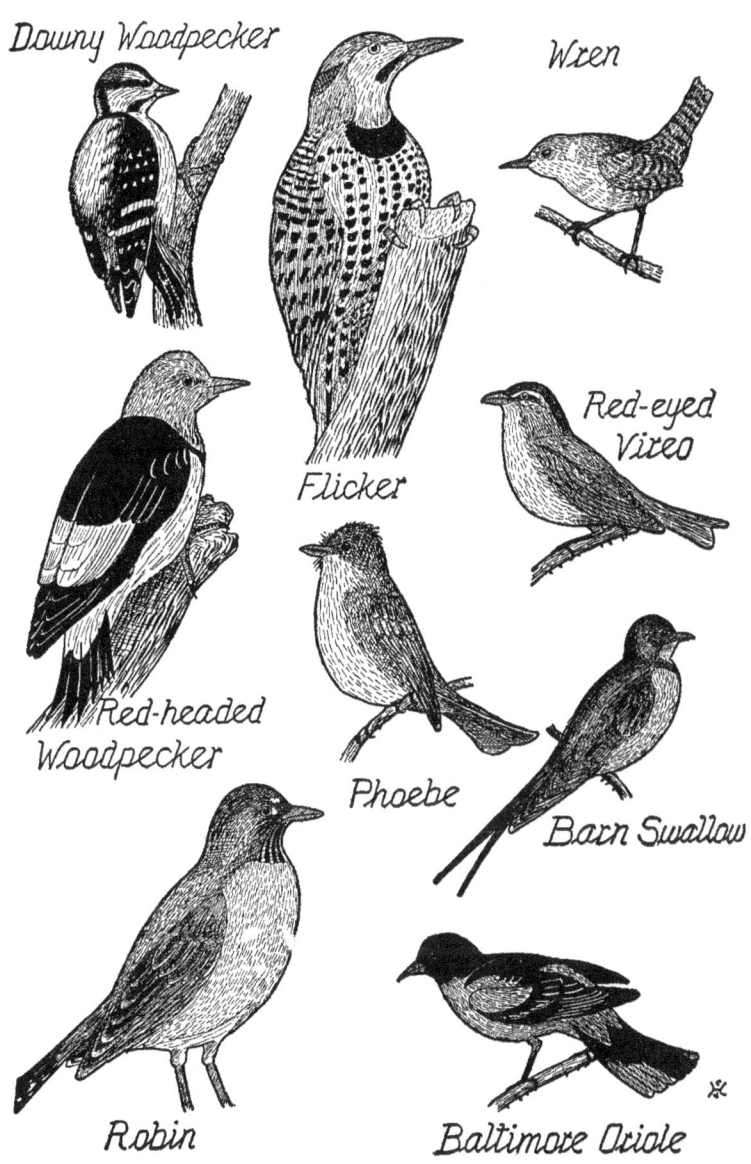

BIRDS OF TOWNS AND FARMS

and made of down and bits of ferns, and so covered with lichens that it is almost invisible on the supporting branch. The nest contains two white eggs, each about half an inch long.

We must find some old barns and woodsheds if we want to find the nests and homes of the graceful BARN SWALLOW. Plastered against the woodwork, in any convenient dark corner, are the mud nests, in which may be found four to six white eggs, slightly speckled with brown. The Barn Swallows fly rather jerkily because they catch their food—insects—in the air; they dip and dive and coast about in the air, speedily and gracefully, while they are feeding. The dark blue back and tail are in contrast to the reddish-brown breast. An easily recognized peculiarity is the deeply forked tail. Like the Hummingbirds, the Barn Swallows arrive in April when spring is well-advanced.

The PURPLE MARTIN is a swallow which has adapted itself to occupying boxes and bird houses. It will live in colonies of hundreds; so that if one family takes to a particular home provided for it, soon there will be many more there. The Martin, or the White-bellied Swallow as it is also called, is the first Swallow to come north, early in April. He feeds on flies, mosquitoes and beetles. Groups of Martins form a lively and pleasing picture; their song is a liquid, gurgling chorus. Each straw-woven nest holds four or five white eggs.

There was a time, before man began building chimneys, when the CHIMNEY SWIFT built his saucer-like shelves of glued twigs in hollow trees. But now this sooty-gray bird chooses the dark recesses of chimneys in which to construct his nests, where four or five white eggs are laid each year. He is a very active and tireless bird, remaining on the wing most of the day

THE BIRDS RETURN

in his endless search for flying insects. In this way he differs from the Swallows, who often will settle down in great flocks on the telegraph wires. The song of the Swift is merely a rapidly repeated "chip," very forcibly sounded. A peculiarity we might remember is the stubby tail, ending in two spiny points to aid in climbing; the feet are absurdly small and weak.

Late in March the PHOEBE comes back to us; this trustful little mouse-colored bird builds its nest of moss and hair under the eaves, under a bridge or on a supporting beam of the porch. The half dozen white eggs are sometimes spotted with yellowish-brown. Year after year, Phoebes will return to the same spot to rear their babies. As they alight on a twig, notice the peculiar twitch of the tail; this flicking of the tail sideways and upwards is as characteristic of the Phoebe as the simple notes of his "Phee-bee, phee-bee-bee."

The RED-EYED VIREO is an abundant and widely-distributed member of the Vireo family; but due to its modest coloring and to its having no striking characteristics, it is often overlooked. It comes to lawns and orchards, to look for its favorite insects. The Red-eye has a greenish-gray back, whitish breast, and a distinctive white streak over each eye. The nest is a hanging basket of bark and pine needles, sometimes varied with bits of newspaper. In this nest we can find three or four white eggs, each egg marked with dark brown at the larger end. This Vireo arrives in May and remains with us until August.

The WARBLING VIREO does not come as close to the ground as the common Red-eye; it seems to prefer the tops of our shade trees. It arrives and departs at the same time as its better known relative. The Warbling Vireo has a grayer and greener breast, and in general harmonizes so well with its leafy perch that we may often hear him without finding the owner of the sweet musical warble. His nest and eggs are much like those of the Red-eye.

The NUTHATCHES—those agile climbers of the trunks of trees—are with us in summer as well as in winter; they will be introduced to you in the chapter on Winter Birds, as will the Bluebird and Chickadee.

The BALTIMORE ORIOLE brings us a touch of tropical brilliance in coloring, much as did the Hummingbird. In May this orange and black songster arrives, and is soon busy constructing the familiar hanging nest from the bending tip of an elm limb or the drooping branches of any convenient tree. The four to six eggs are marked with brownish-black lines over a white background. The adult birds invade the orchards of cherry trees and hungrily search for cankerworms, caterpillars and other pests in the opening blossoms.

The ORCHARD ORIOLE is a beautiful bird which suffers by comparison with its flashier relative. This brownish-red and black bird loves to live in our fruit orchards; and his lively notes may be heard coming from a mass of apple blossoms. Its eggs are bluish-white, and four of them are laid in the suspended nest.

Last but not least, allow me to introduce to you the industrious little WREN. The brown body, barred with black or gray, seems the very essence of busy-ness. While many of the other birds are quite sociable, and go about in flocks, the Wren prefers to live alone. In her tiny house, in a crack of a stone wall, or in any other chance nook, she brings up her family of half a dozen babies which hatched from brown and white eggs. The Wren returns to us from the South in May, and does much good by eating harmful insects and spiders.

THE BIRDS RETURN

BIRDS OF FIELDS, MEADOWS AND SWAMPS

Having become friends with all these birds which venture about our homes and gardens, let us take a walk into the country. Here are some sunny fields where the grass is knee deep; so we jump over a rambling stone wall and find ourselves in a meadow, apparently deserted. But if we remain quiet, and walk carefully we may find Bluebirds and Indigo Buntings; Goldfinches, Palm Warblers and Meadow Larks; Bobolinks and Kingbirds; Song Sparrows, Chipping Sparrows, Vesper Sparrows, Fields Sparrows and even some Bob Whites. At that pond which we see at the far end of the fields, may be Red-winged Blackbirds, Belted Kingfishers and little long-legged Sandpipers.

The BLUEBIRD will at times become sociable enough to appear in the trees about our homes, but his favorite fence posts and low bushes are more likely to be found on the edges of the meadows. In central and northern New England his appearance is as much a sign of spring as the coming of the Robins to New York and nearby southern states. The nest made of grass and feathers is usually found in a hole in a fence post; in it are four to six light-blue eggs. The Bluebird eats beetles and other insects, as well as berries.

The INDIGO BUNTING is our only entirely blue bird; and even this gay little Finch has black markings on his wings. We see one flitting in and out of those briar bushes in a corner of the field. Here in the bushes we see the nest, made of leaves and grass; and in it, the five pale bluish-white eggs. The Bunting arrives about the first week in May.

The fields are often enlivened by the bright yellow and black of the common GOLDFINCH, or Wild Canary. We will find this bird with us as a winter bird also, in slightly less colorful costume.

Often we have heard the melodious notes of the MEADOWLARK floating over the fields early in March. We may be fortunate enough to see one, as it stands in the grass, stretched to its full ten inches of length, or perches on a fence rail. Being a large and short-tailed bird, the flight of the Meadowlark is made up of flapping efforts followed by soaring glides. His yellow breast, marked with a black bib under the throat, offers a recognizable trait. The nest is on the ground, hidden in the grasses; and in it are laid four to six speckled brown eggs. The Meadowlark feeds almost entirely on insect pests.

Sun-swept fields and hillsides are the natural background of the rollicking song of the BOBOLINK. His black and white coloring, with a flash of yellow on the back of his head, is very brilliant in early summer during the mating season. Most of the food of a Bobolink consists of spiders, crickets and other insects of the grasses. The nest is a bed of dry grass on the ground, and in it are laid a half dozen grayish or brownish eggs.

Another dweller in the fields and grassy orchards is the pugnacious KINGBIRD. This fairly large bird is often accused of eating bees, but this slight damage is offset by the great numbers of insects it devours. A Kingbird has a slaty-gray or blue-black back and a lighter colored breast. The nest is located rather noticeably in the branches of a low tree; it is made of twigs and moss, to take care of four white eggs, spotted with brown. The Kingbird is such a fighter that it will even attack and drive away Hawks and Crows.

Our roly-poly friend the BOB WHITE can often be seen in

BIRDS OF FIELDS AND ORCHARDS

the fields, followed by his little brood of babies. His piercing notes sound as much like a whistle as that of any bird.

The friendly little CHIPPING SPARROW is often found about the fields when he is not venturing into our back-yards. His reddish-brown head, its streaks of black, and the gray marking over each eye, are his distinguishing features.

In the dry and overgrown fields we also find the FIELD SPARROW, with his chestnut-brown back and yellowish-brown breast.

Then there is the more familiar SONG SPARROW, which is larger than the two already mentioned. The light gray breast streaked with brown, the streaked brownish-gray back, and the three lengthwise gray bands on the brown head mark this little songster of the fields and roadside fences.

All the time we have been treading our way quietly through the grasses of the fields, we have had our eye on the swampy margin of that little pond. Now we are close to it, and see a RED-WINGED BLACKBIRD; as much a part of the cat-tail growth in the swamp as the cat-tails themselves. Perched on the side of a swaying reed, he looks a shiny black; but as he flies away we see a flash or orange and red at the shoulder of each wing. This beautiful bird arrives early in March, when the Skunk Cabbages have opened their hoods and the frog's eggs are floating in jelly-like masses in the chill water. The food consists of insects found near the water; and while resting between food forays, the noisy "con-quer-ee" echoes over the stretches of swamp and meadow. The coarse grass-lined nest in the low bushes contains four to six pale blue eggs marked with black.

In the sandy banks of the other shore of the pond we see the familiar holes of the BANK SWALLOW. A few of the slaty-gray individuals can be seen hovering over the water.

THE BIRDS RETURN

Perched on an overhanging limb, a towsled-headed KINGFISHER is looking keenly down into the water. With his large strong bill he can pierce any of his fishy prey which he wishes for his dinner. He is a large bird, bluish-gray in color with a breast of brown and white.

We may catch sight of a long-legged little brown and white bird running like a streak over the sandy beach. This SPOTTED SANDPIPER is an interesting bird to watch; and if we do not startle him, he will continue patrolling the beach in his search for aquatic insects.

BIRDS OF WOODS AND ROADSIDE THICKETS

Leaving the open fields and orchards and other signs of civilization behind us, we wander along a winding country road. On both sides of us are scattered clumps of trees and bits of dense underbrush. In such places we are likely to come across White-eyed Vireos, Yellow-breasted Chats, Redstarts, Catbirds, Maryland Yellowthroats, Chestnut-sided Warblers, Tree Swallows and Thrashers, with perhaps a rare Cardinal.

Of these birds, the noticeable ones are the Redstart, Catbird, Maryland Yellowthroat and Cardinal—each having a distinctive color marking.

The back and orange-red bird which is darting busily from bough to bough is the REDSTART; he has often been called the butterfly of the birds. The Redstart carries on an endless search for leaf-eating insects and flies. This member of the Warbler family arrives in May and stays with us until October. His nest is built of bark and soft cottony material, quite high up in a tree; in it are laid four white eggs spotted with brown and purple.

From a thick mass of shrubbery and young trees we hear

a regular symphony of bird notes; we think there must be at least ten different birds hidden away. But to our surprise out hops a sleek gray bird, who shows a bit of brownish-red under his tail as he flicks it impatiently. The CATBIRD is our eastern Mockingbird; though its charming imitation of the songs of other birds is generally concluded with a cat-like "mew." The Catbirds reach us in May, and soon afterwards build their nests in the thick bushes near the ground. The four or five eggs are a shiny blue-green. Even though the Catbird often raids fruit trees, it also does a lot of good by eating worms and caterpillars; for this reason it ought to be protected, even though the harm done in a few instances seems great.

The MARYLAND YELLOWTHROAT can often be found around the thickets of swampy places and wooded streams. In leaving the road for a moment, and exploring the damp fastnesses of a scrubby thicket, we see several of these yellow-breasted and green-backed birds perched on the leafy boughs. On either side of the head is a distinctive black marking. Like most of the Warblers, this gay little singer of the damp thickets arrives in May after most of the other birds have appeared on the scene.

As we glance upward through the limbs of, perhaps, an oak, we see a bright red bird, perched with crest erect and alert eye. It is a CARDINAL or Redbird. He is entirely red except for some black around his beak and throat; this, added to the crest, makes him an easy bird to recognize. He is quite rare north of New Jersey.

Like the Catbird, the BROWN THRASHER is quite experienced in hiding his long body and long tail in the underbrush. We recognize this Thrush-like bird of brown and white by his long tail, clearly seen as he hops out of the thicket at the side of the road. The Thrasher does not often venture into familiar

BIRDS OF ROADSIDE THICKETS

relations with man, but leads a wild and fearless life in the open woods. The nest is in some brush pile or hedgerow, near the ground; and in it we may find three to six eggs, white with light brown markings.

BIRDS OF THE DEEP WOODS AND FORESTS

A walk early some morning into the deep shades of some nearby woodland will disclose many birds not found in more open country. For instance, we will find in such undisturbed places the Wood Thrush, Hermit Thrush, Veery Thrush and Oven Bird; the Towhee and the Pewee; the Black and White Warbler, Pine Warbler and Black-throated Green Warbler; the Scarlet Tanager; and perhaps a Blue-headed Vireo or a Yellow-throated Vireo.

The Thrushes are ground-feeding birds found in the shade of quiet forests. They are all brown-backed birds with a white breast which is spotted or streaked with brown. The largest is the Wood Thrush and the smallest is the Hermit Thrush; the Veery Thrush is the commonest.

The HERMIT THRUSH is the earliest of the Thrushes to arrive in spring; any time after April we may surprise him as he is running silently about on the forest floor. The Hermit Thrush likes to pour out his melodious song from the top of some evergreen tree, in the stillness which follows sunset. It is difficult to tell anyone who has not seen him how the Hermit Thrush differs from the other Thrushes; in general he is a more stocky, chubby bird with quite a greenish tinge to the brown of his back. Three or four eggs are laid in a nest of mosses and grass, built on the ground.

The VEERY THRUSH is a dweller of the moist woodlands and overgrown swamps. His creamy breast spotted with light

BIRDS OF WOODS

streaks of brown is not as distinctly marked as that of the other Thrushes. The Veery feeds on insects, berries and anything else of that sort which he can find in the swampy woods. Like the other Thrushes, the eggs are bluish-green and are laid in a nest on the ground; the Veery's nest is likely to be built of roots, leaves and bark.

The WOOD THRUSH can be found in forest groves and rocky ravines near streams. He reaches New England in May; and soon afterwards his powerful and effective singing may be heard during the day. All day long he is running about the ground, like a Robin, looking for beetles, snails, spiders and any unwary insect. His eggs are similar to those of the other Thrushes.

Like the Meadow Lark, the OVEN BIRD is more often heard than seen. His resounding notes which sound like "teacher, teacher, teacher" echo through the depths of the woods. If we are patient, we follow the sound until we see a little Thrush-like bird running nimbly about among the ferns and mosses, searching for some particularly juicy caterpillars or berries. The Oven Bird has a greenish-brown back and a white breast somewhat spotted with brown. The nest is built on the ground, and well hidden by a cover built above it, of leaves and pieces of bark. In the nest are laid four to six brown-spotted white eggs.

Three of the woodland birds are colored inconspicuously gray or black; these are the Pewee, the Towhee and the Black and White Warbler.

The PEWEE returns to our woods late in May for a short stay until August. He is a mouse-colored bird of gray and greenish-brown whom we may see, if we have sharp eyes, perched on a twig or limb of a low-growing tree. He is ever on the watch for flies and other insects. His song is a somewhat sad and plaintive series of rising and falling notes. Three creamy white eggs, marked with a few splotches of brown at the larger end, are laid in a saucer-shaped lichen-covered nest attached to a branch.

In the bushes at the edge of the woods we catch a glimpse of a strange bird somewhat like a Robin, colored black on his head and back, white on his breast, and with a reddish-brown stripe between the black and white. This is the TOWHEE, or Chewink. He can be seen industriously scratching about the ground, from the middle of April to October. In the nest of leaves and grass, built on or near the ground, are laid four speckled white eggs.

If we see a distinctly black and white little bird climbing up and down the trunks of the trees, after the fashion of a Creeper or a Nuthatch, we are looking at the BLACK AND WHITE WARBLER. He is the first of the Warblers to reach us in April, and once here he generally hides away in the deep woods. The nest is hidden on the ground near a stump or a rock; in it we may see four or five brown-spotted eggs.

The flight of a SCARLET TANAGER through the leafy tops of the Oaks and Hickories is a sight worth seeing, the red body and the black wings offering a brilliant contrast to the green foliage. The Tanager eats more injurious insects than any other bird of the woods, his meals consisting of caterpillars, gypsy moths, leaf beetles and weevils. From May to September they frequent our deciduous woods, during that time mating and building a loosely constructed nest of twigs and stalks of weeds. The eggs are greenish-blue, marked with brown spots.

THE YEAR 'ROUND

And so we have concluded our bird walks in both nearby and far away haunts of these gaily-colored animal friends of man. We have had to limit ourselves to finding out how to tell these birds from each other, and so have had to leave out what is perhaps the most interesting part of the bird study—the little human-like habits and traits which make bird life so interesting.

But if you have learned to know a few of the birds of fields and forests, you will be all the more eager to find out about the family life of these birds. There is no field of Nature reading, either in magazines or books that is more completely covered than is this.

HOW TO RECOGNIZE THE BIRDS

WITH RED OR ORANGE MARKINGS READILY SEEN

I. If the bird has a crest, it is . . . . CARDINAL
II. If the bird has no crest,
  1. And if the color is orange or reddish-brown,
    A. And the bird is small, 5 inches long,
      it is . . . . REDSTART
    B. And the bird is larger, 7 inches long,
      it is . . . . ORIOLE
  2. And if the color is red,
    A. With the red color on the head only,
      it is . . RED-HEADED WOODPECKER
    B. With the red color on throat and breast,
      it is . . ROSE-BREASTED GROSBEAK
                or HUMMINGBIRD
    C. With the red color on head, back and
      breast, it is . . . . . PINE GROSBEAK
    D. With the whole body red, except for black
      wings, it is . . . SCARLET TANAGER

THE BIRDS RETURN

HOW TO RECOGNIZE THE BIRDS
WITH BLUE MARKINGS OR BLUE COLOR READILY SEEN

I. If the body is almost all blue, with little other color,
    1. And if the body is small, bright blue,
      it is . . . . INDIGO BUNTING
    2. And if the body is large, dark blue, it
      is . . . . PURPLE MARTIN

II. If there is considerable other color with the blue,
    1. And if the other color is reddish-brown, on the breast,
      A. With short tail, light blue coloring,
        it is . . . . BLUEBIRD
      B. With long forked tail, dark blue,
        it is . . . . BARN SWALLOW
    2. And If the other color is gray and white, head with a crest, it is . . . . . . BLUE JAY

HOW TO RECOGNIZE THE BIRDS
WITH GRAY OR BLACK AS THEIR CONSPICUOUS COLOR

I. If the shoulders of the wings are marked with red and orange, it is . . . RED-WINGED BLACKBIRD

II. If there is no red or orange on the shoulders,
    1. And if it is a large bird, 12 inches or more long, it is . . . . CROW, GRACKLE
    2. And if it is a small bird, 10 inches or less in length,
      A. With a white throat, it is . CHIMNEY SWIFT
      B. Without a white throat,
        1. And all gray, it is . . . . CATBIRD
        2. And all purplish-black, it is
          STARLING-COWBIRD

HOW TO RECOGNIZE THE BIRDS
WITH YELLOW MARKINGS READILY SEEN

I. If the other color, beside yellow, is black,
   1. And if the black is on the wings,
      A. With no black elsewhere on the body, it is
         PINE WARBLER, YELLOW-THROATED VIREO
      B. With some black also on the head, it is
         GOLDFINCH
   2. And if the black is only on the head and throat,
      A. With black markings on cheek only, it is
         MARYLAND YELLOWTHROAT
      B. With black marking on throat, it is
         BLACK-THROATED GREEN WARBLER
II. If the other color is not black,
   1. And if the breast is striped with brown, it is
      YELLOW WARBLER
   2. And if the breast is not striped, it is
      YELLOW-BREASTED CHAT

THE BIRDS RETURN
HOW TO RECOGNIZE THE BIRDS
WITH BROWN OR BROWN AND WHITE MARKINGS

I. If the bird is 10 inches long, or longer,
  1. And if there is a red spot on the back of the head, it is . . . . FLICKER
  2. And if there is no red . . . . .THRASHER

II. If the bird is medium sized, 6-8 inches long,
  1. And if the breast is spotted or striped,
     A. With olive green back, it is . . . OVENBIRD
     B. With brown back, it is
        VEERY THRUSH, HERMIT THRUSH, WOOD THRUSH, VESPER SPARROW, SONG SPARROW
  2. And if the breast is not spotted or striped, it is
     TREE SPARROW, WHITE-THROATED SPARROW, SNOW BUNTING

III. If the birds is small, 5 inches or less in length,
  1. And has a light brown breast, it is . . . . .WREN
  2. And has a white or whitish breast,
     A. With a black line through the eye, it is   . . . . CHIPPING SPARROW
     B. Without the line through the eye, it is
                         BROWN CREEPER

THE YEAR 'ROUND
HOW TO RECOGNIZE THE BIRDS

WITH GRAY AND WHITE OR BLACK AND WHITE MARKINGS

I. With red marking on the head,
   1. And if the bird is 6 inches long, it is
          DOWNY WOODPECKER
   2. And if the bird is 9 inches long, it is
          HAIRY WOODPECKER

II. With no red markings,
   1. And if there is yellow
      A. On back of head, it is . . . . . . BOBOLINK
      B. On both sides of body, it is
   WHITE-EYED VIREO, BLUE-HEADED VIREO
   2. And if there is reddish-brown on breast or sides
      A. And a long bill and crest, it is
          KINGFISHER
      B. And a short bill, no crest,
         1. If 10 inches long, it is . . . . ROBIN
         2. If 4-8 inches long, it is
        TOWHEE, RED-BREASTED NUTHATCH,
        CHESTNUT-SIDED WARBLER
   3. And if there is no other color than the gray or black and white,
      A. And if a large bird, 10 inches long, it is
          SHRIKE
      B. And if a smaller bird, 5 inches or so long, it is
        WHITE-BREASTED NUTHATCH,
        CHICKADEE, PHOEBE, BLACK AND
        WHITE WARBLER, JUNCO, PEWEE,
        RED-EYED VIREO

CHAPTER 4
PIONEERS AMONG THE FLOWERS

DURING March and April, if we have not been too intent on our frog hunting and looking for blossoms on the trees, we can discover many brave little pioneers among the flowers. They push their way through the brown cover of dead leaves, in search of whatever little warmth there may be in the spring sunlight.

There are some four hundred flowers that bloom throughout the year in the northeastern United States. Of these, about one hundred and twenty belong to that bold band of adventurers who follow hard on the heels of the melting winter snows. These are the first bits of color to greet us amid the dreary stretches of brown. From the middle of March until the end of June these hundred or more flowers can be found in great numbers in the fields and woods about any town. We haven't time to meet every one of these; but let us take a few walks and get acquainted with thirty or forty of the most common ones.

To many people a flower is just a single bit of Nature, placed in a hit-or-miss fashion wherever the seed may have happened to fall. But this is far from true. For just as certain races of people prefer to live in certain regions, just so do certain kinds of flowers like to grow in special surroundings. If the seed of a Cowslip should by chance be carried to a sunny hillside, it would die without growing into a Cowslip plant. Most plants are quite particular where they grow. Some can stand a lot of water and will grow with their feet standing in puddles. Such water-loving plants are the Violets and Forget-me-nots. Other plants can stand the dry and dusty roadside banks—such as Mullein or Fleabane, but never Violets or Forget-me-nots!

Flowers are particular about other things besides water. Some retreat from the sunlight and are happy in the cool deep shade of the forests; such a shade-loving plant is the Wood Sorrel. Others—like the Buttercups—revel in the blinding sunshine of the open fields.

As a result of such likes and dislikes we can group the flowers into communities or societies. Wherever the living conditions are the same, there we will find the same kinds of flower which we saw in another place of similar surroundings. If we group the spring flowers into such communities, it will make it easier to remember their names. At the same time it will make the plants seem more sociable in their relations with one another.

There are really only three such communities. There is the group of water-loving flowers who prefer to form little sociable groups in swamps, along streams and rivers, and around the shores of ponds and lakes. Then there is the community of wood flowers who like just a medium amount of water about their roots; these are the plants of thickets and forests, where the shade keeps the soil fairly moist. Lastly there is the community of field flowers who can thrive in the dry and sunny situations of fields, meadows, hillsides and roadsides.

Just a word of explanation before we start searching for spring flowers. There are always some people who are brave enough to venture far from home and live in places where other people of their kind are not found. All Chinese are not in

PIONEERS AMONG THE FLOWERS 53

China, any more than all Negroes are in Africa. Some of the flowers manage to get a foothold in a place where they seem to have no business living. So if you find a flower or two in some situation different from those here described, just remember that what I have to say is true for *most* of the flowers *most* of the time.

FLOWERS OF SWAMPS

If you wish to find the earliest of the spring flowers you must take a walk with me to the nearest swamp or swampy margin of a stream or pond. It is here that we will find the silvery catkins of the Pussy Willows, already mentioned. And it is here that we will find:

> Skunk Cabbage
> Jack in the Pulpit
> Cowslip
> Marsh Blue Violet
> Blue Flag
> Forget-me-not

It is always surprising to many people when it is pointed out to them that the maroon and green hoods of the SKUNK CABBAGE are flowers. These pointed caps which push their way through the frozen mud and water in late February can hardly be compared with roses or violets. But to the Skunk Cabbage plant they are just as efficient flowers; inside that hood are the egg-producing and pollen-producing organs which are so necessary for the production of new Skunk Cabbage plants. The disagreeable odor connected with these flowers is Nature's way of making sure that the pollen will be carried to the eggs—by a certain kind of fly to whom such a vile smell is most delightful. In March the rich green of the large Skunk Cabbage leaves gives to the awakening lands a real summery touch.

There is another plant with a greenish-brown flower—the JACK IN THE PULPIT. It does not like to grow in quite as wet places as the Skunk Cabbage. Sometimes it retreats to the moist ground at the edges of swamps and streams. The purple-streaked green flower with its unusual protecting flap bending over the "Jack" with the "pulpit" can be found in April and May. The flower is sometimes all green streaked with a lighter green. Even when not in flower, we soon learn to recognize the plant by the one or two large leaves each of which is subdivided into three leaflets.

As we explore the swampy spots about the course of that tiny stream, we see brilliant masses of golden yellow scattered here and there in big clumps. These are COWSLIPS, sometimes called March Marigolds. The plants have short stout stems and very large leaves, thus being different from the swamp Buttercup. The stems branch a number of times, and at the end of each branch is a closely packed cluster of the large yellow flowers. We first see these in early May, and sometimes come across them even towards the end of June.

The other spring flowers we find in the swamps are all blue. Nestling among its leaves, the BLUE VIOLET seems to reflect bits of the sky amid the abundance of green and the muddy water. When the roots and leaves are half submerged in the water, the flowers grow at the ends of long slim stems.

The FORGET-ME-NOT is a larger plant. The bushy growths seem to prefer the edges of little streams. In May the plants are covered with the little light blue eyes of the Forget-me-nots. One boy once said to me, "My, how pretty the flowers are!

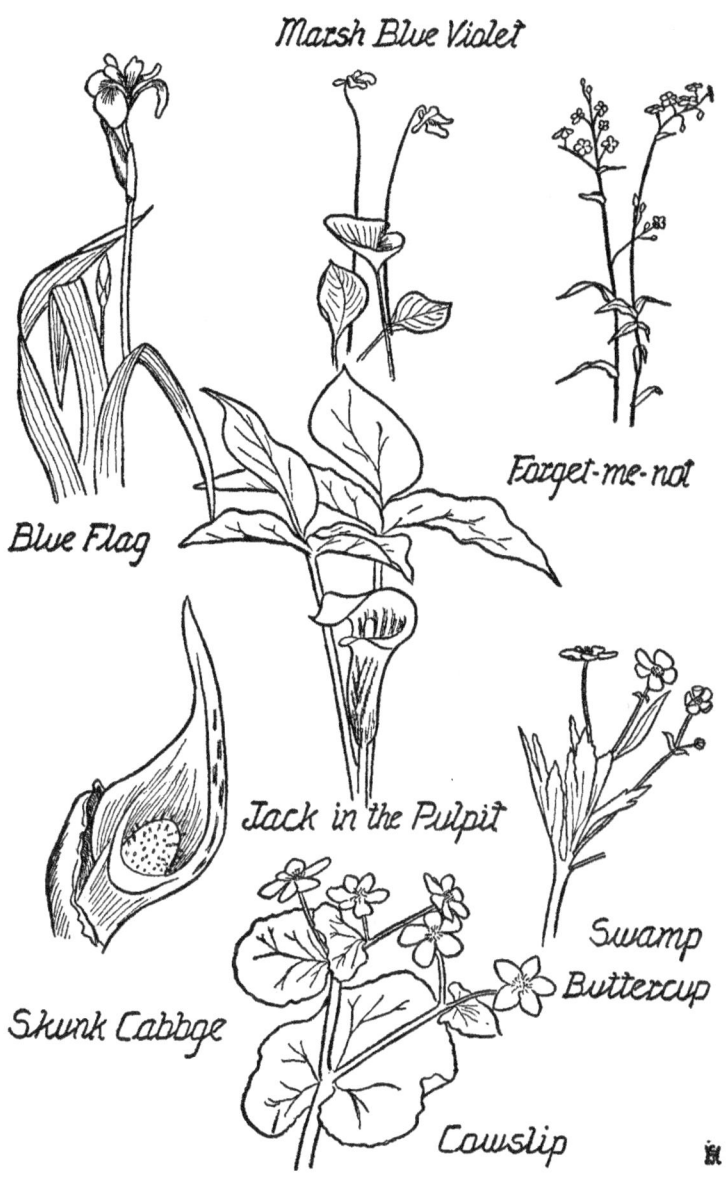

SPRING FLOWERS OF WET WOODS AND SWAMPS

They're so perfect that they look like artificial ones!" No other flower seems to be so obviously made of colored cloth in a regular pattern.

The tall grass-shaped leaves of the BLUE FLAG (or Wild Iris) may form solid walls about the swamps or streams. If we are at all acquainted with the fields and meadows, we have seen these bayonet-like leaves crowned with blue and purple flowers. The curved petals make up one of the most ornate of our wild flowers.

This completes our flower community of the wet places. It is not a large one; yet it is quite commonly repeated with very few variations. Side by side will be found dozens of Skunk Cabbages in varying stages of poking their pointed caps above the ground. On the better drained slopes the Jack in the Pulpit will be growing in great numbers, while down in the wetter situations yellow bits of Marsh Marigold will vie with the blue of Violets and Blue Flag. Less common is the Forget-me-not, which haunts the grassy fringes of tiny streams.

FLOWERS OF THE WOODS

Woods are not just woods. There are open thickets where the sun may shine for part of the day; there are the dense forests of the northern Evergreens. There are the sandy woods, the rocky woods and the level stretches of woodland where the soil cover is a foot deep with leaves and humus. The flowers of the woods are hardly one large community; there are really a number of little societies within this larger social group. But for a beginning, we will consider the woods as just one big family of wild flowers.

Classified by colors, we will find in the woods:

PIONEERS AMONG THE FLOWERS

Greenish-white	*White*	*Blue*	*Yellow*
Bunchberry	False Solomon's	Hepatica	Yellow
Bellwort	Seal	Blue Violet	Violet
Meadow Rue	Canada Mayflower	Lupine	Wood
Solomon's Seal	Rue Anemone		Betony
	Wood Anemone		
	Spring Beauty		Dutchman's
	Blood Root		Breeches
	Saxifrage		
	White Violet		Dog-tooth
			Violet

Red
Columbine
Trillium

As we start out through the woods let us look first for the greenish-white flowers.

In passing through an opening where evidently some old forest monarchs have been cut down, we find the ground covered with a carpet of erect little plants, each less than six inches high. About half a dozen Dogwood-like leaves surround the top of the stem; and within the leaf circle is a little flower with four greenish-white petals and a yellow center. Really these are not the petals, but whitened leaves; the true flowers are in the central compact mass. This is the DWARF CORNEL, or BUNCHBERRY—a relative of the Dogwood whose berries we will discover in winter.

We leave the open space carpeted with Bunchberries and pass again into the cool shady depths of the woods. If we have sharp eyes, we can spot the BELLWORT plants that are hiding away amid the scattered clumps of other flowers. Each Bellwort seems too weak to hold up its head; the upper third of the light green stalk droops so that the clasping grass-like leaves and the yellowish-green flower hang downwards. It is a flower easy to overlook, due both to this drooping habit and the inconspicuous color.

Amid the rocks of a sloping bank we see a loosely-spreading plant which interests us. A short scramble and we are beside some EARLY MEADOW RUE—which however does not live up to its name. All that I have ever seen have been comfortably at home in the open woods and on the banks of wooded roads. The leaves are small and round, with rounded notches in their margin. The flowers are yellowish-green and in numerous clusters of drooping bunches. Like the other greenish flowers we have seen, they are easily overlooked in the shadows of the woods.

Certain woodland flowers are usually connected in my mind with rocky ravines and fern-covered boulders. One of these is the delicate stemmed SOLOMON'S SEAL. It does grow elsewhere in the rich woods. But it seems more at home presiding, in an inch-wide crack, over some mossy rock, with its gracefully arching stem and double row of oval pointed leaves. The flowers are very small and green, hanging in pairs from the joining of leaf to stem. The hanging groups of bell-shaped flowers look more like pods than blossoms.

It seems as though the favorite color of the wood flowers is white, just as that of the field flowers is some shade of yellow. The number of white woodland flowers is very great; but we can hurry along and catch a glimpse of a few of them.

Late in March the first of these white flowers appears. It is the SPRING BEAUTY, that lowly white flower whose petals are often streaked with delicate lines of pink. Hidden by the

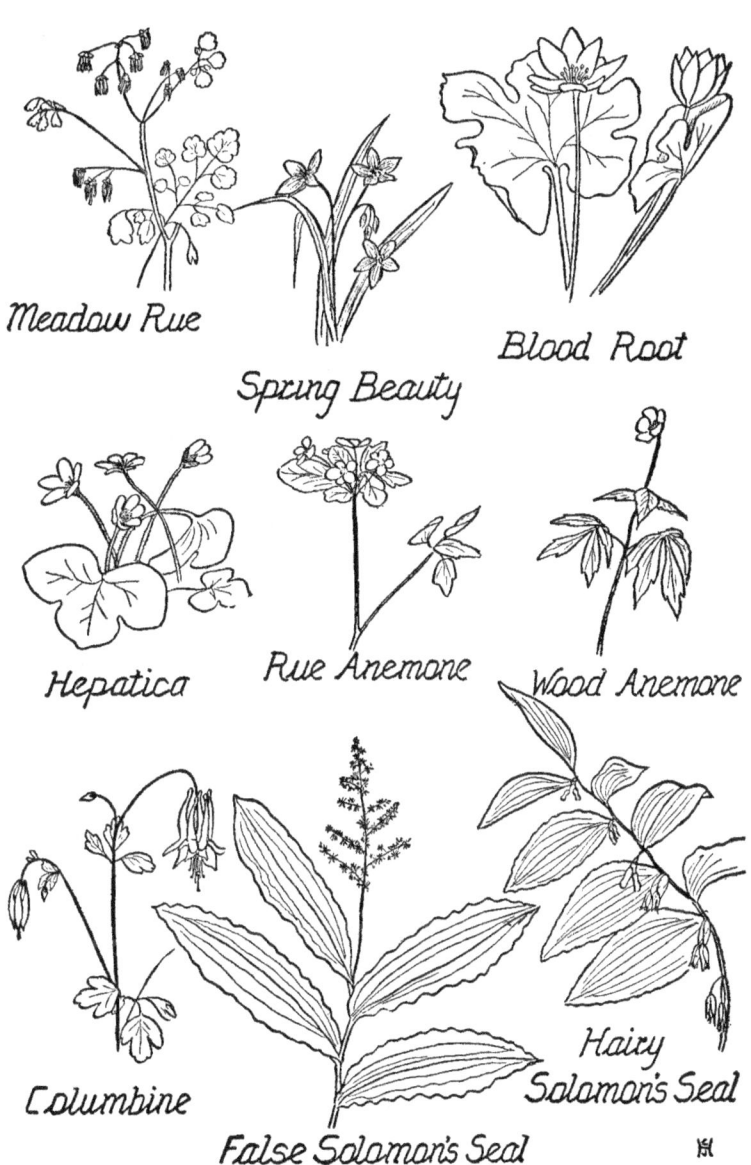

SPRING FLOWERS OF WOODS

surrounding growth of dead grasses and leaves, this little spring flower blooms often undiscovered. The leaves are long and slender, much like those of the grasses.

At about the same time, in March or April, the floor of the open thickets is dotted here and there with clusters of white RUE ANEMONES. The Rue Anemone has without doubt the daintiest stem of any flower; it seems so frail that we wonder how it can support such a cluster of leaves and flowers. Usually there are four or five little white flowers—often tinted with pink. The leaves of the Rue Anemone are almost the shape of small hearts.

A month later the WOOD ANEMONES greet us in the moister portions of the woods. Unlike the Rue Anemone, with which it is often confused, the flowers generally occur singly at the top of a stouter stem. They also are occasionally streaked with pink. The leaves of the Wood Anemone are long and narrow, ending in three or four large teeth.

Another white flower which appears early in the spring is the SAXIFRAGE. You have to be a good rock-climber to reach the home of this sturdy little plant. It loves to sun itself on the narrow shelves of rock on the side of a steep bank. The leaves are small and flattened out at the bottom of the flower stalk, which rises sometimes to six inches above the ground. The flowers themselves are borne in compact white clusters at the top of the stems.

Coming back to the moister and shadier parts of the woods we see numerous erect shafts of leaves, coiled about a hidden stem and bud. Some of these shafts have uncoiled their large leaves to disclose a single large white flower with a golden yellow center. Nothing is more beautiful than a bed of BLOODROOTS with the large white flowers forming a living

PIONEERS AMONG THE FLOWERS 61

snowbank on the wooded slope. The name comes from the orange-red sap which flows from the root when the plant is picked. The Bloodroot can be found blooming early in April.

At the base of the trunks of large trees we see the ground covered with a small erect plant which reminds us of the Lily of the Valley. The CANADA MAYFLOWER is indeed called Wild Lily of the Valley. It is a relative of the Solomon's Seal. The short zigzag stalk bears at its tip a fluffy cluster of little white flowers. Hundreds of these plants may carpet the ground beneath Hemlock and Pine trees.

While we are talking of the Solomon's Seal, we might mention the FALSE SOLOMON'S SEAL. This is a rather large plant, reaching several feet in height which often forms a solid thicket of coarse stems and oval leaves. The flowers are clustered at the end of the stalk, in an ungainly mass of white. It is common enough to be considered a weed in many wooded areas.

If our walk happens to take us through the moister and richer parts of the woods, we may find the sweet-smelling WHITE VIOLET. This retiring little flower is often well hidden by its larger neighbors; but a little search is well worth the trouble, as anyone knows who has discovered the fragrance of this tiny-flowered Violet.

Then there are the blue flowers:

Of course we have with us the BLUE VIOLET, our friend of the marshy places we explored earlier in the chapter.

Chief of the spring flowers is the bold HEPATICA. Every March it is a race between these and the Spring Beauties, Anemones and Bloodroots to see which will be the first to bloom. More often than not the Hepatica will be the winner. The brown-spotted, three-lobed leaves are frequently still hidden by twigs and brown leaves when the hairy stems push their buds up to the sunlight. The flowers may be white, blue, purple or rosy pink. In any case, they are a pleasing forerunner of spring.

Some day when you may be wandering through woods of scattered Pitch Pine and grassy sand banks, you may find bits of brilliant blue adding color to the otherwise drab landscape. The WILD LUPINE is the plant which contributes such touches of blue to dry and sandy woods. It blooms late in the spring, usually in May. The compound leaves are arranged like the fingers of a big hand; and the flowers are clustered about an erect stalk which may grow to a height of several feet.

There are two red flowers which are very common in the woods. One is the RED TRILLIUM, a plant which has all its parts in threes; three leaves, three sepals, and three dark red petals. This Trillium, often also called Wake Robin, blooms throughout April and May.

The other red flower is a brighter and gayer color. The graceful and dainty COLUMBINE can be found clambering up the rocky ridges and ledges in woods as well as in more open locations. The strong yet slender brown stems bear leaves which are subdivided into many small rounded leaflets. The flowers are nodding bells of yellow and red which appear in the latter part of April.

So far in our walks through the woods we have passed by many yellow flowers. Now that we have become acquainted

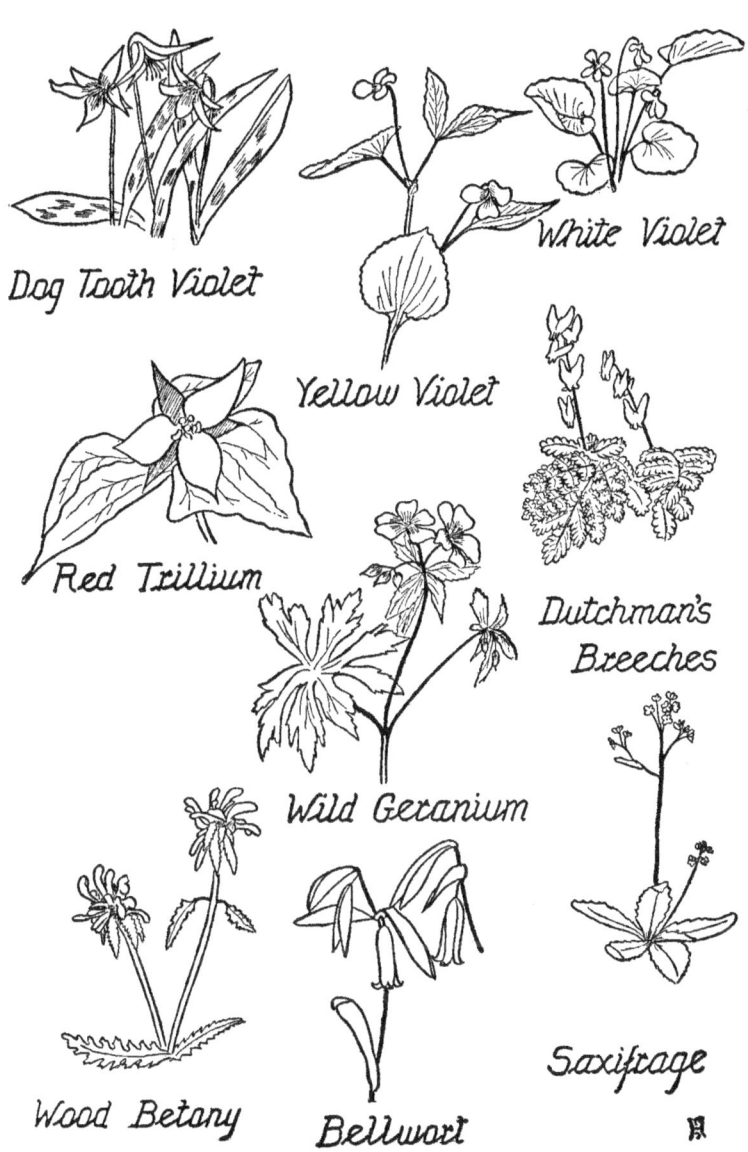

MORE SPRING FLOWERS OF WOODS

with the greenish, white, blue and red flowers let us look for a few of the yellow ones—of which there are about five.

We wander down towards the moister lower portions of a wood, and soon catch glimpses of bashful little yellow flowers poking their heads up here and there from the underbrush. These are YELLOW VIOLETS, whose flowers are borne at the tips of long and branching stems. These violets appear early in May.

Then there is the familiar ADDER'S TONGUE, also called Dogtooth Violet. It really is not a violet at all, but a member of the lily family. These grow in the moist areas surrounding swamps; frequently they form solid beds around the bases of the tree trunks. The inconspicuous light-yellow flowers droop diffidently from the tops of frail stems. The numerous pointed leaves all grow up around the stem where it leaves the ground; and it is the speckled brown and green color of the leaves, with their resemblance to some snakes, which may have helped start the Adder comparison. They flower in April and May.

No other flowers appear in the wet low areas of the wood, so we retrace out steps to higher and drier regions. Soon we spy clumps of large oval leaves, light green in color, springing right out of the ground. In the center of each group of leaves rises a long stout stem, bearing three to six small yellow flowers at its tip. This is the DOGBERRY, otherwise known as Yellow Clintonia. It is found in May in the more northern parts of New England and New York, far from the warmer southern portions of the Atlantic coast. It continues flowering through June.

A thickly shaded rocky ravine opens up ahead of us, and we lose no time in exploring its inviting recesses. We see a great number of leaf clusters which at first sight look like some

PIONEERS AMONG THE FLOWERS

dwarfed fern. But there are flowers rising up from the fern-like leaves. These are DUTCHMAN'S BREECHES, whose nodding clusters of flowers, each with a yellowish-white coloring in its petals, resemble its cultivated relative, the Bleeding Heart.

In the drier portions of the woods above the ravine we find WOOD BETONY. This is sometimes called—rather inelegantly—Lousewort. This also has a dense mass of fern-like leaves growing close to the ground. The flowers themselves are born on a short stalk, forming a dense tuft of yellow-brown blossoms. Both Wood Betony and Dutchman's Breeches bloom in April.

FLOWERS OF FIELDS AND ROADSIDES

These are the flowers that are very familiar to all who have walked or been driven along the ordinary country road. They are not as elusive and fussy about their living conditions as some of their cousins in the woods. Some of these flowers grow in dry, grassy, dusty situations where one would think that only a cactus could thrive. Unlike the woodland flowers, few of these are white; the majority of them are yellow.

Of the white flowers, there is the WILD STRAWBERRY, which grows everywhere in dry soil. The three-parted leaves and the erect white flowers are perhaps not as familiar to boys and girls as the delicious scarlet fruit found on these plants late in summer.

Of the several yellow flowers, perhaps the commonest is the creeping FIVE FINGER or Cinquefoil. This little plant hugs the grassy bank or field, sending up from the prostrate stem leaves in clusters of five (hence the name) and tiny yellow flowers which may be confused with small Buttercup blossoms.

Then there is the YELLOW STAR GRASS, whose flowers often persist into summer. They are found amid the meadow grasses, where the grass-like leaves bear the small yellow flowers near their tips.

The other yellow flower looks much like a Daisy with the white petals picked off—the TANSY. This sturdy plant with its fern-like lacy leaves gives a spicy fragrance when crushed. The compact heads of the flowers are bright yellow; they persist late into summer, as do most of the spring flowers of roadsides and fields.

The blue flowers we may chance upon in these open and sunny places are the Blue-eyed Grass, the Bluet, the Daisy Fleabane and the Heal All.

The little BLUET makes up for its lack of size by its occurrence in beds of hundreds wherever the plants find a grassy place suitable to them. We may walk miles without finding a Bluet flower; but if we find one we will find a hundred. The four-petaled light blue flower appears in April, and blossoms through June. The narrow small leaves are often hidden by the abundance of flowers as well as by neighboring grasses.

While the Bluets hide away close to the ground, the grass-like blades of the BLUE-EYED GRASS raise their deep blue flowers high up above the surrounding grasses. The six-parted flower appears in May and continues blossoming on into July.

The DAISY FLEABANE is a slender-stemmed plant which grows to a height of several feet. There are a few small leaves scattered along the stem; at the top are a few lavender flowers with yellow center. The flowers, sometimes an inch in

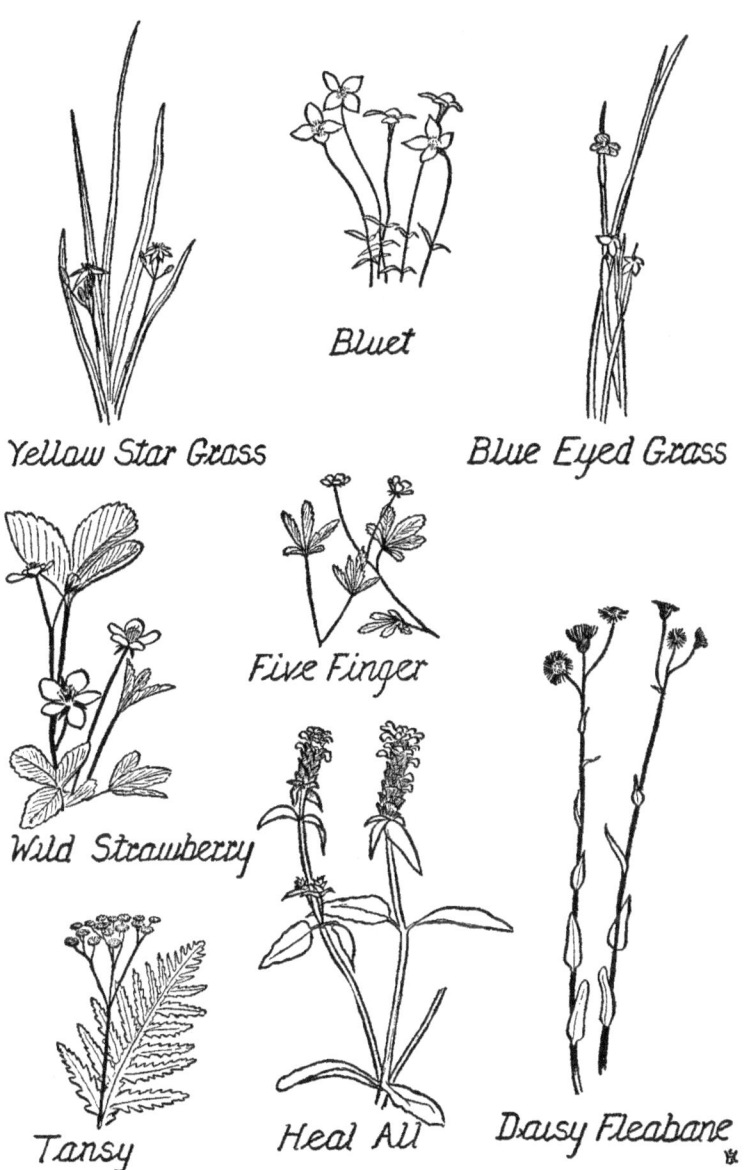

SPRING FLOWERS OF FIELDS AND ROADSIDES

diameter, look like small daisies and grow in similar situations. The Daisy Fleabane is a late spring flower which blossoms late into August.

The HEAL ALL is a common little weed found in fields and waste places; its flower consists of a dense cylinder covered with deep blue petals. It is usually a lowly plant, hiding away in the grasses.

And so we have wandered through swamps and wet meadows, roadside thickets and deep woods, open fields; we have explored all the haunts of spring flowers, catching glimpses of the bravest of the pioneers when they appeared in March, as well as the stragglers which are well content to live amid the heat of July. I hope that now we will have many old friends to greet, and be able to recognize them by name the next time we take a spring walk in similar locations.

HOW TO RECOGNIZE THE FLOWERS

WHICH ARE GREEN OR GREENISH-BROWN IN COLOR

I. If there are none of the usual petals,
    1. And if the flower is without a stem, and cone-shaped, it is . . . . .SKUNK CABBAGE
    2. And if there is a stem, it is. JACK IN THE PULPIT
II. If there are the usual petals,
    1. And if the flowers are at the ends of the stalks,
        A. With drooping flowers half an inch long or longer, it is . . . . BELLWORT
        B. With drooping flowers in clusters, less than half an inch long, it is . . MEADOW RUE
    2. And If the flowers hang at the place where the leaves join the stem, it is. SOLOMON'S SEAL

PIONEERS AMONG THE FLOWERS

HOW TO RECOGNIZE THE FLOWERS

WHICH ARE WHITE IN COLOR

I. If the whole plant is small, less than six inches high,
  1. And if the leaves are long and grass-like, it is
                        SPRING BEAUTY
  2. And if the leaves are broad and large,
    A. With the leaves, or most of them, flattened on the ground below the flower stalk,
      a. With one flower on each stalk, it is
                      HEPATICA (also blue)
      b. With many small flowers on the long stalk, it is . . . . SAXIFRAGE
    B. With the leaves along the stem, or growing up beside it,
      a. Petals an inch or more in length, it is
                      BUNCHBERRY--BLOODROOT
      b. Petals much less than an inch long, it is
                RUE ANEMONE, WOOD ANEMONE, CANADA MAYFLOWER, WHITE VIOLET, WILD STRAWBERRY

II. If the whole plant is larger, more than six inches high
  1. And if the leaves are delicate and fern-like, it is
                  YARROW, QUEEN ANNE'S LACE
  2. And if the leaves are not fern-like, it is
             WHITE DAISY, FALSE SOLOMON'S SEAL, CALICO ASTER, WHITE TOPPED ASTER, SILVERROD

For keys to red, orange, yellow and blue flowers, see Chapter 11.

CHAPTER 5

THE STORY OF THE CATERPILLAR

TO many people, caterpillars are nothing but fuzzy, squirmy "worms" which appear where they shouldn't appear at picnics in the woods.

But when one comes to know them, and understands the remarkable events which take place in all caterpillars' lives, they become the most interesting of animals.

For after all, a caterpillar is but a butterfly or moth in disguise.

When a chicken lays an egg and the egg hatches out, you expect something resembling a chicken to appear. And when your dog has a litter of little ones you are hardly surprised that they look like dogs and not giraffes. But there are some cases where you would be surprised if you could see the very little ones which develop from the eggs.

This we found out in the case of tadpoles, where the fishlike babies look quite different from frogs; but still are really frogs, and will become frogs some day.

In the same way, a caterpillar isn't a bit like a moth or a butterfly; yet it is a baby stage in the development of these insects.

THE EGGS ARE LAID

Late in summer or early in autumn you may have found one or more tiny eggs stuck to the under side of a leaf or attached

THE STORY OF THE CATERPILLAR

to a small twig. Each egg is about the size of a small drop of water; and may be greenish-white, yellow, blue, brown or green. Some of the eggs are round and smooth, while others are barrel shaped and covered with spines and ridges. These are the eggs of some butterfly or moth, and the mother was careful to lay them near the favorite food plant upon which the young baby, soon to hatch out of the egg, could feed.

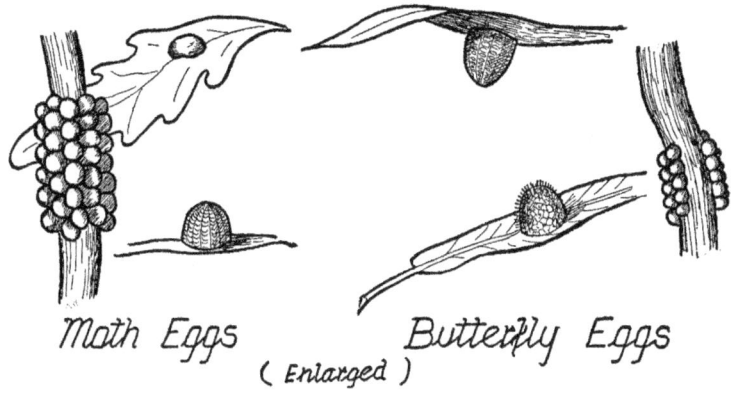

Moth Eggs   Butterfly Eggs
(Enlarged)

No sooner is the egg laid than marvelous changes begin to take place within that thin shell. The soft contents form into the necessary parts of a tiny worm-like animal, which in a few weeks begins to wiggle about and increase in size. Soon it takes on the shape of the ordinary caterpillar.

This awakening of the caterpillar after hatching out of the egg may take place in late summer or fall, or in spring.

THE CATERPILLAR

As the caterpillar grows in size he sheds his skin four or five times, and each time he puts on a larger coat. But with each change his shape stays the same, a long soft body made up of thirteen sections, each section like an inflated automobile tube. Inside he is nothing but one huge stomach except for the three small sections right behind the head. And what an appetite the caterpillar has! He eats his way through life, nibbling leaf after leaf, for a glorious two or three months of existence. That big stomach simply has to be filled. This is why caterpillars (inch-worms, cutworms and the like) do so much damage to trees and crops.

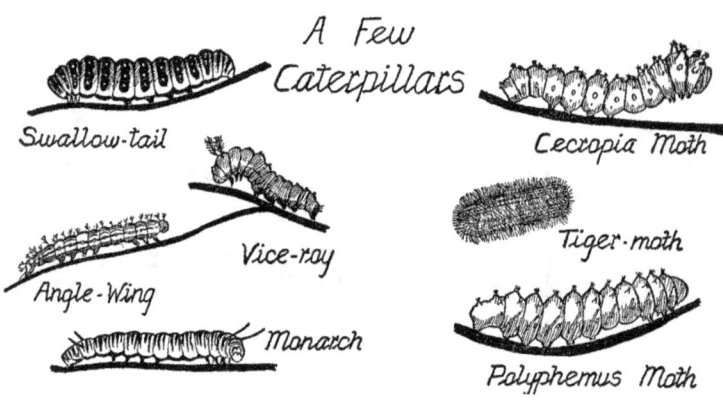

Pick up a caterpillar some time and look at him. He is really quite harmless, no matter how horny and dangerous he looks. All those horns and spines and brilliant spots are only tricks to scare his enemies; or to protect him by a likeness to the surroundings. Each of the three sections behind the head has a pair of real legs which correspond to the three pairs of legs on the butterfly. On some of the remaining sections there may be other pairs of "false" legs. The head—and it is not easy, sometimes, to tell which is the head and which the tail—is small and has a mouth provided with effective eating parts, spinning organ and tiny eyes.

THE STORY OF THE CATERPILLAR

THE RESTING STAGE

After this delightful period of stuffing itself with leaves, the caterpillar feels an urge to curl up and go to sleep. If it is a butterfly caterpillar, it attaches itself by the tail to some stick or overhanging stone; it may even sling itself in a cradle of its own manufacture to the under surface of some branch. A hard coat of armor then develops over the small and shrunken caterpillar so that the brown or green object looks like some dead thing. This is called a chrysalis.

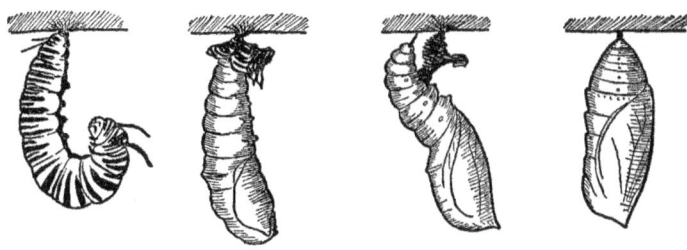

The Butterfly Caterpillar Becomes a Chrysalis

If it is a moth caterpillar, on the other hand, it burrows into the leaves and earth or hides itself under the loose bark of a tree. Here, well protected from foraging enemies, the caterpillar surrounds itself with the same coat of armor as its butterfly cousin's. But in addition it spins a cocoon out of silk, produced in its spinning glands. Only moth caterpillars make cocoons.

Under this drab covering, miraculous changes soon take place. The worm-like caterpillar, curled up in darkness and without any contact with the outside world, feels strange impulses creep over him. As the days pass, he changes so that he looks less and less like a caterpillar and more and more like a butterfly. Beautifully colored wings of the most delicate gauze, long graceful antennae and a compact little body develop out of those thirteen sections of caterpillar.

Then one fine day the walls of the prison break open and there creeps out a wet and forlorn looking insect. A few hours in the sun and he is ready for the new life. This period of change, within the chrysalis or cocoon, usually lasts through the winter.

THE ADULT STAGE

When the moth or butterfly first breaks out of the protecting shell the wings are wrinkled and the antennae lifeless and cramped. Then the wings dry and become stiff, as the livening blood circulates through them. And after a few preliminary trials the insect sails off on his long-awaited flight through the air.

Butterflies and moths, like all other insects, have jointed bodies and jointed legs; unlike fishes, frogs, snakes, birds and mammals, they have no skeleton of bone inside them to keep their shape. The skeleton is really outside the body, instead of inside of it; and consists of a hard celluloid-like armor.

The body has three sections: a head, with two large brilliant compound eyes, several more simpler eyes, a mouth and very sensitive antennae, or feelers; a thorax or middle section, to which is attached wings and legs; and an abdomen. The wings are delicate structures, made up of a framework of strong veins, covered with thousands of very small overlapping colored scales. If you carelessly touch a butterfly's wings, these scales become rubbed off easily.

These insects feed in a most delicate fashion on the honey and water found deep down in the petals of a flower. To do this they have a special kind of tongue, which is like a long flexible spring; when not in use it is coiled up out of the way, but when straightened out it can reach the depths of a flower without difficulty. The honey is pumped up into the tube by automatic bulbs which act like a syringe.

We could go on for a long time telling of the interesting habits of the adult butterflies. But instead we had better become acquainted with a few of them by name.

But before we do this, it might be well to decide how we can tell a moth from a butterfly.

In living habits, there is a very marked difference. The moths like to fly about after dark and are night-hunting insects. The butterflies are creatures of daylight and sunshine, always to be found about the gay flowers of the fields and roadsides.

In appearance, the antennae of the butterfly usually ends in a knob or club while that of the moth is feathery; in addition the body of the butterfly is much slimmer and less hairy than that of the moth. The butterflies are generally more brilliantly colored.

SOME COMMON BUTTERFLIES

There are more than two hundred different kinds of moths and butterflies commonly met with in eastern United States. It seems hopeless to pick out a few as examples of what we might discover in some field. The best we can do is to get acquainted with those that are widely distributed and frequently met with.

Let us start with the most strikingly colored of them all— the Swallowtails. These are large butterflies, about three or four inches in width, possessing a curious tail-like projection from the end of each hind wing. The Swallowtails live at the border of woodlands, and often flutter in gay companies about some choice morsel of food which chances to lie in the sandy country road.

The TIGER SWALLOWTAIL is a bright yellow with blue black stripes extending a short distance into each of the fore wings. The borders of the wings are dark blue also.

The EASTERN SWALLOWTAIL is a dusky blue-black fellow with a lengthwise yellow band bordering each wing. On the very margin of each wing there may be a series of yellow spots.

The SPICE BUSH SWALLOWTAIL is the most somber of the trio. The wings are a lustrous black, tinged with brown and blue. There are a few small yellow spots along the margin of the front wings, and a few larger pale blue spots along the margin of the hind wings.

The MONARCH butterfly is slightly smaller than the Swallowtails, usually averaging about two or three inches in wingspread. It is also called the Milkweed butterfly, for good reason; find a purplish cluster of Milkweed blossoms by the roadside, and you will see one or more of these very common insects hovering over them. The reddish-brown wings are edged with black; the veins too are outlined in black. This butterfly is quite socially inclined; and at times great flocks of them, numbering thousands, may be seen passing over the countryside in their annual migration.

The VICE-ROY butterfly is a most remarkable example of color imitation; the reddish-brown wings, marked with black, seem at first glance to be an exact duplicate of the Monarch. It is smaller in size than the Monarch; and if you have

SOME COMMON BUTTERFLIES

an observant eye you can see an extra black line running lengthwise through each hind wing.

The BANDED PURPLE butterfly has a wing spread of two and a half inches; about the same as that of a Vice-Roy. Its color is a rich purple or black, with a broad white band lengthwise on each wing.

If you are at all acquainted with meadows and fields on hot sunny summer noons, you have seen numerous kinds and sizes of speckled brown and white butterflies. These FRITILLARY butterflies flutter about by the dozens, ranging in size from an inch to two inches, The larger varieties, with aluminum colored spots on their under sides, are called SILVERSPOTS.

The MOURNING CLOAK is a fairly large butterfly, the size of some of the Swallowtails. Each wing has a golden yellow border to the brownish-blue of the remainder of the wing; on the darker portion of the wing, near the yellow margin, is a row of pale blue dots.

The WOOD NYMPH is a graceful little butterfly whom we must not pass over. It is brownish-gray, like some little modest nymph of the forest; its color matches the dim shadows of the woods. On each front wing is a yellow spot in which there are two black marks looking like little eyes painted on by some mischievous spirit of the forests.

Then there are the vast host of yellow and white butterflies of the SULPHUR family. Some of these little butterflies have black spots on the wings, others are unmarked. They are frequently found around vegetable gardens; hence some of them are also called Cabbage butterflies.

The ANGLE WINGS are little butterflies, averaging two inches in length, conspicuous in the ragged outline of their wings. The edge of the wings project in an irregular series of rounded

THE STORY OF THE CATERPILLAR

points. In color they usually are some shade of golden brown, with darker brown or black spots.

The RED ADMIRAL is a common little butterfly, the size of the Angle Wings but with a smoother wing margin. Its brown wings are streaked with orange-red, and have a cluster of white spots in the upper corner of each front wing.

SOME COMMON MOTHS

Some evening when you hear countless moths bumping against the windows or screens as they try to reach the light, go out and collect a few of these unbidden guests. You will be surprised by the variety and charm of these night flying insects.

The LUNA moth is the largest and showiest of them all, reminding us of the Swallowtail butterflies in its long tailed projections on the hind wings. The Luna moth is pale green or peacock blue, with a yellowish-white eye spot in each wing. They are large for moths, measuring three inches in width and four to five inches in length.

There are three other large moths, easily recognized by their size and coloring. These are the Cecropia, Cynthia and Polyphemus moths; all of which are at least four or five inches in wing spread.

The CECROPIA moth has a dark reddish-brown background, with a lighter red streak running across both wings. A half moon shaped spot is in the middle of each wing, between the streak and the body; and between the streak and the edge of the wing is a complicated mass of wavy lines and spots. This is a native silk-moth, whose caterpillar (after feeding on willow and maple leaves) wraps itself up into a cocoon which is quite commonly discovered by observant young naturalists.

The POLYPHEMUS moth has a lighter, yellower background; the streak across the wings is fainter, often incomplete on the front wing; and the spots in the center of the wings are more distinct. The spot in the hind wing looks like a painted eye, yellow and blue with a black border. Its caterpillar is a most beautiful object—being colored a grass green and decorated along the sides with straight lines of silvery white.

The CYNTHIA moth shades into a grayer brown, with a yellower tinge to the streaks and spots. Otherwise it is marked much the same as the Cecropia.

Of the great number of smaller moths, most of them are a neutral grayish-brown in color which makes it difficult to describe in words. We can best omit them, and mention only those smaller moths that have some distinctive color marking which makes then easy to identify.

The IO moth is a yellow moth, brightly tinged with light red. In each of the hind wings there is a large black eye-spot. The caterpillar of this moth is one of the few caterpillars which really is able to sting. The green body is covered with spiny hairs which inflict painful stings when handled.

The ROSY MAPLE moth is a small and delicately colored insect, pale yellow and rose. It is about an inch or two in wing spread, much smaller than the Io moth.

Another moth which is rarely more than two inches in size is the TIGER moth. It gets its name from the network of light yellow stripes which marks the otherwise black fore wings. The hind wings are a rosy red, marked with a few black spots.

The UNDERWING moths make up a large and easily recognized group. They have a drab gray front wing which is the only wing visible when the moth is at rest. But when flying,

SOME COMMON MOTHS

the under wing is strikingly in evidence, being marked by several cross stripes of red or yellow.

The SPHINX moths are unusual in the large size of their hairy bodies and in the long pointed fore wings. The hind wings are very small. Some of the Sphinx moths are light brown or tan, with rosy streaks and dark brown spots; while others are a more yellow or more gray color, with greenish shades and blacker spots.

Larger moths of this same type go under the name of HAWK moths. One common Hawk moth is about three inches or more in wing spread, and is colored a mottled gray and brown in a most inconspicuous fashion. The abdomen has yellow spots along the sides.

THE STORY OF THE CATERPILLAR

HOW TO RECOGNIZE THE BUTTERFLIES

I. If the wing spread is 2 inches or more,
  1. And if the hind wing has a tail-like projection,
     A. Color chiefly yellow, it is TIGER SWALLOWTAIL
     B. Color dark blue-brown, it is EASTERN SWALLOWTAIL, SPICE BUSH SWALLOWTAIL
  2. And if the hind wing has no tail-like projection,
     A. With the color chiefly brown,
        a. Striped with black, it is
                              MONARCH, VICE-ROY
        b. Spotted with black and silver, it is
                              SILVERSPOT
     B. With the color chiefly dark blue,
        a. Yellow marginal stripe, it is
                              MOURNING CLOAK
        b. White band across wings, it is BANDED PURPLE

II. If the wing spread is less than 2 inches,
  1. And if the chief color is yellow, it is one of the
                              SULPHURS
  2. And if the chief color is light blue, it is one of the
                              BLUES
  3. And if the chief color is brown,
     A. And there are two black spots in a yellow mark on each front wing, it is   WOOD NYMPH
     B. And there are many black spots all over the wings, it is. . . . . CHECKERSPOT, CRESCENTSPOT, ANGLE WING, RED ADMIRAL, PAINTED LADY, FRITILLARY

SUMMER

CHAPTER 6

DWELLERS IN THE DAMP AND SHADE

When the word "plant" is mentioned, most of you think of "flower" or "tree." It is true that the most familiar plants are trees and flowers; but there are many other kinds of plants, some of them very unusual and for that reason very interesting.

There are four kinds of plants that seem to avoid the sunlight with its heat and dryness, and therefore are not found in any great numbers in fields and along unshadowed roadside banks. Instead, they hide away in the cool and dimly-lighted recesses of the woods where there is always abundant moisture in the ground. In the nooks under overhanging ledges of moist rocks, on the walls of caves, on the rocky sides of shaded ravines and on the damp forest floor itself, these plants have made themselves at home.

These are the mosses, ferns, lichens and mushrooms. Some brave members of each of these groups have migrated to the open swamps, to the borders of lakes and streams and even to the drier locations of fields and meadows. But still the majority of them are to be found "at home" in the sort of places just described in the paragraph above.

In many ways these plants are quite different from trees and "flowers." They are smaller in size, for one thing; though in the case of the ferns that has not always been true. The ancestors of the ferns, living in the days when the coal we burn was being formed (millions of years ago), were trees fifty and sixty feet high! The tallest ferns, excepting the tree ferns of the tropical countries, now rarely grow higher than five feet.

Another difference is in the way they make new plants. Trees and shrubs and all flowering plants make eggs inside of a flower; this grows into a seed, as we have already seen. But these ferns, mosses, lichens and mushrooms never produce flowers or seeds; instead they make very tiny particles, about the size of grains of dust, called spores. These spores are blown to new homes and there grow into new plants.

MOSSES

No mosses grow in salt water; the red, brown or green plants which grow in the ocean and are often found tossed up on the beach after a storm, are, in spite of their common name of Sea Mosses, not real mosses. These seaweeds belong to another class of plants which we will learn about in the chapter on Seashore Life. Some mosses do grow in the fresh water of ponds, and particularly in streams where we see them clinging to the stones in the swiftest currents. But the mosses we are interested in grown on trunks of trees, on stones and on the soil in the damp and shady parts of the woods.

Mosses are very sociable plants; one rarely finds a *single* plant. They huddle together in tufts and hummocks and dense mats, thousands of them in such a compact mass that it is hard to separate a single plant. But let us do so, for a moment, to see what a moss plant is like.

The root system is very small, and really is not made up of true roots but of little hair-like growths called rhizoids; these anchor the moss to the ground and absorb mineral food when

DWELLERS IN THE DAMP AND SHADE 89

it is available. Above the rhizoids is a vertical stem, thin and frail and green; the delicate little leaves, thin as tissue paper and almost transparent, clothe this erect stem closely with green. At the tip of the green leafy plant there are produced very small eggs which do not become seeds, but stay where they are formed even when they start growing.

At certain seasons we see long brown stalks growing up from the top of the green plant; these stalks are really other plants, germinating from the tiny eggs. And after a while, at the end of the stalk, there develops a sac in which millions of brown spores are born. When this spore sac opens, the wind carries the spores for many miles. Eventually these spores will settle to the ground and if the soil is moist enough they will germinate into new green moss plants.

Next time you find a clump of shiny green moss, covered with a mass of stalks like spears of a Lilliputian army, pass your hands lightly over them; and if the spores are ripe you will see a cloud of yellowish brown dust arise from the spore sacs. You have merely helped Nature release millions of these little specks which may grow into new moss plants, miles away.

Now as to names of some common mosses.

Unfortunately, most of the mosses are neglected by ordinary people; for this reason, they have never been given common names. Perhaps you don't know that all plants and animals have names, given them by the scientists who discovered or studied them. These names are in Latin, and often are more ponderous than the object named. If you had to call a White Oak "Quercus alba" every time you saw it, or Jack in the Pulpit "Arisaema triphyllum, you wouldn't be very enthusiastic about studying trees and flowers. For this reason, people give them easier-to-pronounce common names. The disadvantage to this is that the same animal or tree might have a different common name in every state where it was found.

However that may be, I think that is one reason so many boys and girls lose their interest in identifying mosses and mushrooms, and even seaweeds. It certainly is no fun, even for some grown-ups to remember "Physcomitrium" or "Dicranella." I have tried to select those mosses to which I could give common names; you will find many others, quite commonly—and will have to give them your own names until you get old enough to study them in a moss guide which uses the scientific names.

PEAT MOSS forms beautiful pale green or pinkish yellow carpets on the damp slopes of ravines and around the edges of swamps; it often forms solid beds of green in the oozy bottoms of bogs and ponds. The leaves are thin and pale, and so constructed that they absorb tremendous quantities of water. Thus Peat Moss is more absorbent than cotton; and no matter how dry it may seem, one can always squeeze some water out of it. Its scientific name is Sphagnum.

MNIUM MOSS also grows in very wet and swampy places, especially about shaded springs. It has very large, semi-transparent leaves; and the clusters of erect plants are not as closely grouped in clumps as the other mosses. The rich green plants grow to a height of two or three inches.

If we leave the wet and swampy parts of the woods, we come across many other kinds of mosses which are satisfied with what moisture they can take out of the air or get from an occasional drip from an overhanging ledge. They clamber over trunks of rotting and fallen trees; they cover the rocks with

DWELLERS IN THE DAMP AND SHADE

shining green carpets; and the damper and more shady the place, the more the mosses seem to thrive.

Here most of the mosses form creeping mats on rocks and tree trunks; these mosses have a prostrate stem from which grow upright brown spore stalks.

FEATHER MOSS is a plant of this type; its dark green leaves form branched masses of foliage similar to a dense tangle of feathers.

CEDAR MOSS is like the Feather Moss, only the leaves are flattened in rows, giving the plant the appearance of a cedar spray.

TREE MOSS has a matted growth of stems also, but from it projects upwards a number of leafy stems which are branched like little evergreen trees.

Elsewhere in the woods, we see rich green cushions of moss, especially thick and luxurious about the bases of trees. The FORK MOSSES grow after this fashion, their glossy green leaves in twisted silky masses from which the beaked spore cases project like so many geese with outstretched heads.

Some of the mosses grow in the open thickets and together with the grasses in the meadows. Such mosses are the Pincushion (or White) Moss, the Hairy Cap Moss, and the Catharine Moss.

The PINCUSHION MOSS forms highly arched greenish-white cushions, with the moss plants so crowded that it is impossible to detect the individual plant.

The CATHARINE MOSS forms dark velvety cushions along roadside banks and around the bottoms of trees; the erect plants bear curly brownish-green leaves which have bright red tips to them in autumn and winter.

And then, last but not least, there are the HAIRY CAP MOSSES.

These are the common brownish-green mosses which straggle over the rocky ledges in fields, and occupy all sorts of waste places where nothing else could grow. When not too much dried out, the leaves at the top of each erect Hairy Cap plant form a star-shaped cluster. The moss gets its name from the hairy covering on the spore case.

FERNS

Mosses are fairly common everywhere in the United States; but ferns increase in abundance as one goes northward into the cool moist forests of New England and northern New York.

Like the mosses, the ferns grow new plants by means of spores and not seeds; but they have developed several ways of producing these spores instead of the one usual spore case of the moss. Some ferns have the spores in clusters of brown dots on the underside of the leaves, as in the Lady and New York Ferns. Others have the spores under a rolled-up margin of the leaf, as in the Brake Fern. Others have the spores born on special leaves, part of which looks and acts like an ordinary leaf, while another part has taken over the duty of making spores, as in the case of the Interrupted and Royal Ferns. And lastly, some of the ferns have entire leaves which are not green, but are devoted to the one responsibility of making spores; so the whole leaf functions as a large spore stalk. This can be seen in such ferns as the Sensitive and Cinnamon Ferns.

No matter how the spore is formed by the leafy fern plant, it eventually reaches the ground and germinates. But something takes place which is quite like the butterfly's egg hatching into a caterpillar, which in turn becomes a butterfly. The spores grow into a small heart-shaped flat green plant never larger

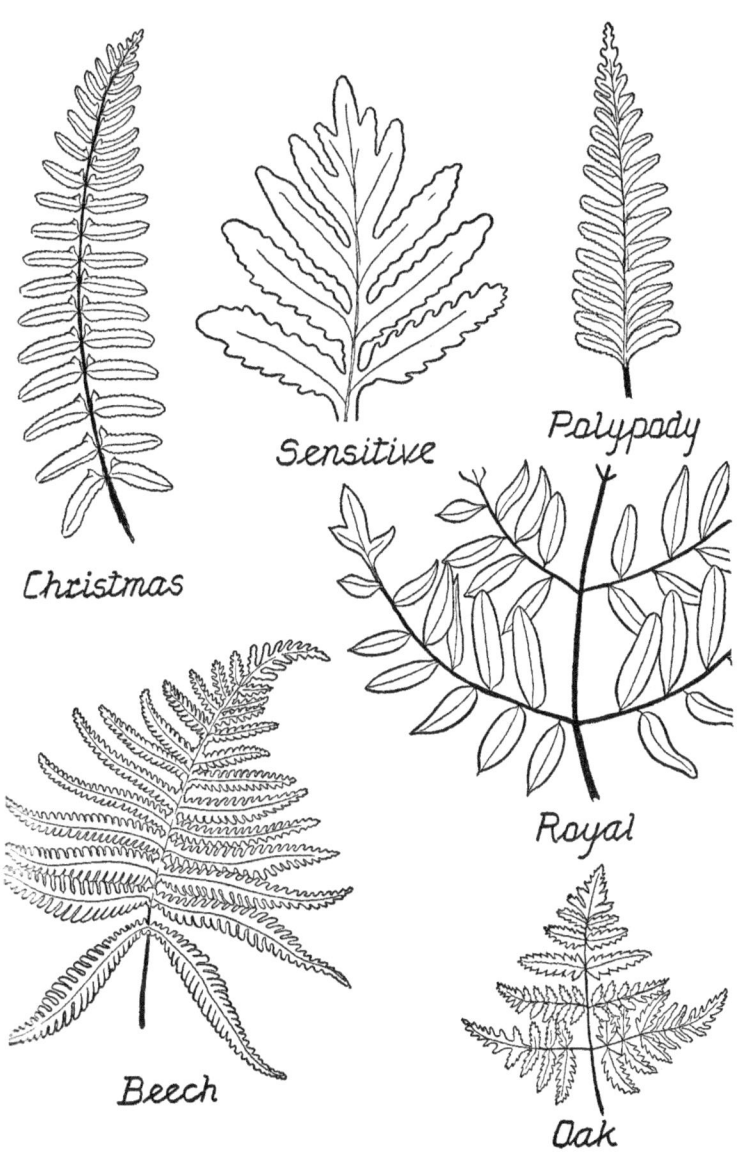

SOME COMMON FERNS

than a quarter. This hides away in the damp spots beneath the grasses and bushes; and after a time there grows out of it an erect stalk which soon forms a new fern plant.

But let us get out into the woods and meet a few common ferns face to face.

Before we reach the woods, we find, as we did in the case of the mosses, certain individuals who wanted to be different; these ferns have become accustomed to much drier and sunnier situations than is usual for members of this family.

Alongside the road, marching in solid ranks of dusty yellow-green, down to the very sandy margin of the highway, are dense growths of a delicate lace-like fern. This is the LADY FERN, which grows to a height of one or two feet; its unbranched leaves are divided into leaflets, and the leaflets in turn are subdivided into smaller ones. The margin of the little leaflets is toothed like a saw. The spores are born on the underside of the leaves in oblong spore groups (known as sporangia).

Before reaching the wooded portion of the hillside we have to cross through a grassy field where Hawkweeds, Heal All and Queen Anne's Lace are flowering in summer brilliance. Hardly the place for a fern, yet we see scattered groups of little fern-like plants. This is the SENSITIVE FERN, which attains a larger size when it grows along stream margins, though it is rarely more than a foot in height. The leaves are broad and short; and are divided into leaflets by indentations which do not quite reach the main stalk. The spores, instead of being formed on the underside of the leaves, are produced at the tips of brown leafless stalks which rise upright in the center of the cluster of triangular leaves.

The Cinnamon Fern and Interrupted Fern are two of the

DWELLERS IN THE DAMP AND SHADE

largest ferns of ordinary moist woods. They both form vase-shaped clusters which look like graceful plumes of green, from three to five feet high.

The CINNAMON FERN has large thick-stemmed leaves which are subdivided into deeply toothed leaflets. The center of each clump of fern leaves contains one or more brown stalks bearing the spores. Cinnamon Ferns often form tussocks in swamps and bogs.

The INTERRUPTED FERN is slightly smaller, and is more often a plant of the open woods. The large coarse leaves are also subdivided into leaflets; but the leaflets instead of being cut into sharp toothed lobes, are edged by rounded overlapping lobes. It is the easiest fern to recognize when it is forming spores, for the spores are on withered brown leaflets part way along the stalk of the leaf. Green leaflets grow out both above and below the spore stalk, hence the "interrupted" name.

As we pass through a sunny glade in the woods we have to wade knee deep through a bed of light green delicate ferns; they give out a fragrant scent when crushed under our feet. These are the HAY SCENTED FERNS; which look like Lady Ferns, but can be recognized by the spores rolled under the margin of the leaf, instead of being in spore cases in the middle of the underside of the leaf.

The other side of the glade we find ourselves along the overgrown margin of a small stream; the water gurgles over stones green with streaming moss. And with its very feet in the water, a large fern-like plant forms a graceful covering for the bank of the stream. This is the ROYAL FERN, a fern with sturdy brown branching stems, and leaves divided into stalked leaflets which look more like a flowering plant than a fern. Some of the leaves have queer wrinkled up swellings at their upper extremities. These bean-like masses will soon form brown spore cases, from which the millions of spores will be released to find new homes.

After struggling through thickets of thorny bushes and sprouting maple clumps, we find ourselves in another open glade; but this one is filled with a tall shoulder-high fern which has tough brown stems, branching into three parts to form an umbrella-like top portion. These three-branched leaves are characteristic of the BRAKE FERN. The Brake is one of the commonest ferns; and can be met with anywhere in open woods, borders of fields, roadsides and pastures. The spores are formed on the inrolled margin of the leaf.

All the remaining ferns are small plants, rarely growing more than a foot high. Two of these are evergreen, and have dark-green glossy leaves; these are the Boulder, or Polypody Fern and the Christmas Fern. The others disappear in winter; the Wood Fern, Maidenhair Fern, Beech Fern and Oak Fern.

The CHRISTMAS FERN is well known; its spreading clumps of dark green can be found in any forest, usually clustering about stones or rocky ledges. The leaves are subdivided into leaflets with very small teeth along the margin.

The POLYPODY FERN is one of our tiniest ferns. It grows on rocks and tree trunks, often covering them with a miniature forest of green. A huge boulder covered with Polypody, seen in the dim light of the forest, presents an unforgettable picture. Each leaf is erect, and subdivided once into leaflets which grow together to form an overlapping edge to the main stem.

The WOOD FERN is one of the most delicate looking of all the ferns, considered from the viewpoint of the lacy subdivision of the leaf into leaflets which are again subdivided

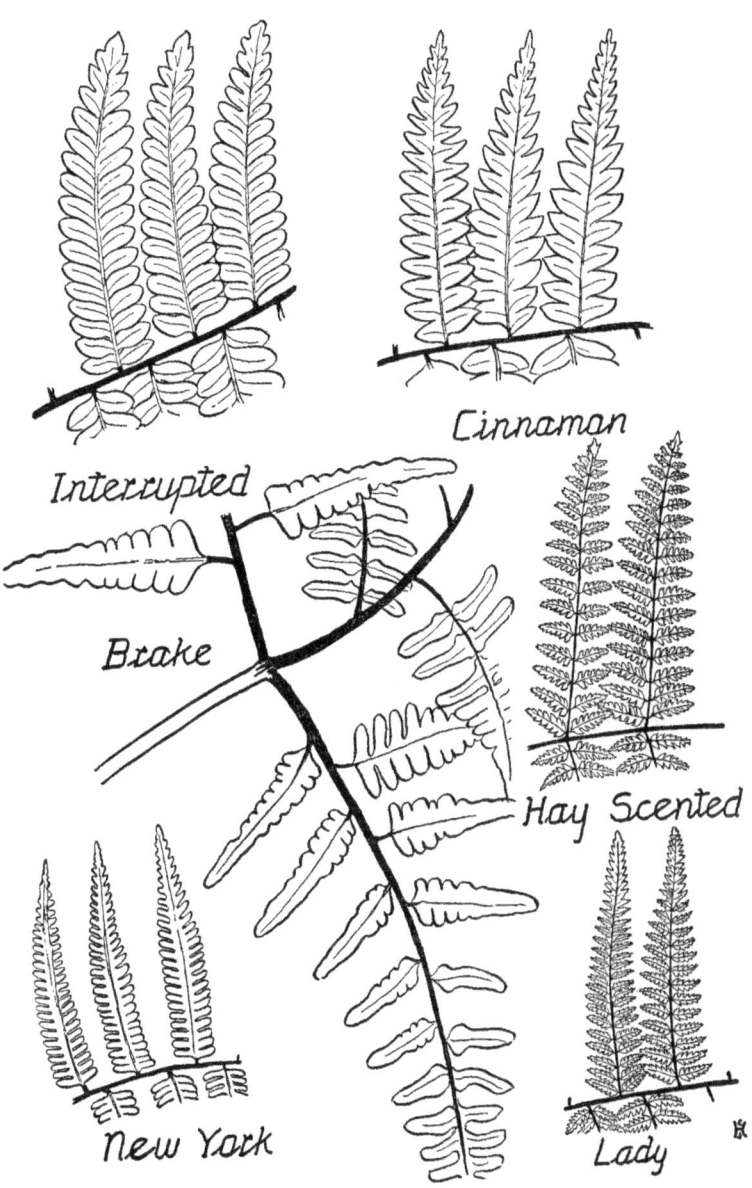

MORE COMMON FERNS

Both the Polypody and the Christmas ferns have the spores formed on the underside of the leaves, as is also true of the Wood Fern.

The MAIDENHAIR FERN is very common in the southern portions of New England and New York, but more rare farther north. It is a very delicate and graceful fern, likely to be found in rocky and shady woods. It grows to a height of a foot or two, and its erect main stem, which is very brown and still, branches into a series of shorter stems bearing rounded leaflets. Like the Royal Fern, its leaves look more like those of a flowering plant than a fern.

The BEECH FERN is a small fern, rarely more than six inches in height. We can find it is scattered groups in the open spaces about the bases of the large trees and boulders. Its leaf is broad and triangular, like one of the three subdivisions of a Brake Fern; its habit of having the last two large leaflets curved back like a pair of horns, makes it easily recognized.

The OAK FERN is our tiniest fern which is at all common. It grows to a height of three or four inches. The main stem is stiff and brown, and branches into three parts (like a miniature Brake); each of the three parts of the leaf is subdivided into leaflets. The Oak Fern likes to grow on the slopes of wooded hills, where it is often overlooked due to the tangle of plants growing above it.

SOME FERN RELATIVES

Relations sometimes don't look alike, as we all know. Brothers and sisters, more often cousins and uncles and aunts, may hardly resemble each other at all. The relatives of the ferns, belonging in the same family with them, are common but are often not considered ferns.

THE DWELLERS IN THE DAMP AND SHADE 99

These are the Scouring Rushes, Horse-tails (or Section Grass), Club Moss, Running Pine (or Creeping Pine), Ground Pine and Ground Cedar.

The SCOURING RUSH is a peculiar fern, looking more like a cylindrical grass than anything else. It has no leaves in the usual sense, the long slender main stem being green and doing the work of the leaves. The Scouring Rush grows in shallow bays and swamps around ponds, as well as on moist banks and wooded hollows.

The HORSE-TAIL also has no leaves; but the green main stem is not as thick as that of the Scouring Rush, and branches regularly. While the Scouring Rush resembles a long spear shooting up out of the ground, the Horse-tail looks like a little tree with foliage growing out in a series of circular umbrella-like layers, one above the other. Horse-tails grow in waste places as well as in moist woods and pastures; their favorite home seems to be along railroad embankments.

The CLUB MOSS is small than either of the preceding; rarely growing to a height of more than six inches. It has a running underground stem from which many erect stems form a cluster of rich dark green. The short pointed leaves grow all about the stem in dense masses, resembling the habit of mosses. For this reason it is called a moss, though it is really a fern.

The RUNNING PINE is a smaller edition of the Club Moss; like it, it prefers to grow in deep woods and has a long underground stem from which grow short erect stems clothed with short-pointed leaves. This is also called CREEPING PINE.

The GROUND PINE looks like a diminutive evergreen tree. It is an erect little fern, branching the way a tree does; and all the leaves are tiny scales which completely cover the stems.

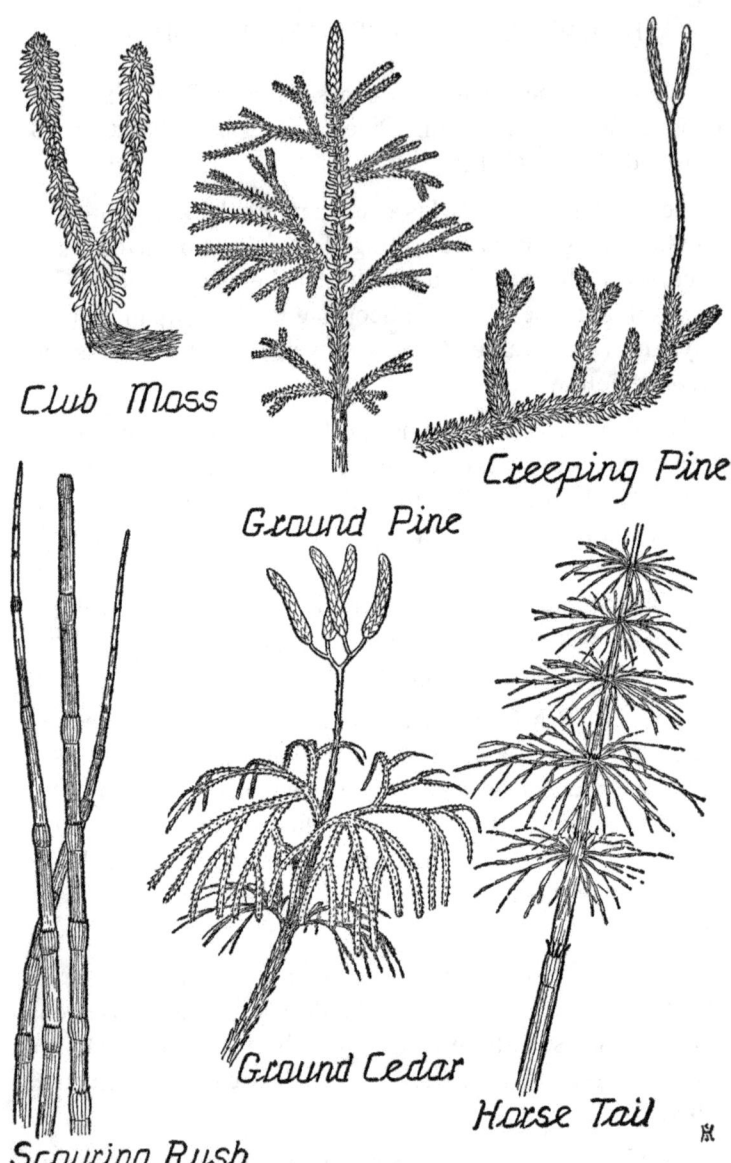

SOME FERN RELATIVES

DWELLERS IN THE DAMP AND SHADE 101

Together with the Running Pine and Club Moss, it often may be found as a rich green carpet on the forest floor—especially in mixed evergreen and deciduous forests. When the spores are formed, they appear in golden yellow club-shaped projections from the tops of the plant, looking like so many candles attached to the tops of little Christmas trees.

The GROUND CEDAR is a similar evergreen fern, but more creeping and less erect than the Ground Pine. The main stem branches frequently and regularly; and all the stems are covered with very small scale-like leaves.

These last four ferns, being evergreen and lending themselves well for purposes of wreath-making and general decoration are often uprooted carelessly for Christmas decorations. This habit should be stopped, as in a short time these attractive ferns of our woods will become destroyed completely.

MUSHROOMS

All the plants we have so far become acquainted with have had some green parts—either leaves or stems. It is very important to a plant to be green, for as we will find out in later chapters this green color is what makes a plant able to live on air and water and soil. If a plant does not have this green color, it is unable to live the way honest-to-goodness trees, flowers, ferns and mosses live; instead it has to *steal* its food from dead and decaying material, or even from living things.

Mushrooms are plants of this type. They lack the green color and therefore have to absorb their food from other materials; so we find them growing on humus—which is nothing but a concentrated mass of dead leaves and twigs—on decaying trees or on living trees. They are unable to stand very dry and sunny conditions, due to their frail structure; most of the mushroom plant is water. So the damper and rainier the season, the more mushrooms we find on our lawns and in the forests.

The familiar mushroom consists of a stalk and an umbrella-like cap. This is really only the "flower" of the mushroom plant. For just as plants have flowers to form seeds, so the stalk and the cap are only for purposes of producing and scattering spores. The spores are grown in partitions on the underside of the cap.

The part of the mushroom which corresponds to the roots, leaves and stem of an ordinary plant is all under ground. It is made up of a branching mass of white threads which anchor the mushroom to the ground, as well as absorb nourishment from the place where the plant grows. This underground mass of fibers grows in size until the time comes for spore-formation. Then one of the fibers gets a little swelling on it; this swelling grows upwards until a little white "button" forces its way through the ground. If there is plenty of moisture, the button grows in size rapidly—sometimes several inches over night. As it lengthens out, the skin breaks around the middle, the top spreads out as a cap and the rest of it forms a fleshy stalk. Mushrooms are short-lived, and cannot be "picked"; they lose their watery strength very quickly, and wither up into an offensively smelling mass.

The color of mushrooms is white; but in many cases the spores are a variety of colors, as are the caps. It is by the color of the spores and the cap, as well as by the type of structure producing the spores, that we can recognize mushrooms.

The ordinary mushroom, with cap and stalk, is the most common and familiar; so let us learn the names of a few of them first.

The BOLETUS MUSHROOM has a thick yellow stem, and

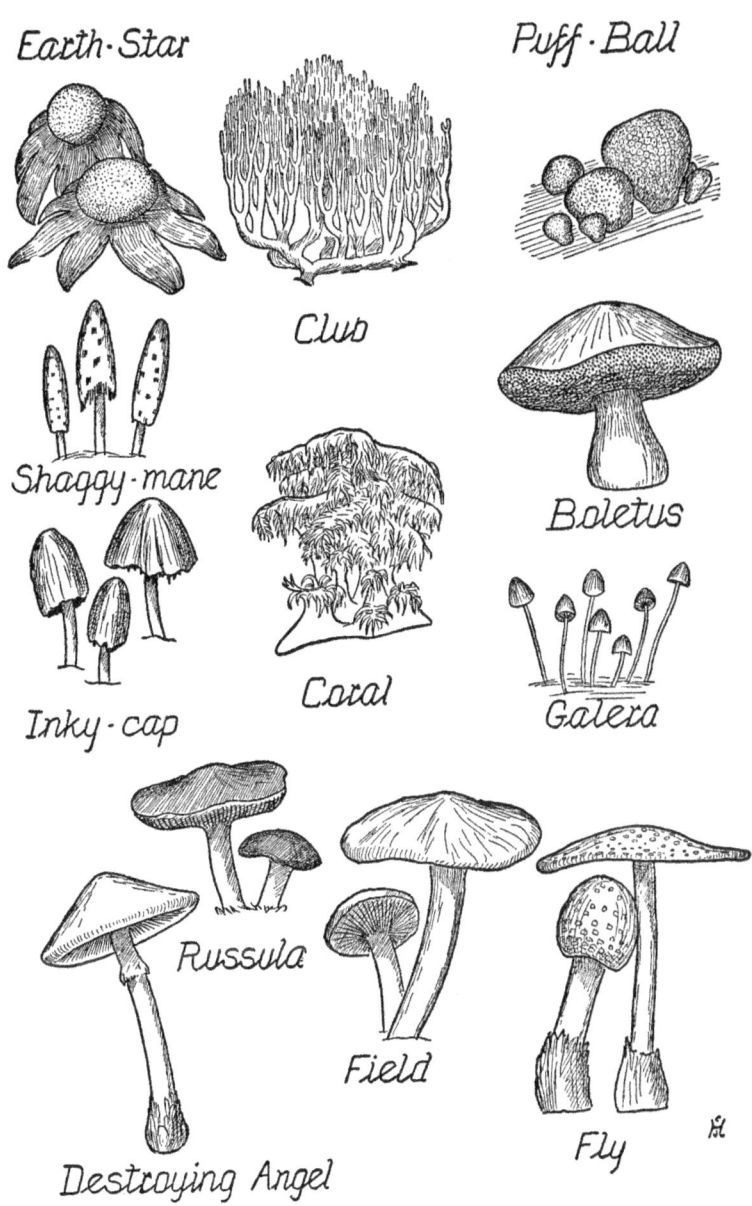

SOME COMMON MUSHROOMS

brown cap; it differs from other cap-mushrooms by having pores on the underside instead of rows of partitions radiating out from the center. It grows in woods during July and August.

The common FIELD MUSHROOM has a broad silky cap and white stem; it is common in open locations such as on lawns and along roadsides. When the spores are ripe, the underside of the Field Mushroom is brown or black.

The INKY-CAP, and its close relative the SHAGGY-MANE MUSHROOM appear from May to September, whenever there has been warm wet weather. They force their way through grass and undergrowth, pushing their egg-shaped caps to the light. The color of the cap is some shade of gray or brown; when the spores ripen they drop to the ground in an inky, sticky mass which gives one of these mushrooms its name.

The FLY AMANITA is a poisonous mushroom with a distinctive color. The cap, at first rounded, changes to a flattened umbrella; but the color remains a red or an orange, covered with sticky substance. White spots of irregular sizes are scattered over the surface of the cap. This mushroom has white spores. The Fly mushrooms appear in July and may be found through October, more commonly occurring about the bases of trees.

The DESTROYING ANGEL, another Amanita, is pure white, both as to cap, stalk, and spores.

The very tiny fairy-like mushroom with bell-shaped cap and slender stem which appears in great numbers on lawns after rains, is the SLENDER GALERA. The cap varies from brown to silvery buff, and the spores are dark rust colored.

But not all the mushrooms have caps and stalks. Some of them, like the Coral Mushroom, form the spores in erect club-shaped and branching masses. Others have stemless sacs, close to the ground, in which the spores are grown; this is the case with the Puffballs and Earth Stars. Still others have corky and woody spore producing parts, instead of fleshy ones; this is what we find in the various shelf-fungi and bracket mushrooms.

The CORAL MUSHROOM is white or light tan, forming coral-like growths on decaying wood.

The PUFFBALLS are so well known that they need no description; the dust which comes out of them when they are squeezed is the spores.

The EARTH STARS are like little Puffballs growing on a star-shaped brown base. Both of these brown mushrooms grow on decaying stumps and logs in woods, or on soil.

The BRACKET FUNGI are very common sights on tree trunks, whether the trees are alive or dead. The Gray Birches have a particular Bracket Fungus all of their own; other larger and woodier forms grow on other trees.

LICHENS

I would not be surprised if many of you never had heard this word; it is pronounced "likens."

They are strange gray-green plants which are half fungus and half something else. The fungus part makes up the outside of the plant; it consists of a mass of white threads similar to the underground portion of a mushroom plant. Towards the center of the lichen there are many little green balls held in the meshes of these white threads. These are very simple green plants known as Algae; other Algae are the sea-weeds and the green coating on the north side of trees.

Thus the lichen is really not one plant, but two; these two plants live peaceably together for each other's benefit.

Because of the ability of the fungus threads to dissolve rock and absorb mineral food, lichens can live where few other plants can gain a foothold—on bare rock; they also prevent the bright light and dry air from injuring the more delicate green Algae cells.

The green spheres, on the other hand, can do what no fungus can do: make food out of air and sunlight. So between the two of them, life is a fairly safe proposition.

Lichens are a blue gray, sometimes a silver gray, except when wet. After a rain the lichens appear bright green. You have often seen them, without knowing what they were; as curly leaf-like crusts on rocks, as crisp gray moss-like carpets on rocky ledges, or as (in the spruce forests of Maine) gray beards hanging from the limbs of trees.

A walk in the evergreen woods of northern New England will give us a chance to see many varieties of lichens. First let us see how many kinds of the curly crust-like forms there are. These grow on the bark of the trees, on rocks and boulders.

Here is a large dark-gray one, hanging from the side of a vertical cliff; the underside is black, and has a rope-like central stalk which fastens it firmly to the rock. This is ROCK TRIPE, a very common large dark-colored lichen of wet cliffs and boulders.

Nearby, on the trunk of a birch tree, we see a spreading mass of another flat lichen; this one is branched regularly by forking, and the upper surface is lighter and greener than that of the Rock Tripe. A network of ridges covers the upper surface. This lichen has the name LUNGWORT.

The smaller crust lichen of a bright yellow color, common on rocks along the seacoast, is a PARMELIA LICHEN. Some of

DWELLERS IN THE DAMP AND SHADE 107

this bright lichen is mixed with the somber gray of the others on the trunks of the fallen spruces.

Throughout these woods we have noticed gray-green threads hanging from the branches of the trees. OLD MAN'S BEARD is a very appropriate name for this lichen. It is also called BEARDED MOSS.

Old Man's Beard is a good name for this Lichen

A great many of the lichens form small busy growths varying in height from one to three inches, and covering the rocky ledges under foot with a carpet of crisp gray in dry weather and spongy light green in wet weather. These lichens are so abundant in more northern countries that they form the chief article of food for the reindeer; hence the name REINDEER MOSS.

The COMMON REINDEER MOSS forms an erect branching growth like a tiny gray tree without leaves.

The BAYONET LICHEN is a variety of Reindeer Moss, with the long slender branches sticking upwards like a mass of spears or bayonets.

The CORAL LICHEN is another variety which forms egg-shaped and rounded masses of gray, like the coral growths in tropical submarine gardens.

These lichens are all fairly large. Some of the smaller varieties, less than an inch in height, grow on stones and tree stumps; their spore-producing parts are sometimes a bright orange or scarlet.

Reindeer "Mosses" are really Lichens

The SCARLET-FRUITED LICHEN has little club-shaped erect stalks tipped with bright red.

The CUP LICHEN is a more flattened form, with cup-shaped growths on the upper surface.

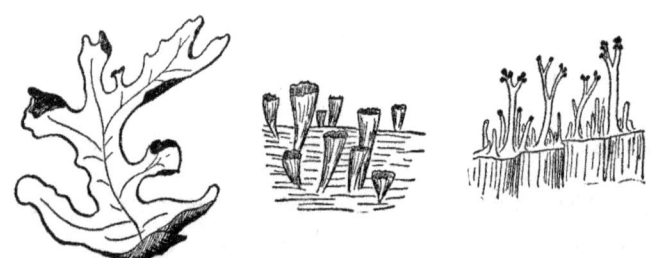

Other Lichens look like leaves, goblets, and red-tipped clubs.

There is nothing more fascinating than the variety of lichens; and I hope this introduction has been sufficient to make you keep your eyes open for them next time you take a walk in the woods, and want to know more about them.

HOW TO RECOGNIZE THE FERNS

I. If the leaf (frond) is branched into three parts,
    1. And if the fern is small; 3 inches or less high,
        it is . . . . OAK
    2. And if the fern is tall; 1 foot to 4 feet high;
        it is . . . . BRAKE

II. If the leaf (frond) is unbranched,
    1. And if the leaves are not subdivided into leaflets separate from the main stem, it is
                           SENSITIVE
    2. And If the leaves are subdivided into leaflets,
        A. With the leaflets themselves entire and finely toothed,
            a. Leaflets overlapping at the base,
                it is . . . . POLYPODY
            b. Leaflets not overlapping at the base,
                it is . . . . .CHRISTMAS
        B. With the leaflets notched deeply, it is
                CINNAMON, INTERRUPTED
        C. With the leaflets subdivided into smaller leaflets again,
            a. 2 to 5 feet tall, it is . . . . ROYAL
            b. Less than 2 feet tall, it is
                BEECH, MAIDENHAIR, HAY SCENTED, LADY, WOOD

CHAPTER 7

ANIMALS CLAD IN ARMOR

EVERY kind of animal has the same problems to solve. But these problems are different from those you find in your arithmetic book, because there often are many different correct answers to the same problem.

For example, all animals need to get their food. In order to get it they have thought out all sorts of methods of walking, creeping, crawling, jumping, flying and swimming. We call these various means of locomotion.

The problem is to get food. The solution of the problem has been worked out by every animal in his own way, and must be satisfactory or the animal would not keep alive.

Another problem is to protect the delicate inside parts of the body from injury. Some animals have solved this by putting their skeleton on the outside of their bodies; this has been mentioned in the case of the insects, and is also true of the shelled animals like the clams and oysters. Such hard parts protect very well, but they have a great disadvantage in keeping the animal from increasing in size while he grows. He has to molt or shed his shell, every time he wants to grow larger, which means getting a larger outside coat of armor.

Thus most animals have found it more satisfactory to have the skeleton inside the body; these animals are called vertebrates. Then how can they protect their delicate inner parts? Some vertebrates have nothing but a thin smooth skin

ANIMALS CLAD IN ARMOR

on the outside of their bodies, as in frogs and ourselves; such animals have to depend upon their ability to quickly escape injury and hide in the water, or to use their intelligence to make protective clothing.

Other animals protect themselves by means of feathers or fur. Animals who must move quickly cannot be encased in clumsy suits of heavy armor. Birds and mammals therefore protect themselves with flexible coverings. These serve the double purpose of retaining the warmth of the body and of protecting it from damage.

An armor of scales, overlapping like the shingles on a roof, has been adopted as a covering by the great group of water animals—the fishes. But there is a group of land animals, some of whom live in the water also, who use scales as a protection. These belong to the group of interesting animals we are to meet in this chapter—the reptiles.

Reptiles are cold-blooded vertebrates who today make up a small part of the animal population of the earth. But years ago they were far more numerous and more powerful. Long before any tiny mammals or timid birds appeared on this planet, reptiles were the rulers of the land, the sky and the ocean. These prehistoric reptiles varied in size from that of mice to whales; some of them were those terrible Dinosaurs. All that is left of these "good old days" of reptile life is the fossil bones of the mighty ones, mounted in our museums; and their living descendants, the turtles, snakes, lizards and crocodiles.

TURTLES

Few animals are as easily identified as the turtles. Nor do many other animals thrive so well in the home as pets.

Turtles require little attention and become quite tame. They eat only once or twice a week at the most, and a diet of lettuce and chopped beef keeps them happy and contented.

Being a reptile, the turtle is covered with scales, except for his head and limbs. The scales are joined together to form an efficient armor, his shell.

Turtles generally lay their eggs in the sand or mud at the edges of ponds and streams. These eggs are long and cylindrical, about an inch or less in length, the unusual softness and elasticity of the shell reminding one of rubber.

The largest of the turtles is the SNAPPING TURTLE. Some day you will find one, as you are exploring a muddy little stream in the open woods or perhaps the marshy margin of a small pond. Half buried in the mud, the olive-brown shell looks like a dirty stone; but from it projects a big ugly head. Like the snakes, this turtle strikes at an offending object with a rapid movement of the head. The powerful beak-like jaws can inflict dangerous wounds; so pick it up cautiously by the tail and with due respect stand beyond striking distance of the sharp jaws. Even though the Snapping Turtle may get its food on land, in the form of small animals and birds, it has to swallow and digest them entirely under water. It grows to a length of two feet or more, and may weigh thirty pounds. The shell is raised into three lengthwise ridges; and the rear margin of the shell is toothed. The tail has a ridge of spines along its upper surface.

All the other turtles are six inches in length or less. So if the Snapping Turtle is an adult, there is little danger of mistaking him for any other. Of the six other turtles we may find in northeastern United States, four live in the water and two are land dwellers. The four water dwellers are the Musk,

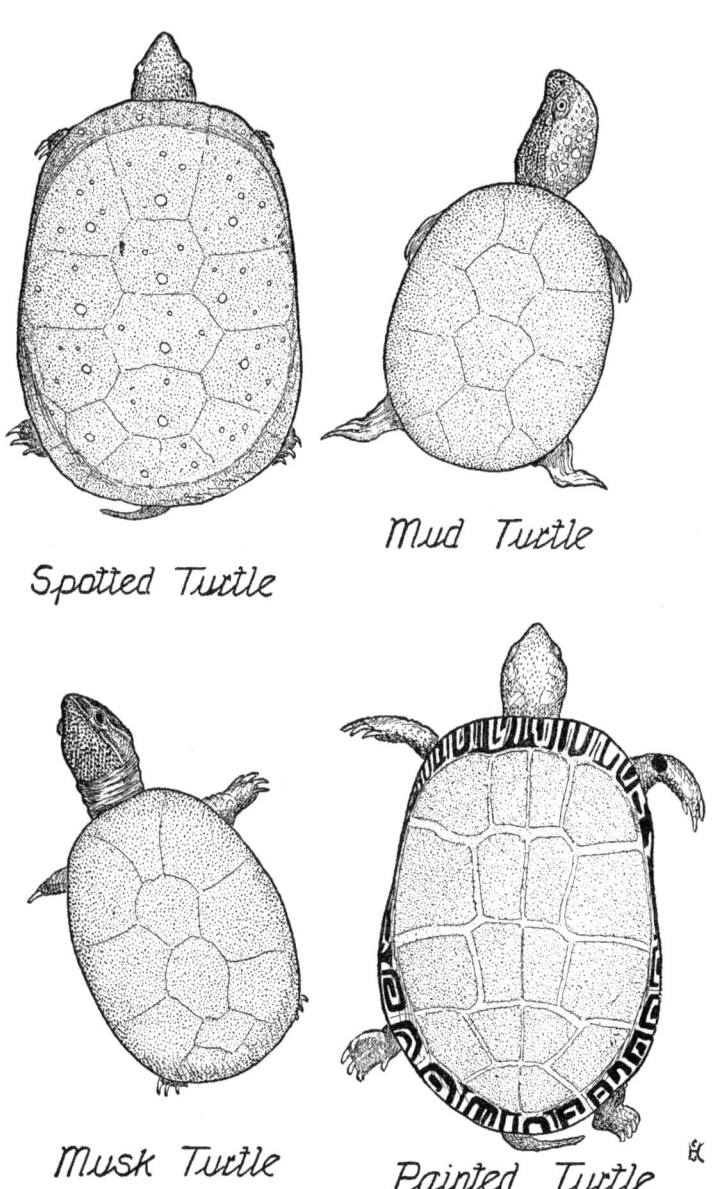

SOME COMMON TURTLES

Mud, Painted and Spotted Turtles; the two land dwellers are the Wood and the Box Turtles.

The MUSK TURTLE is a dull brown little turtle, about four inches long and inhabiting the muddy bottoms of slow streams. The fact that there are two yellow stripes on each side of the dark brown head makes it easy to recognize. At times, like the other aquatic turtles, it comes to the sunny banks or floating logs to bask and dream. Then it may be seen, and caught—if you are spry in your movements. Catching sleeping turtles isn't as easy a sport as one might imagine. They wake at the slightest sound; there is a splash, and a rocking log seems to make fun of your failure. Once a turtle is in the water it is very difficult to catch him; he is a good swimmer, and will burrow down into the muddy bottom, leaving an effective smoke screen behind him.

The MUD TURTLE is very much like the Musk Turtle in color, size and habits. Its distinguishing marks are found on the head; where, instead of yellow stripes, there are yellow spots on either side of the head and neck.

The PAINTED TURTLE is a dweller of clear ponds and lakes. The dark-greenish brown shell has a colorful border of crimson and black. The underside is a bright yellow and black. Painted Turtles make fine pets; but in an aquarium containing goldfish or newts they raise havoc. For these are the choice food of the turtle. Aquatic insects, tadpoles, fishes and water plants make up his diet in his natural surroundings.

The SPOTTED TURTLE is another pond turtle. The shell is black, marked with yellow spots. In captivity this turtle will eat lettuce leaves and raw beef. Its natural food consists of insects, caterpillars and fish. If our wanderings happen to take us to the grassy marshy meadows where streams widen

MORE TURTLES

out into quiet inlets, we may surprise many of these Spotted Turtles enjoying an afternoon nap.

The land turtles, apart from the fact that they are not found in the same places as the turtles just mentioned, are different in that their shells are marked with circular ridges in each section of the shell.

The WOOD TURTLE has raised ridges forming a sculptured pattern in each section of the shell. The top of the turtle is brown, the under parts yellow, and there is considerable red on the fleshy parts of the head and limbs. We may come across this handsome land turtle if we explore the damp woods near some swampy pond. It feeds on berries and leaves (it devours strawberries by the pound!), sometimes on insects. It can swim if need be and will retreat into the water if pursued.

Finally there is the common yet interesting BOX TURTLE. The dark brown shell is marked with yellow in an irregular pattern. The shell is much higher at its middle than that of the other turtles. Its habit of pulling in its head and limbs and closing up the hinged portion of the under shell protects it completely from its enemies. We come across Box Turtles in grassy fields and open woods. They feed on berries and leaves, but will also eat earthworms and other soft-bodied animals of like size.

SNAKES

There are no animals more universally avoided and misunderstood than snakes. Of all the popular misconceptions concerning them, let us settle two, for once and for all. They are not detestable things, slimy to touch. Instead, if we touch them, we find that they are smooth and dry; perhaps they feel cold and creepy to some people who are

ANIMALS CLAD IN ARMOR 117

not used to cold-blooded animals. Indeed, snakes are far cleaner than many animals more frequently accepted as pets. The other mistaken idea is that the forked tongue is the fangs. The red or black tongue which keeps darting in and out as the snake moves along is merely a sense organ; it can do no damage, as you can prove by letting it gently touch the palm of your hand. The fangs are specially long teeth, found in the jaws of poisonous snakes.

Of course, some snakes are dangerous, because they are poisonous or can squeeze a man to death. And there are parts of the world where such snakes are common. But in our nature ramblings along the northeastern part of the United States we do not find the snakes which inhabit the Florida swamps, the Texas deserts or the Orient. There are only two poisonous snakes, and those two are not frequent except from southern New England southward. These are the Copperhead and the Eastern Rattlesnake. Some of the other snakes are spunky enough to put up a good fight, and may strike and bite, but they have no poison fangs; and their bite is not more dangerous than that of a cat or a dog.

All snakes are entirely covered with small overlapping scales, arranged in such a way that the free edge slips over the underlying scale when the snake is in motion. Snakes are really fascinating. If you have never brought home one of these limbless reptiles and kept it as a pet for a while, you have missed observing one of the most graceful of the wild animals.

Snakes are quicker to hear you than you are to see them. So you will have to have keen eyes and a quick hand to catch the snake before he slips away in the grass or burrows his way under a pile of stones. Some people can hike all day through fields and woods and swamps and never see a snake. Perhaps they prefer not to!

The easiest way to become familiar with the snakes is to recognize them by their color. Some of them are a uniform color on their backs—such as the Black Racer, the Pilot Black Snake, the Grass Snake, the Ground Snake, the Red-bellied Snake and the Ring-necked Snake.

The BLACK RACER is the common Black Snake, which grows to be the largest of any of our eastern snakes. Specimens five and five and a half feet long are commonly seen. The color is an even slaty black, both on top and underneath, with a satin-like finish. If we are in the habit of scrambling over rocky ledges and through the underbrush of rock-strewn ravines we will have a good chance of coming across this slim and extremely swift-moving reptile. It can travel over bushes, branches, rocks and earth with lightning speed. The Black Racer eats snakes of lesser size and small mammals. When cornered, it will thrash about and fight gamely, striking at its enemy; but after a few weeks in captivity it becomes quite tame. Like most snakes, it lays its eggs (six to eight) in early summer under stones or in the soft soil of sunny banks. In September, the young snakes hatch out.

Often confused with the Black Racer is a less common snake, the PILOT BLACK SNAKE. Although black above and below, its scales are shiny and the edges are marked with white. The size is the same as that of the Black Racer, but the head is broader and more square. This snake is usually found only in rocky places, and hides in crevices of the ledges as soon as he is surprised. The Pilot Black Snake is a constrictor, that is, he kills his prey (sometimes as large as a

SOME COMMON SNAKES

cotton-tail rabbit) by squeezing it to death in his coils. This snake is of great value to farmers as a means of keeping down the numbers of rats and mice.

As we walk along a narrow wood path with the branches of the trees meeting overhead, we brush past a limb and are amazed to see one of the smaller branches become alive and glide noiselessly away. The GRASS SNAKE is a beautiful leaf green above, shading to a lighter green on its under side. It is an excellent example of how color can protect an animal. In the bushes or amid the grasses, its green color makes it invisible. It is a small, slender snake, about a foot long, and perfectly harmless. Yet I have seen big "brave" men pound one of these little snakes into pulp, with the mistaken idea that they were ridding the world of a dangerous animal. Unlike the other snakes, this Grass Snake eats insects (grasshoppers and crickets), spiders and caterpillars.

As we walk late in the evening along an overgrown wood road we may surprise a little slender gray snake slipping through the grass to escape us; he isn't more than a foot long. This is the EASTERN RING-NECKED SNAKE, a ring of yellow about his neck giving him his name. He is a retiring individual who likes to hide under flat stones during the day, and prowls about at night looking for earthworms and salamanders.

The GROUND SNAKE and the RED-BELLIED SNAKE are the smallest of our common snakes, rarely growing longer than ten or twelve inches. They are usually likewise not found in the daytime, though we have often uncovered dozens of them by turning over the stones in a rocky pasture. The abdomen of the Ground Snake is pinkish-white, while that of the Red-bellied Snake is a polished and bright red. Both these snakes eat earthworms, slugs and other soft animals.

ANIMALS CLAD IN ARMOR

All the snakes so far described have been of a uniform color—black, gray, green or brown. The remaining snakes are banded crosswise or lengthwise, or a covered with irregular spots.

There are two snakes with lengthwise yellow stripes on their otherwise brownish-black bodies. The RIBBON SNAKE, marked in this fashion with three lengthwise stripes along its back and sides, is one of our most slender snakes. Even though it grows to a length of two feet and more, its diameter rarely exceeds half an inch. We are not likely to come across this snake near civilization; it withdraws to the borders of streams and lakes in the more mountainous and unsettled parts of the country. In the damp places where it likes to live, it finds plenty of frogs and tadpoles, which make up its diet.

The common GARTER SNAKE has likewise three lengthwise yellow stripes on a black body; but it is twice the diameter of the Ribbon Snake, and grows to a slightly larger size (2 ½ to 3 feet in length). This snake is found everywhere; and there is hardly a boy or a girl who has not at some time seen these snakes in a grassy field, crossing a country road or basking on a rocky ledge. When roughly handled it will give off a milky secretion which smells offensively, but it is harmless. The Garter Snake does not lay eggs after the fashion of most of the reptiles, but has its young born alive. As many as fifty young snakes have been found as the "litter" of a mother Garter Snake. They all are fond of earthworms as a steady diet, but adults will eat frogs and toads.

The QUEEN WATER SNAKE is a brown snake with three narrow black stripes on its back, and a yellow stripe along the lower part of each side; but usually the stripes are very indistinct and the whole snake looks a dingy black or brown. The yellow abdomen has two lengthwise black stripes at the center. This snake likes to fasten itself around the limbs of low trees which grow over streams and brooks, where it can pounce upon its food of frogs and toads.

Then there are the snakes that are striped and banded crosswise. Under this heading come the common Water Snake, the Milk Snake, the Hog-nosed Snake, the Copperhead and the Rattlesnake.

The BANDED WATER SNAKE, or so-called "Moccasin," is often mistaken for a dangerous, poisonous snake because of its stout and pudgy body (an inch and a half thick to a length of three feet). One must admit that it is not a beautiful snake, but that is no reason for stoning it to death at sight. The pale brownish or gray body is crossed by wavy dark brown bands; these bands are broader on top than on the sides and bottom. It lives near the edges of streams and ponds, and makes a hasty retreat into the water when disturbed. Its food consists of fish and other water animals.

Like the Ring-necked and Ground Snakes, the MILK SNAKE is fond of hiding under stones during the brighter hours of daylight; and can be found moving about usually only towards evening. A stroll along a wood path on the outskirts of a town may make it possible to see one of these rather large and colorfully marked snakes. The gray of the back is regularly marked by brown areas edged with black; the bottom of the snake is a glossy white, spotted with black. Because this snake is commonly found around farms ad stables, where it searches for its favorite food of mice and rats, it has been slandered by the farmers as being a thief of milk from the cows. Another superstition without foundation!

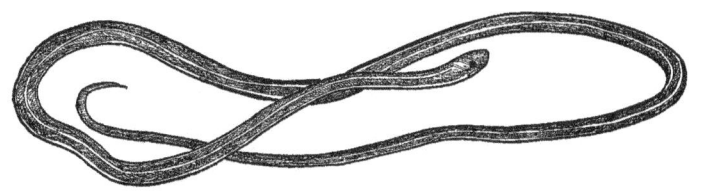

Ribbon Snake

Ground Snake

Red-bellied Snake

Ring-necked Snake

Grass Snake

MORE SNAKES

The HOG-NOSED SNAKE is a peculiar and ugly snake which may be found from southern New England southward. It is an unpleasant sight with its thick body of over an inch in diameter yet only two feet long, and with its habit of hissing, coiling and striking. Yellowish-brown in color, with irregular patches of dark brown and black, it looks uninteresting. But it has one unusual habit—that of feigning death. This is uncommon among snakes.

All the snakes thus far considered are not dangerous, even though they may assume threatening attitudes and strike or bite. There are left only two poisonous snakes common to northeastern United States—the Copperhead and the Rattlesnake.

In a hike through the swampy glades of a thickly overgrown forest where there are rocky glens and stony ledges, we may find the COPPERHEAD SNAKE. This is a moderate sized snake, usually two or three feet long, with a stout body. The body color is light reddish-brown, marked with bands of darker brown which are wider on the sides than across the top. The head often has the coppery brown color from which this snake gets its name. The Copperhead is not a vicious snake, and will try to glide away into some crack or burrow as soon as it is disturbed. Its food consists of other snakes, birds, mice and frogs. A bite by a full-grown Copperhead, if not treated, might result disastrously.

The BANDED RATTLESNAKE is a member of a notorious and widely distributed family of snakes. Our northeastern variety grows to a length of three or four feet, and thus is a moderate sized snake, as is the Copperhead. Usually the body color is yellow with wavy dark brown or black cross bands and splotches. Like the Copperhead, this snake likes mountain ledges and rocky slopes. So it is only in such localities that you will be likely to encounter one of these snakes. Unless angered or injured, neither of these two poisonous snakes will attack you; their first thought is of escape. But naturally it is well not to try to add these to your collection—unless you aspire to be a second Ditmars!

The rattle is an interesting organ, whose use has never been clearly understood. It begins as a small button on the tip of the young Rattlesnake's tail, and sections are added to it (three or four a year). It is commonly supposed that you can tell the age of a snake by the number of sections to the rattle, but this is merely another superstition. Most of the snakes thrash and vibrate their tail when disturbed, so the Rattlesnake is merely following snake custom in doing so. With the loose button inside of the section of the rattle, a loud whirring noise is produced which perhaps brings curious animals within reach.

The fangs are two large teeth which can be bared of their covering of flesh when the snake wishes to do so. The poison is contained in little sacs above the hollow fangs. Thus the poison is injected in the prey as the fangs pierce the flesh.

It is unfortunate that, because of a few members of the group, the whole class of snakes should be considered dangerous and deadly. As we have seen, most of our snakes are harmless, beautiful and interesting. So even if you do not become a snake-enthusiast after reading this chapter, let us hope that you will at least restrain yourself—and others—from killing every snake you chance to meet.

HOW TO RECOGNIZE THE TURTLES

I. If the turtle is more than eight inches long, with a ridge of spines on the tail, it is . . . . . SNAPPING TURTLE

II. If the turtle is six inches or less in length, with no spiny tail,
   1. And if the shell is smooth,
      A. With no other color than black on the shell
         a. With yellow stripes on the side of the head, it is . . . . MUSK TURTLE
         b. With yellow spots on the side of the head, it is . . . . MUD TURTLE
      B. With spots or margin coloring,
         a. With a border of orange and red, it is . . . . PAINTED TURTLE
         b. With yellow spots all over the shell, it is . . . . SPOTTED TURTLE
   2. And if the shell is rough, and raised into sculptured ridges,
      A. With the turtle able to close up its shell like a box, it is . . . . BOX TURTLE
      B. Without being able to close up its shell, it is, ... WOOD TURTLE

ANIMALS CLAD IN ARMOR

HOW TO RECOGNIZE THE SNAKES

I. If the color is uniform, without stripes or spots,
    1. And if the color is black, it is
        BLACK RACER, PILOT BLACK SNAKE
    2. And if the color is bright green, it is . . . .
        GRASS SNAKE
    3. And if it is brown, on the back,
      A. But bright red on the stomach, it is . . . .
        RED-BELLIED SNAKE
      B. But not red underneath, it is . . . .
        GROUND SNAKE
    4. And if it is gray, with a yellow ring around its neck, it is . . . . RING-NECKED SNAKE

II. If there are stripes or spots on the snake,
    1. And if the stripes run lengthwise,
      A. On a body half an inch in diameter, it is . . . . RIBBON SNAKE
      B. On a body an inch in diameter, it is . . .
        GARTER SNAKE
    2. And if the stripes run crosswise,
      A. On a thick, clumsy body, it is . . . . . .
        BANDED WATER SNAKE
      B. On a more slender, graceful body,
        a. With rattles on the tail, it is . . . . .
          RATTLESNAKE
        b. Without rattles, but with a coppery brown head, it is . . . . COPPERHEAD
        c. Without rattles, but with a gray head, it is . . . . MILK SNAKE

CHAPTER 8

OUR FURRY FRIENDS

IT is a rare treat in these days of the rapid disappearance of our wild life to come upon some furry animal in the woods. Insects, birds, an occasional frog or turtle or snake, greet us on our rambles through forests and fields. But the furry animals are distrustful of man—and rightly so, perhaps. So as man invades the woods with his camps and summer homes, the large fur-bearing animals disappear.

These furry animals are called mammals. To many people, the two words are the same. We hear people say, for instance, that they saw some fish, some birds and a few animals on their nature walk. All living things which are not plants, are animals; so that a starfish or an earthworm is as much an animal as a whale or a lion.

Mammals are a particular kind of animal; an animal with fur. Thus they are contrasted with the Birds, which have feather; or the Reptiles and Fishes, which have scales. Some mammals have fur only when very young, as the Elephant or the Whale. But they all feed their young with milk from the mother; this is really the true test of a mammal. Another characteristic of a mammal is that in general it has greater intelligence than any other animal. Though perhaps if insects or reptiles had schools and wrote books, they might dispute this claim.

Mammals live in all three kinds of surroundings which are

OUR FURRY FRIENDS 129

possible for animals; on land, in the water and in the air. Since only one mammal which we will discuss is in each of the last two groups, let us consider them first.

The SEAL is a mammal which has become adapted to living in the water. As a result its feet and legs have changed into flippers and the shape of the body has become that of a streamlined water dweller. In the water he is very much at home, being able to swim and dive perfectly. But having lungs, he has to come up to the top for air every so often; which is something a fish does not need to do. Perhaps some of you have been able to get near enough to a seal family sleeping on the rocks of the Maine coast, so that you could hear their dog-like bark when they were aroused, and could see their awkward shuffling over the wet rocks in their haste to reach the water. Grown-up seals are deep brown or black, but the babies are white and have large black eyes which stare at you curiously if you are lucky enough to get close to them.

The BAT is a mammal which has become adapted to living in the air. Its front limbs, or arms, form the framework of leathery wings; and the whole body is made as light as possible, thus resembling that of a bird. Bats sleep during the day, hanging upside down in some dark corner of the roof. But at night they become very active, and fly about very well when one realizes that they are blind. Hairs about their head are so sensitive to slight movements of the air, that the bat feels an object before he reaches it; and dives suddenly up or down, or dodges to the right or left, to avoid it.

The surface-dwelling land mammals, some of whom, like the Beaver and Muskrat, have adapted themselves to a partial water existence, are separated into different groups according to their teeth and feet. The grass-eating hoofed mammals which one might meet in the woods are the Deer and the Moose. The majority of the wild mammals belong to the Cat and Dog family, or to the family of gnawing mammals known as Rodents. They have clawed feet and are either vegetarians or meat eaters.

The DEER needs no description. Enough to say that the nature wanderer who has not caught a glimpse of an alert head with erect ears, above the bushes in some forest glade, and the flash of golden brown as the fleet animal takes to his heels, has missed one of the real treats the animal world has to offer.

The Raccoon, the Weasel, the Skunk, the Fox and the Wild Cat are members of the Cat and Dog family, known as carnivorous animals. This long word means flesh-eating.

The RACCOON is a southern mammal, with coarse brown and white fur which is often made into coats for people. Raccoons like to stay up in the trees, and often make their homes in hollow trunks.

The WEASEL is a long slinky animal with short legs; it is the natural counterpart of the Dachshund. The Weasel is a killer, and does considerable damage to chickens and other small domesticated animals of the farm. In summer his coat is brown, but in winter it changes to a spotless white; thus nature helps her own to protect themselves from their enemies. It can often be caught running into the convenient hollows in broken-down stone walls.

The SKUNK is a mammal as much misunderstood as the snakes among the reptiles. This "pussy" with its long black hair, marked by stripes, is often seen (or smelt?) in the woods. Unless startled or pursued, it does not give off the evil-smelling liquid which has given the Skunk such a bad name.

OUR FURRY FRIENDS

Many persons have tamed Skunks, and say that they make excellent pets.

FOXES, particularly the Red Fox, are less common than they were ten or twenty years ago. Their dens may often be found in rocky sides of ravines; or the penetrating odor of the bodies may be perceived along a forest trail. But it is rare good luck to be able to get a close-up view of Mr. Fox himself; he really is quite as clever an animal as stories make him out to be.

The WILD CAT, and its close relative the Canada Lynx, look like a big overgrown cat; it has an unusually small head, and the gray and white stripings of the domestic tiger cat. This mammal, also, has retreated to the wilder parts of our New York and New England mountain regions; and is rarely seen about civilized resorts.

Most of the familiar mammals, however, belong to the Rodent group. These have shark gnawing teeth, with which they do considerable damage in girdling trees and destroying shrubs and crops. In this group there are such old friends as the Red Squirrel, the Gray Squirrel, the Chipmunk, the Flying Squirrel, the Meadow Mouse, the Jumping Mouse, the Rabbit and the Porcupine.

The RED SQUIRREL is the common squirrel of the more northern woods; he is smaller and more destructive of birds' eggs than his southern gray cousin. The noisy chatter with which he greets any human intruder, and the neat little piles of cone scales which he leaves on stones and stumps in the forests, are familiar to anyone who has explored the woods of northern New England.

The GRAY SQUIRREL is the common squirrel of southern New England, New York and states farther south. Instead of feeding on spruce and pine cones, he chooses acorns and other nuts.

Both of these squirrels are clever climbers, and their sharp claws aid them in running up and down tree trunks, and in landing without falling when they leap from tree to tree. But the FLYING SQUIRREL goes them one better; he spreads out his hind legs after he jumps, and a flap of skin from the front to the hind leg, close to the body, acts as a plane and helps him to glide farther than his two relatives could hope to get.

The CHIPMUNK is a tiny dweller of the dark forests, differing from the Red Squirrel by having black stripes along his back; in addition he is a smaller animal. Chipmunks do little harm, and are interesting companions in a summer camp.

The common MEADOW MOUSE, sleek and gray underneath and brown above, is more often seen than caught. Once we captured a whole family, one winter, entirely by accident. A large dead chestnut, several feet in diameter, was being sawed into lengths for fireplace wood. When one of those sections was split in half, after being brought in the cellar, a cozy little nest made of down and fiber was uncovered. In it were curled up three sleepy-eyed and much surprised little Meadow Mice.

The JUMPING MOUSE is a peculiar little fellow, reminding one of a tiny kangaroo. The hind legs are very long; so long that when he is "sitting" he rests on half of his leg. As well as scurrying about, he jumps, covering unexpectedly long distances in each hop.

The PORCUPINE makes life interesting—and miserable—for all hikers and campers in the woods. The long black hair, with the sharp spines scattered among the fur, distinguishes him from all other mammals. Contrary to popular stores, he does not shoot his quills; but he can stiffen them so suddenly, and they are so loosely attached at their bottom ends, that if your hand is near the porcupine when he does raise his quills, the chances are they will stick in you and leave him. Porcupines are very inquisitive, and love domestic fare; thus they are easily caught and can be kept a short time in captivity.

CHAPTER 9

SOME TELL-TALE LEAVES

THE most obvious part of the woods and fields in summer, is the leaves. Here and there flowers and fruits appear amid the leaves; a few twigs and tree trunks show themselves. But summer is almost entirely a disguise of leaves.

Let us try to collect these leaves into groups, so that there will be some rhyme and reason to how we would go about identifying the common trees and shrubs by the leaves, alone.

In a later chapter we will talk about the evergreen leaves of pines and cedars; so for now let us consider only the broad, thin, flat leaves of the trees which are leafless in winter.

The first thing we notice is that some leaves are a single broad blade, while other leaves are subdivided into leaflets. The former leaves are called "simple," and the latter "compound." The leaves of a maple or an oak are simple; those of a sumac or a locust are compound.

Then there is another big difference in leaves; some of them have edges which are notched and toothed like the cutting edge of a saw, while others are smooth. We can call the former "toothed," and the latter "toothless." Simple leaves may be either toothed or toothless; and compound leaves may be either toothed or toothless. Dogwood is a simple toothless leaf; Maple is a simple toothed leaf.

A third difference between leaves is whether they are attached to the stem or twig singly, or in pairs. If only one leaf

SOME TELL-TALE LEAVES

grows out of the twig, it is called an alternate leaf. If two or more leaves grow out at the same level on the twig, they are called opposite leaves.

In identifying trees by the leaves, it is well to keep these three characteristics in mind. Decide first whether the leaves are alternate or opposite; then whether they are simple or compound; and lastly whether they are toothed or toothless. That will give us an outline to follow, something like this:

Leaves alternately arranged on the stem—
1. Leaves simple—
   a. Leaves toothless
   b. Leaves toothed
2. Leaves compound—
   a. Leaves toothless
   b. Leaves toothed

Leaves oppositely arranged on the stem—
1. Leaves simple—
   a. Leaves toothless
   b. Leaves toothed
2. Leaves compound—
   a. Leaves toothless
   b. Leaves toothed

As we collect the leaves, let us try to fit them into these eight groups.

ALTERNATE SIMPLE LEAVES

In this group we find, among the toothless leaves, the Oaks, Tulip, Sassafras, and Tupelo; among the toothed leaves the Willows, Poplars, Hazel, Birches, Elm, Mulberry, Sycamore, Cherry, Pear and Apple.

The OAK leaves are all lobed; that is, there are projecting parts of the margin with incurved portions between. Some of the Oaks have bristle-like points at the tips of the lobes; this is true of the Red Oak, Pin Oak, Scarlet Oak and Black Oak. Other Oaks, like the White Oak, Swamp White Oak, Post Oak and Chestnut Oak, lack these bristles at the tip of each lobe.

The RED OAK leaf is four to seven inches long, and the many-pointed lobes are not separated by as deep notches as in the case of the following three oaks:

The PIN OAK leaf, three to five inches long, is very deeply cut into two or three narrow lobes on each side.

The SCARLET OAK leaf is the same size as the Red Oak, but is more deeply notched and is divided into seven narrow lobes, each one many-pointed.

The BLACK OAK leaf is also the same size as the Red Oak, but is divided into only three lobes on each side, and the lobes are not as many-pointed.

The preceding four oaks have bristle-tipped lobes; the following ones lack these bristles.

The WHITE OAK leaf, four to seven inches long, is shaped like a long ellipse; and the margin is divided into seven to nine rounded lobes. The base of the leaf is wedge-shaped.

The SWAMP WHITE OAK has the largest leaf of all these oaks, reaching a length of eight inches. It is broad at the base and tapering towards the tip; the margin is scalloped into shallow rounded lobes.

The POST OAK has a peculiar leaf, which, though the size of the White Oak leaf, is strikingly different in being wider at the top than at the bottom. There are five or seven broad lobes, wavy along their margins.

The CHESTNUT OAK has a leaf like the now rare Chestnut tree; it is five to seven inches long, and elliptical. The edge of the leaf has a wavy series of shallow scallops.

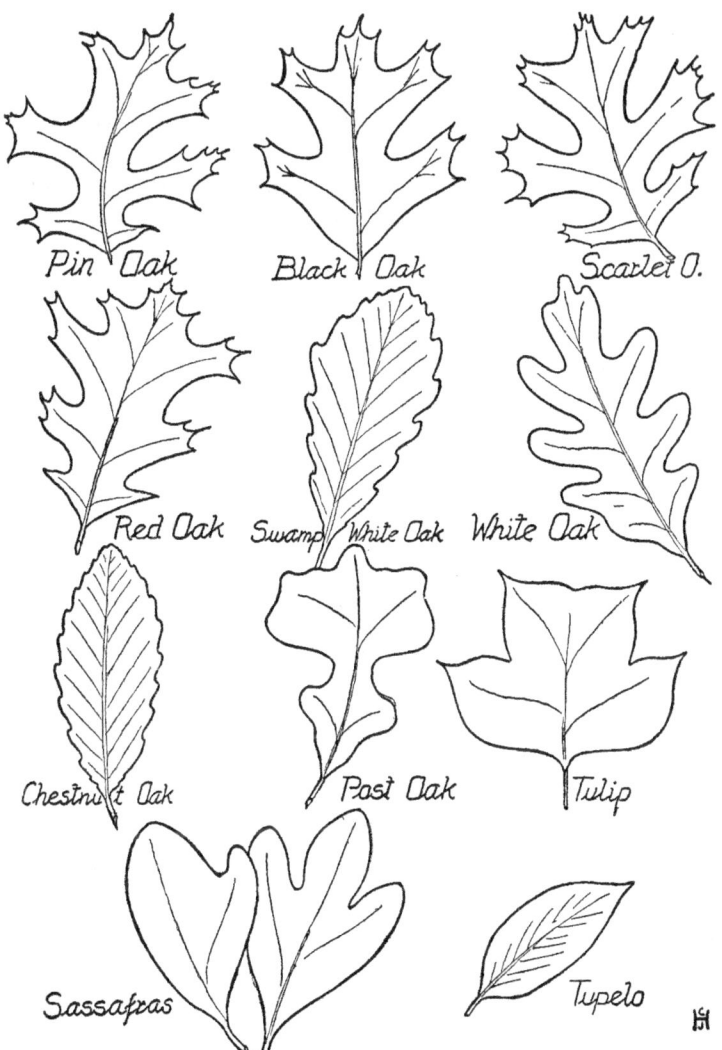

SIMPLE ALTERNATE LEAVES WITHOUT TEETH

The TULIP TREE leaf is a lighter and yellower green than most leaves; it is divided into four sharply defined lobes, the two upper ones being square across the top.

The SASSAFRAS leaf seems to have some difficulty about making up its mind as to what kind of a leaf it is going to be. Some Sassafras leaves are oval and have no lobes at all. Others have a large and a little lobe, making them look like mittens. While still others have three lobes.

And the last of these simple alternate leaves which are toothless, is the TUPELO or SOUR GUM. These leaves are oval and small, with a pointed tip; generally there are not even slight scallops along the margin, which is therefore called "entire."

Those simple alternate leaves with teeth along their margin include a great many of the common trees, as we have already mentioned.

The BLACK WILLOW has long narrow leaves, two to four inches long; rounded at the base and quite pointed at the tip. The teeth are very small and fine.

The shrubby PUSSY WILLOW has leaves three to four inches long, broader than those of the Black Willow. The teeth are not so sharp and are so far apart that at times they give a scalloped edge to the leaf.

The HAZEL NUT is a shrub, sometimes a small tree, with heart-shaped leaves which are abruptly pointed and edged with irregular notches as well as fine teeth.

The WHITE POPLAR has leaves two to four inches long, with a wavy edge divided into five or more dull points. The heart-shaped leaf is somewhat flattened at the base.

The ASPEN POPLAR, also called the QUAKING ASPEN, has a small broadly heart-shaped leaf with a fine toothed

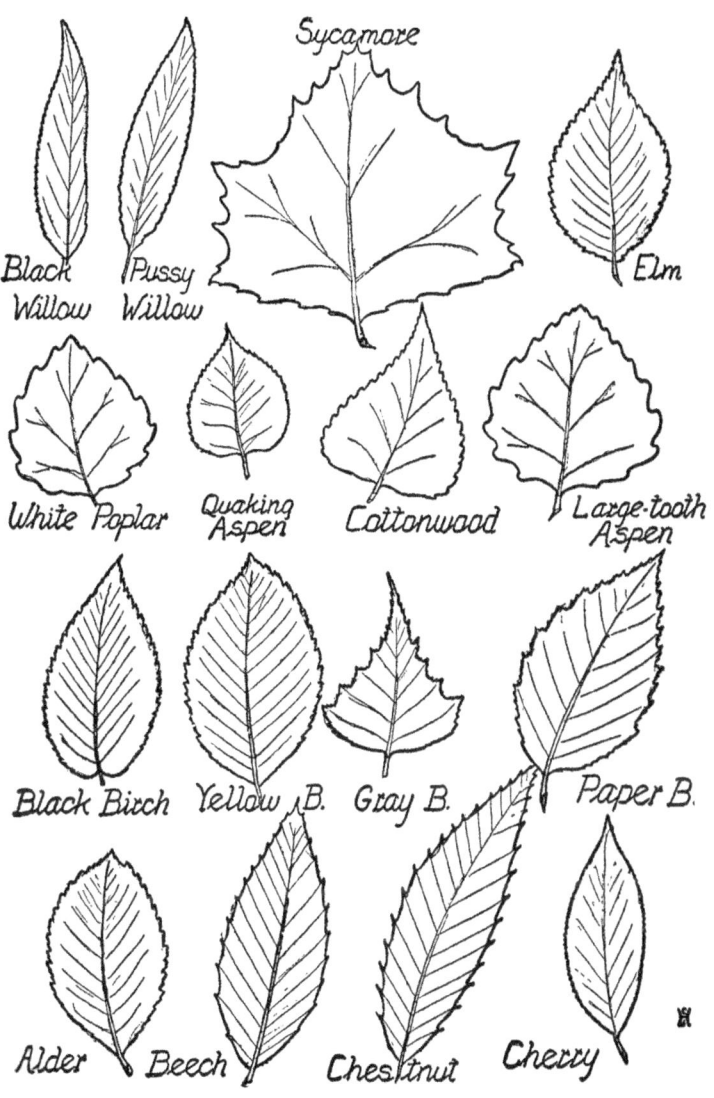

SIMPLE ALTERNATE LEAVES WITH TEETH

The flattened stems allow the leaves to tremble in the slightest breeze; hence the name.

The leaf of the LARGE TOOTHED ASPEN is twice the size of the preceding leaf, with larger and coarser teeth forming a wavy margin.

The COTTONWOOD POPLAR has a triangular leaf, broad and flat at the base; the edge of the leaf is divided into coarse rounded teeth.

Then there are the leaves of the Birches. If we can see the trunk of the tree, we rarely are mistaken; for the horizontal marks which occur on the bark, whether it peels or not, are very distinctive. The leaves of the Black and Yellow Birch are much alike; they are both oval and pointed at the tip. The leaves of the Gray and Paper Birches are triangular with a flat base.

The BLACK BIRCH leaf is heart-shaped at the base, and has a double-toothed margin.

The YELLOW BIRCH leaf has the same double-toothed margin, but is broader and shorter than that of the Black Birch.

The leaf of the PAPER BIRCH, also called WHITE BIRCH, is broadly oval and pointed at the tip, rounded at the base. The margin is cut up into six notches, each of which is edged with fine teeth.

The GRAY BIRCH has the smallest leaf of all the Birches; it is triangular, with a five-notched margin, which has a saw-tooth edge like that of the Paper Birch.

The very familiar ELM leaf is oval, and ends in an abrupt point; it is smaller than most leaves, being two to four inches long. The margin is regularly double toothed.

The ALDER is a shrub, sometimes a small tree, with a broad elliptical leaf which is irregularly double toothed.

SOME TELL-TALE LEAVES

Perhaps the largest of all the leaves which are simple and alternate, are the leaves of the SYCAMORE or Buttonball Tree. They are four to nine inches wide, and divided into five angles; between the angles are several coarse teeth.

The CHERRY has a long elliptical leaf which is sharply pointed and edged with fine rounded teeth.

ALTERNATE COMPOUND LEAVES

Only two trees have compound leaves which are alternate and toothless; the Locust and the Poison Sumac.

The HONEY LOCUST leaf has 18 to 22 small leaflets; each leaflet being a long oval with a wavy edge.

The POISON SUMAC leaf has 17 to 23 small leaflets; each leaflet being elliptical and pointed, with a toothless wavy margin. This shrub grows in low wet places, such as swamps and poorly drained meadows; the common Staghorn Sumac is the one usually met with, and fortunately has no poisonous effects.

The alternate compound leaves which have toothed margins are the Staghorn Sumac, the Mountain Ash, the Butternut, the Walnut, the Hickories and the Horse Chestnut.

The STAGHORN SUMAC leaf is subdivided into 11 to 21 long leaflets, pointed and with sharply toothed margins.

The MOUNTAIN ASH leaf has 13 to 15 elliptical leaflets, which taper to a point and are double-toothed along their margins.

The BUTTERNUT leaf usually has 11 leaflets, but the number may vary from 7 to 17. Each leaflet is rather bluntly lance-shaped, with shallow teeth along the margin.

The BLACK WALNUT has a compound leaf which may have from 11 to 17 leaflets, each leaflet being more or less heart-shaped

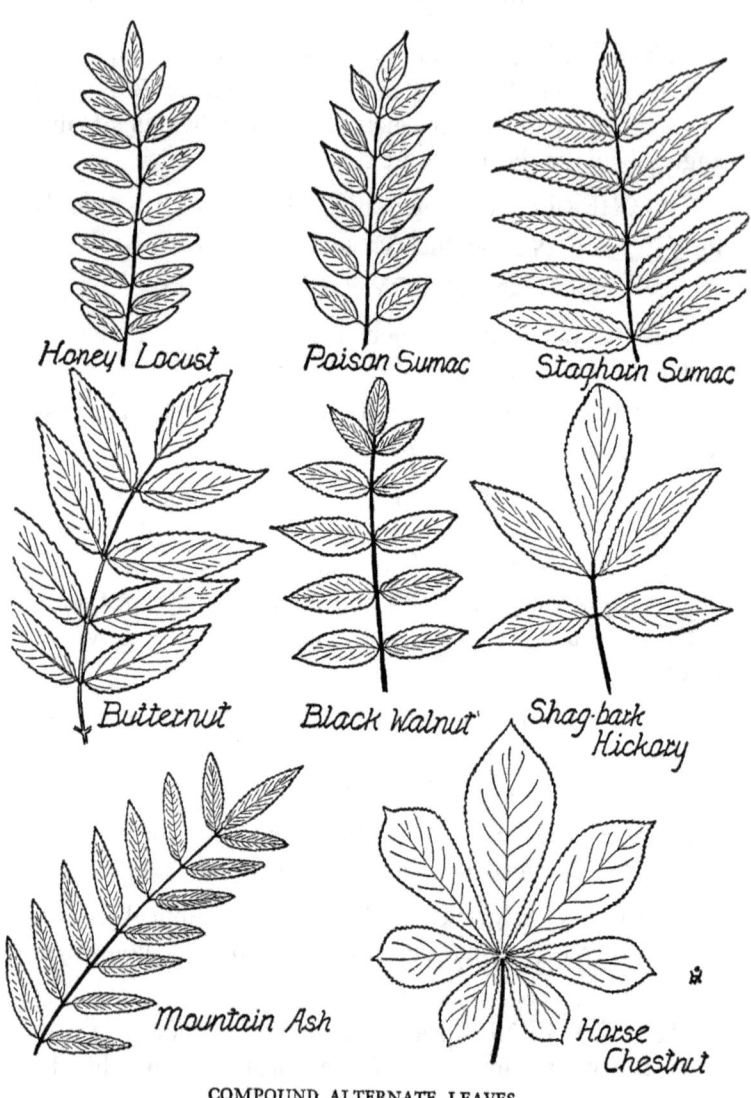

COMPOUND ALTERNATE LEAVES

SOME TELL-TALE LEAVES

at the base and broader than those of the preceding trees. The margin of the leaflets is very slightly toothed.

The SHAG-BARK HICKORY has a broad and large compound leaf divided into 5 to 7 leaflets; the three upper leaflets usually look different from the others, being more tapering towards the base and less oval in outline. The edge of the leaflet is delicately toothed.

The HORSE CHESTNUT is the only tree of this group with its compound leaf circular in outline rather than long and narrow. The seven wedge-shaped leaflets radiate out from the center; they are coarsely toothed.

OPPOSITE SIMPLE LEAVES

Not many trees have leaves of this type; the toothless varieties are found in the Dogwood and Catalpa, and the toothed ones among the Maples.

The FLOWERING DOGWOOD leaf is gracefully oval in outline, ending in a prolonged tip; the margin is without teeth or scallops.

The CATALPA leaves are very large, averaging six inches or more in length. They are distinctly heart-shaped, ending in a long point.

The STRIPED MAPLE, or Moosewood, is a tree of the more northern woodlands. Its leaf is large—four to six inches long; usually divided into three sharp lobes, with the entire margin sharply toothed with many fine small teeth.

The MOUNTAIN MAPLE is a tall shrub which sometimes grows to the size of a small tree; its leaves are a lighter yellower green than those of the Striped Maple, and are smaller. Usually three-lobed, the leaves at times have two additional small

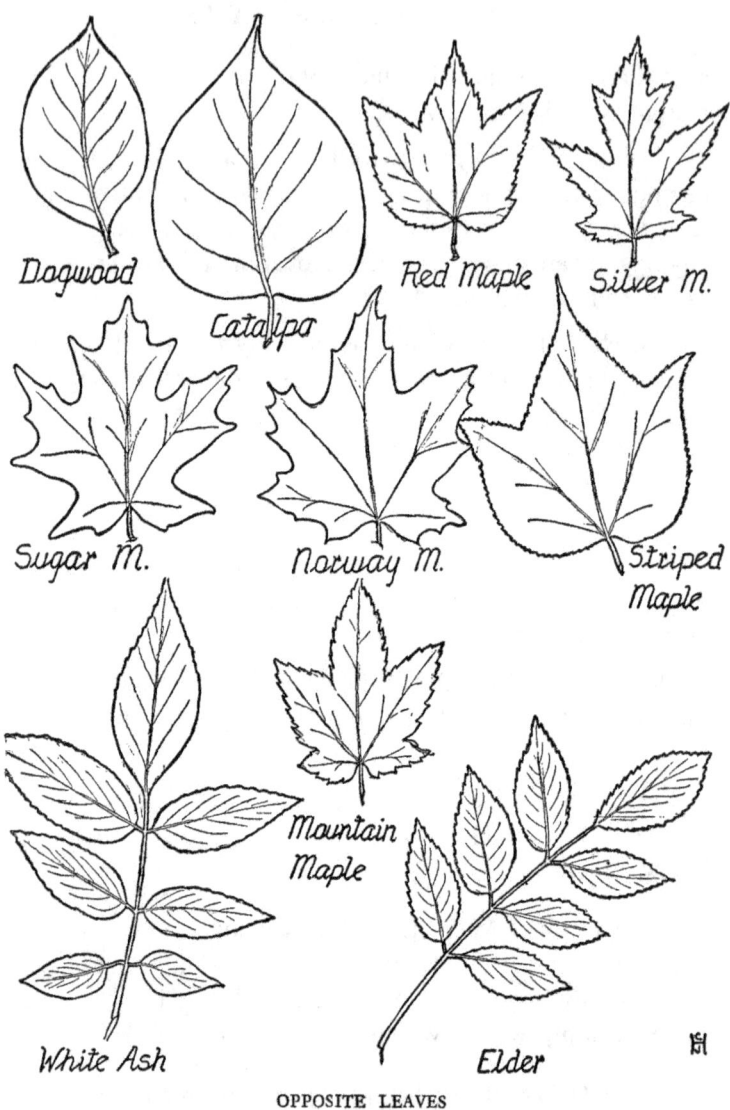

OPPOSITE LEAVES

SOME TELL-TALE LEAVES

lobes at the base of the leaf. The edge is made up of large rounded teeth.

The SUGAR MAPLE leaf is usually five-lobed, sometimes three-lobed. Each pointed lobe is divided into shallow scallops and rounded projections.

The SILVER MAPLE has five-lobed leaves, with the notches between each lobe very deep; the result is a less solid-appearing leaf than the other maples. The margin of the leaves is sharply toothed.

The RED MAPLE, or SWAMP MAPLE, leaves are three-lobed and broad, sharp pointed and double-toothed. These leaves are a bright red when in bud; and also form a great part of the solid masses of red found among the swamp trees in autumn.

The NORWAY MAPLE is a European tree which is so common about towns that we ought to mention it here. The leaves are broad and five lobed, like those of the Sugar Maple.

OPPOSITE COMPOUND LEAVES

There are only two common trees with leaves of this type.

The WHITE ASH leaf is made up of 5 to 9 leaflets, the margin of each leaflet being barely irregular enough to call it "sparingly toothed."

The ELDER is a big shrub with compound leaves, made up of 5 to 11 leaflets which are broader and more noticeably toothed than those of the Ash.

In reading over this chapter, I feel that it is most uninspiring and unexciting. However, it cannot be helped; to make a list of leaves, putting them into related groups, is hardly a thrilling pastime. But I am sure that if you make a leaf collection, and identify the leaves as I have suggested, your walks in the future will reveal to you many friends among the trees and shrubs hitherto unknown to you.

CHAPTER 10
EXPLORING AT THE SEA SHORE

THE plant life of the ocean is very different from that of the land. On land, the plants need roots to absorb mineral food; need woody stems to act as a skeleton and keep the plant from collapsing; and have specialized parts like leaves to make food for the rest of the plant. Most of the land plants also have flowers and seeds.

The plants of the ocean live in a narrow zone from high tide mark down to perhaps a hundred feet or so below tide mark. Deeper than that very few plant are able to live, due to the dim violet light which is too faint to support vegetable life. Because they are buoyed up by the water, these plants need no woody stems; and because they are bathed by water rich in food minerals, they need no roots; and instead of having leaves, the whole plant acts as a leaf. None of them have flowers or seeds; they form spores, as in the case of the ferns and mosses.

These salt-water plants are commonly called seaweeds and sea-mosses; their real name is Algae. All the Algae are green, and can make food the way leaves do it; but in some cases this green color is covered over by brown, red, purple or black pigments. All the green seaweeds grow in the upper regions of the sea, where the sunlight is very bright. They are found therefore around high tide mark; rarely below low tide mark. The seaweeds which are brown in color—sometimes olive brown or black—grow below the green seaweeds; they prefer the light of medium brightness which is found from low tide mark to a depth of ten or twenty feet. It is the brown seaweeds which form a slippery covering completely disguising the rocks around low tide mark. Deepest down in the ocean depths are found the delicate moss-like Red Algae; after a storm they are often found tossed up on the beach in tangled mats.

Just as the plants of the ocean are very different from land plants, so are the animals of the sea. The seals and other marine mammals, as well as the fishes, will have to be omitted from this chapter; otherwise it would become a book instead of a chapter. The rest of the animals belong to the big group known as Invertebrates; that is, they have no bones as a skeleton.

The sea shells are the most familiar of these; the animals which lived in the shells are seldom seen. These shelled animals are called Mollusks. They can be found on sandy and muddy beaches, and attached to the rocks. In like situations we find the crab and lobster animals; these belong to the group known as Crustaceans. But ocean life is not made up merely of Mollusks and Crustaceans; there are worms, starfishes, sea urchins, jelly fish and corals—just to mention a few.

PLANT LIFE AT THE SEASHORE

The GREEN SEA LETTUCE looks more like the torn leaves of a plant, than a plant in itself. It is a thin flat green plant without roots, stems or leaves; it tears into ragged fragments which may drift about in the quiet waters of bays and harbors. When attached, it is found on rocks, wharves and even pebbly bottoms between tide marks.

EXPLORING AT THE SEASHORE

THE GREEN SILKWEED is found in the same sort of places, but instead of being a thin broad leaf-like plant, it resembles a tangled mat of green threads. Some of the threads are thick and coarse. It is generally found floating about in tidal pools or harbors.

THE GREEN MERMAID'S TRESSES, on the other hand, is a silky thread-like mass which is almost always found attached

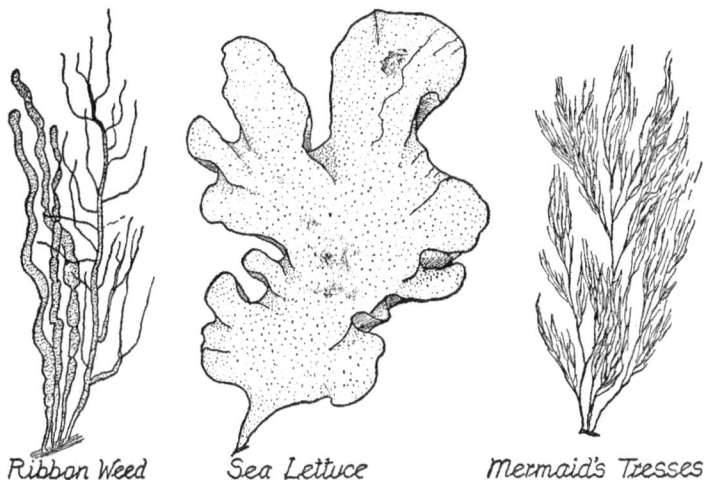

Ribbon Weed   Sea Lettuce   Mermaid's Tresses

Green Seaweeds grow between tide marks.

to rocks and woodwork between tide marks. Mermaid's Tresses form dainty tufts and plumes in the tidal pools left amid rocks when the tide goes out.

A fourth green seaweed which is common in rock pools and on wharves, is the RIBBON WEED. Instead of being made up of thin threads, the plant is a branching cluster of inflated cylindrical tubes. It is like the Sea Lettuce in being thin and glossy green; differing from it in being tube-like instead of flat.

The brown seaweeds are very abundant in cold water; so

the farther north one goes along the coast (or the colder the ocean currents get) the bigger and more abundant are the brown Algae. Most of them are found north of Cape Cod.

There is a silky, thread-like brown seaweed which is the counterpart of the Green Silkweed; only it is a golden brown. This can be called the BROWN SILKWEED. It grows on stones, woodwork and wharf piles mixed with the green seaweeds. Often it forms a plush-like coating on spars and buoys.

By far the commonest seaweed of a rocky coast is the BLADDERWRACK, or ROCKWEED. This olive-green to brownish-black seaweed grows in dense mats around the low tide mark. The swollen bulbs, or bladders, on the forking plant body being familiar to anyone who has explored the seashore. The secretion of a sticky slime which coats the plants makes walking on rocks overgrown with these seaweeds a test of skill. There are two varieties; the FLAT ROCKWEED has flattened branches, while the ROUND ROCKWEED is a darker, tougher plant, of a more stringy appearance due to the rounded branches.

In deeper waters one can find the Kelps; or often they are washed ashore after a storm. This seaweed is of great importance, in many parts of the world being harvested as a source of minerals and for fertilizer.

The COMMON KELP has a long leathery stalk and a thinner banner-like blade which often is ten feet long or more. The base of the stalk forms a root-like clasping organ which very effectively anchors the plant to the stony bottom.

The HENWARE is a Kelp which is readily recognized by the groups of leaf-like blades which grow out from either side of the stalk, just below the long blade which forms the bulk of the plant. The whole plant is usually so torn into fragments by storms and waves that little of the original plant is visible.

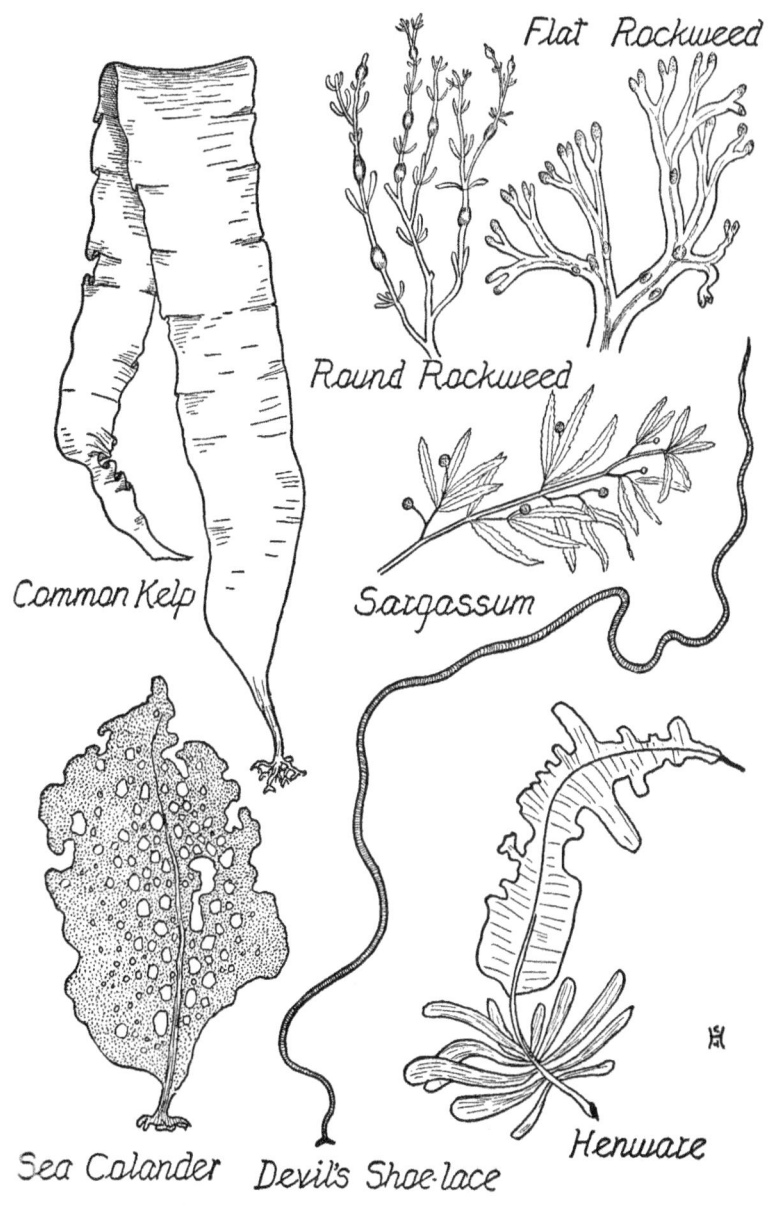

SOME BROWN SEAWEEDS

The SEA COLANDER is another Kelp, of a deeper and blacker brown and very stiff. Its blade is very broad and perforated by dozens of holes of varying sizes. Another name for it is Devil's Apron.

While we are on the subject of Devils we might mention another brown seaweed, the DEVIL'S SHOE-LACE. This is a long rope-like seaweed, less than half an inch in diameter and many feet long. When discovered attached, in waving submarine meadows below low tide mark, it looks like a field of grass.

These green and brown seaweeds can often be found growing attached to rocks and pebbles between tide marks; but most of the red seaweeds either have to be dredged up or collected from the masses of drift which accumulate on any beach.

The exception to this is the IRISH MOSS. This little purplish-brown seaweed forms short busy growths on stones and logs below low tide mark.

The thread-like red seaweeds may be varieties of NIGGER HAIR, PITCHER WEED, or RED THREAD WEED; it is difficult to recognize these smaller and more delicate forms without a microscope.

Some of the red seaweeds are thin flattened leaf-like plants of the Sea Lettuce type. DELESSERIA is such a plant, suffering greatly for the want of a common name.

These are a few of the sea plants upon which the sea animals feed, and among which we will find many of the animals described in the latter part of this chapter. If you are interested in collecting these unusual plants, you can do so without much trouble; for these seaweeds have enough gelatine on them to enable them to stick to mounting paper without the addition of glue or paste. Take the seaweed and float it out in a shallow pan, until all the dirt and extra material are washed off and the seaweed is in the shape you desire. Then slide a piece of glass or sheet of metal with a piece of mounting paper on top of it, under the floating seaweed. Lift the seaweed, paper and glass carefully out of the water, and you will find the plant spread out on the paper. Then place a piece of cheesecloth over the specimen to absorb the surplus water, put between blotting paper and press under a weight. When dry, the pressed specimen will stick to the paper and keep its color for years.

ANIMAL LIFE AT THE SEASHORE

In searching for seashore animals, let us divide our trip into three parts; first, an exploration of the underwater part of wharves and the encrusted poles which support piers; second, a ramble over a rocky headland at low tide; and third, a survey of what can be found on a sandy or muddy beach, also at low tide.

To one who has never before seen any forms of ocean life, a study of the sides of a floating wharf or the dripping piles beneath a pier brings many surprises.

Amid a green and brown profusion of Sea Lettuce, Ribbon Weed and Silkweed, with perhaps some Brown Silkweed and Rockweed thrown in for good measure, we see dozens of Starfish of every size and color; numerous spiny Sea Urchins; delicately colored Sea Anemones; and floating pale Jelly-Fishes and Comb-Jellies.

The COMMON STARFISH is a five-armed animal with his skeleton outside of the fleshy parts; the outer covering is armed with many short spines and bumps, and varies in color from pink, yellow and brown to darker shades. Large specimens reach a diameter of a foot or fifteen inches. This starfish can be found around and below low tide mark from Long Island Sound northwards. South of Long Island, it is replaced by a relative known as FORBES' STARFISH, with blunter tips and swollen arms. Starfish do great damage in oyster beds, for the oyster is their favorite food.

The BRITTLE STAR is a variety of starfish found in shallow water, with long thin snake-like arms and a rounded central disk. Their other name of Sea Spider describes their general appearance. These unusual members of the Star Fish group are found only on the North Atlantic coast.

Sticking to the lower portions of the wharf posts, and covering the muddy bottom of the harbor, are numerous green and greenish-purple rounded burrs. Each one looks like a stone or some other lifeless mass, covered with spiny growth. But these SEA URCHINS can move when they want to; by using the spines on their underside they make fairly good progress in or out of the water. And if you are unfortunate enough to step on some of these when barefoot, the stinging remembrance of the Sea Urchin's spines will be with you for several days.

The Star Fishes and the Sea Urchins are able to move about on the posts and stonework; not so, the plant-like SEA ANEMONES. These peculiar animals are rooted fast by their lower ends. At the top of the cylindrical body is a large mouth opening, surrounded by a fringe of tentacles which look like the petals of a flower. Sea Anemones vary in color from white and pink to red and brown. They are very sensitive, and will shrink into a wrinkled ugly mass, withdrawing their tentacles and contracting their bodies, as soon as they are touched.

The common JELLY FISH needs no description; the white

varieties are usually harmless, while the pink ones are able to deliver an electric shock which is as irritating as a nettle rash. They move through the water by contracting and expanding their semitransparent bell-like bodies. Jelly-fishes have so much water in their make-up that when they dry up on the sandy beach, all that is left is a dark colored sticky spot only a fraction the size of the original animal.

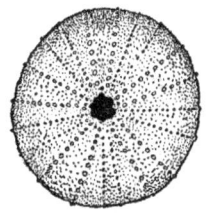

Sea Urchins

The COMB JELLIES are tiny Jelly Fishes seldom more than two inches in diameter; fringes extend down the sides of the highly arched bell.

It is a waste of time to look for seashore life when the tide is high. But at low tide, a tempting expanse of muddy or sandy beach, or a group of exposed rocks and cliffs, will disclose many interesting forms of life.

When the tide recedes, it leaves all the hollows in the rocks filled with salt water; these tidal pools are natural aquaria which present endless combinations of plant and animal associations.

In such rock tidal pools we will find the green Ribbon Weed, Silkweed, Mermaid's Tresses and sometimes young Sea Lettuce plants; reddish Irish Moss; and brown silky threads of Silkweed, perhaps stranded Kelps; and of course a jungle of Flat and Round Rockweed.

Amid these seaweed gardens we may discover our old friends of the wharves—Star Fishes and Sea Urchins. But there are many newcomers. Little blue-black Isopod worms huddle together for safety; greenish Crabs hide beneath the drooping Rockweed; portly Sea Cucumbers stand erect in the quiet water; and a great number of Mollusks move about in a restless search for food—Periwinkles, Oyster Drills, Purple Snails. Motionless Limpet Snails stick to the bottom of the deeper pools with a grip which is hard to loosen. And, of course, all over the rocks are the white and gray masses of encrusted Barnacles.

The SEA CUCUMBER is a brownish-green animal of varying shape, sometimes round and sometimes long and thin. It is attached by a flattened base, but changes its location frequently. The color may also shade into purple. About the mouth end is a fringe of branched tentacles. Once out of the water, if handled roughly, it will squirt water from its mouth; hence its other name of Sea Squirt.

In the tidal pool we are introduced for the first time to the shelled animals—the Mollusks. There are two kinds of Mollusks. Some have a double shell as a protection, hinged at one side and capable of being opened and closed by powerful muscles. These two-shelled Mollusks are called Bivalves. The other shelled animals have a single shell, usually in the form of a spiral (like the Snail); these are called Univalves. All the Mollusks living on the rocks about tidal pools are Univalves.

The LIMPET is a small shell, one half an inch to an inch long; in color it is a mixture of brown and white and green spots. Unless one catches a Limpet by surprise, it is impossible to pry the little cone-shaped shell off the rocks.

The Periwinkle lives amid tidal pools by the hundreds;

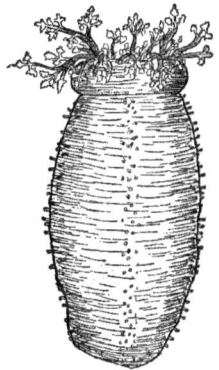

Sea Cucumber

often thousands of them cover the rocks around low tide mark with a black knobby coat. The Periwinkle varies in size from a quarter to a half an inch; its color varies from black to olive green. The shell forms a flattened spiral, not much longer than broad, with horizontal lines paralleling the curves of the spiral.

The OYSTER DRILL is commonly found only south of Cape Cod. Its long pointed spiral shell is a dirty gray, up to an inch in length. In addition to being very common in tidal pools and on rocks, it attaches itself to living oysters, drills into them and feeds on them. A combination of Starfish and Oyster Drills is enough to worry any oyster fisherman.

The PURPLE SNAIL is as abundant a rock dweller as the Periwinkle. It is lighter in color, varying from white and yellow to brown; often it is marked by yellow or red bands. It varies in size from one-half to one inch; and has a larger more oval opening in the shell than the Periwinkle. This Snail gets its name from its Mediterranean cousin, who in ancient times

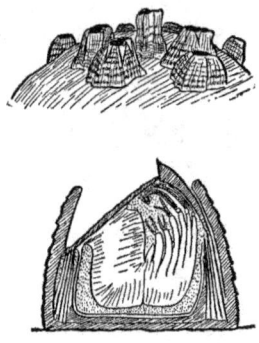

Barnacles

was crushed in order to yield a royal purple dye much prized by the Greeks and Egyptians.

BARNACLES are perhaps the most common sight on any rocky seashore; in addition they attach themselves to the bottoms of boats, pilings of wharves or any other convenient underwater support. The little animal lives inside the sharply-edged shell, attached by the base and with its feathery dainty "legs" projecting out of the opening at the top. The Barnacles are not related to the Mollusks, even though they do have a shell; they belong in the same family (the Crustaceans) with the Crabs and Shrimps. A young Barnacle goes through an interesting life history. When it hatches from the egg, it swims about for a while as a little sea animal with one eye, three pairs of legs

EXPLORING AT THE SEASHORE 159

and a single shell. After molting several times, it has two eyes, two shells and six pairs of legs! When it finds a rock which it considers suitable for its future home, it attaches itself by its front end, makes a cement to hold itself fast, grows its permanent cup-shaped shell and there it is, all ready for an unwary bather to tread on with his bare feet!

There is a bewildering variety of lifeless and living animals along the wet stretches of muddy or sandy beaches. Clam Worms and Bristle Worms hide under the stones and burrow in the mud; Sand Dollars and Sea Urchins are present in the

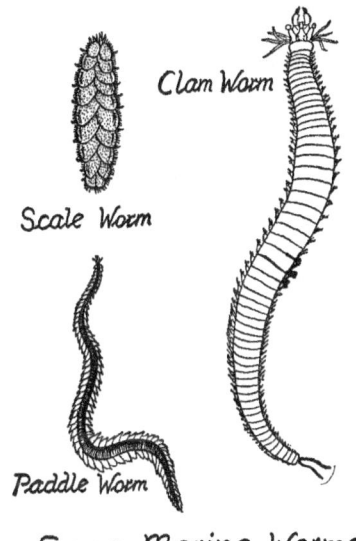

Some Marine Worms

form of their fragile skeletons; Horseshoe Crabs, Blue Crabs, Green Crabs, Sand Crabs, Hermit Crabs, Rock Crabs scurry about in the warm shallow water; Beach Fleas and Sand Shrimps hop about in dry seaweed heaps, and what seems at first a jumble of univalve and bivalve Mollusks, alive and dead.

The CLAM WORM is a bristly looking worm, dark blue-green in color and sometimes reaching a length of eighteen inches. He burrows in muddy sand or hides under the rocks between tide marks. At night he ventures forth and swims about looking like a segmented eel. He is a fierce fighter and devours other worms. When he sticks out his horny jaw, more like a beak than anything else, we are glad that we are not the "other worms."

The BRISTLE WORM is a smaller worm, only three inches long, found in similar places. Its color is dark green with a row of black spots down its back. The thin projections at each side of the jointed body are larger than those of the Clam Worm.

The SAND DOLLAR is a relative of the Sea Urchin, far more commonly found dead than alive. Its round, white shell, flattened and delicately marked, is about three inches in diameter.

The HORSESHOE CRAB, or King Crab, is a common large sea animal of the sandy and muddy shores of the Atlantic coast. Its olive brown shell and long pointed spine, which grows out of the abdomen, are easily recognized. This is really not a crab, but a form half way between the Crustaceans and the Spiders; some scientists put it in the same family with the Spiders.

The Crustaceans are very particular about the temperature of the water they live in; thus south of Cape Cod we come across the Green Crab; the Blue Crab (which is the common one we eat), the Sand Crab and the Fiddler Crab. While north of Cape Cod these crabs are very rare, and we find the Rock Crab and the Jonah Crab, who rarely venture south of the

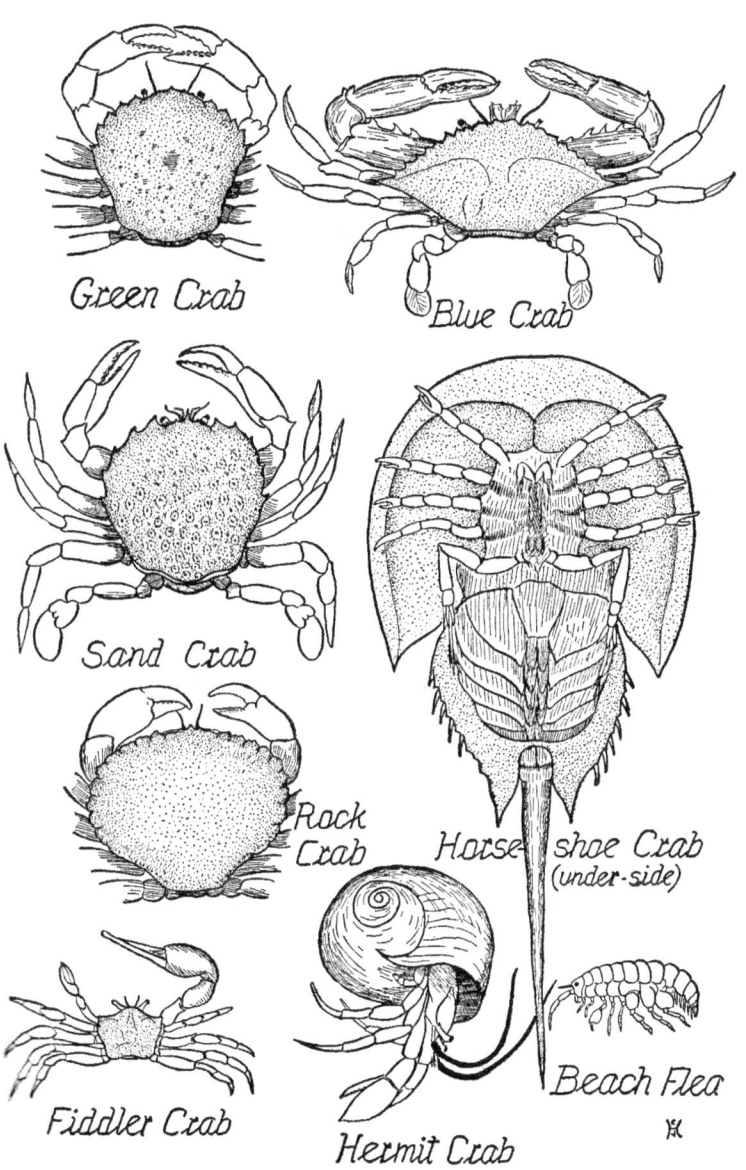

SOME CRABS AND THEIR RELATIVES

Cape. The Hermit Crab is less fussy about his surrounding and is found all along the coast.

The BLUE CRAB has a dark green shell which is much broader than it is long, ending in a long sharp spine on each side. It prefers to live along muddy shores, especially around bays and estuaries. The shell averages six inches across.

The GREEN CRAB is much smaller, its shell rarely measuring more than two inches in breadth, and spotted with yellow on a green background. This crab is often found under stones on beaches and in tidal pools.

The SAND CRAB, or Lady Crab, has a more rounded shell than the others. The shell is a dirty white covered with little rings of red and purple. And as its name shows, it prefers sandy bottoms, where it can burrow and hide with only its eyes and claws projecting.

The little gray-black FIDDLER CRAB burrows into the black mud of eel-grass tidal flats, and can be found scurrying around bays and river mouths. One claw is much larger than the other, making it easily recognizable from all other crabs irrespective of size.

The HERMIT CRAB'S habits are well known. It is born without the hard protective covering over its abdomen which the other crabs have. So it makes up for this oversight on the part of Nature by adopting the shell of some Mollusk and fitting itself into it.

In the colder waters of the North Atlantic coast we find the Rock Crab and the Jonah Crab.

The ROCK CRAB is three to four inches in breadth, and has a shell broader than long, yellow and covered with small brown dots. We can find this crab on sandy as well as rocky beaches, and frequently chance upon him in tidal pools.

EXPLORING AT THE SEASHORE

The JONAH CRAB resembles the Rock Crab, but is larger and has shorter, clumsier feet. The shell is red above and yellow beneath. This crab lives on rocky coasts only, and can be found at low tide amid the Rockweed and Kelps.

The Crustaceans are not all water dwellers; two inhabitants of the sand and dried seaweed are the Beach Flea and the Sand Shrimp.

The SAND SHRIMP is a small, almost transparent animal found among seaweed and in the sand around low tide mark. Its habit of taking long jumps, and its long feelers or antennae distinguish it.

The BEACH FLEA is a smaller animal, dark brown in color; disturb a pile of drying Rockweed on the beach and at once the sand becomes alive with jumping bodies.

And now for the shells.

Let us make our collection and withdraw to some clean bit of beach or polished rock where we can divide the shells into piles. First we can make two big piles; one consisting of the Univalve shells and the other of the Bivalve shells.

In the Univalve pile we have shells of all sizes, many of which are an inch or less in length. So we divide this pile into two smaller ones, into one putting all the shells that are an inch or less in length, and leaving in the other pile all the shells which are two, five and even nine inches long.

The common Univalve Mollusks more than two inches long are the Moon Snail, Ten Ribbed Whelk, Common Whelk, Smooth Whelk, Channeled Whelk and Knobbed Whelk.

The MOON SNAIL grows larger and is more common south of Cape Cod. It is gray or brown, two to four inches in length.

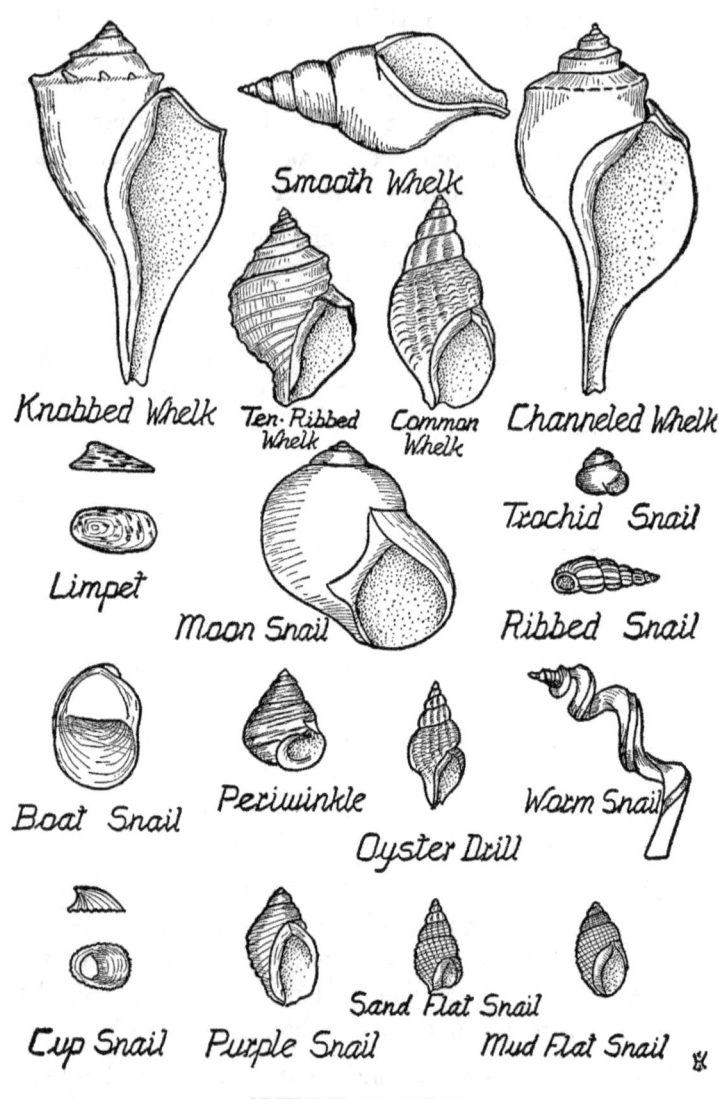

UNIVALVE SEA SHELLS

Its favorite haunts are the sandy beaches where it can bury itself safely. The Moon Snail, in spite of its harmless appearance, is a destructive flesh-eater; in a salt water aquarium it does a lot of damage by killing and eating other Mollusks and marine animals.

The Smooth Whelk, the Common Whelk and the Ten-Ribbed Whelk are found only north of Cape Cod. The Channeled Whelk and the Knobbed Whelk are found south of Cape Cod.

The SMOOTH WHELK is three to five inches long, and a light brown color. Its home is in deep water and is seldom found alive on the beach.

The TEN-RIBBED WHELK is smaller, averaging two to three inches in length. Its gray white shell is marked with ten revolving ridges which mark the shell crosswise. This whelk often lives just below low tide mark.

The COMMON WHELK is found everywhere on rocks and stony bottoms just below low tide mark. Its yellowish-brown shell is the same size as the Ten-Ribbed Whelk, but is more slender and has lengthwise gentle ribs instead of prominent crosswise ones.

The KNOBBED WHELK lives in the sandy beaches south of Cape Cod; its grayish-brown shell has a bright red color around the shell opening. The size varies from four to nine inches. The knobs on the spiral above the opening serve to distinguish it from the following Whelk.

The CHANNELED WHELK is the common Whelk of sandy beaches south of Cape Cod. Its size is that of the Knobbed Whelk, but it lacks the knobs, and in addition has lengthwise ridges and marks in contrast with the smooth shell of the Knobbed Whelk.

So much for the pile of shells more than two inches long.

In the pile of smaller Univalves we find Limpets, Periwinkles, Oyster Drills and Purple Snails; already old friends after our excursion into the tidal pools. In addition there are the Boat Snail, Cup Snail, Trochid, Ribbed Snail, Sand Flat Snail and Mud Flat Snail.

The BOAT SNAIL is a dull white little shell, about an inch or less long, and recognized by a shelf-like partition which forms a little bench across the upper end of the shell, on the inside.

The CUP SNAIL has a similar but smaller shelf on the inside of the shell. It is the same size, but has a circular instead of an oval outline, and has a wavy margin.

The TROCHID SNAILS are very small, usually a quarter of an inch to half an inch long. The shells are red or brown, and are made up of four flattened spirals.

While the Boat and Cup Snails are more often found attached to other shells below low tide mark, this Trochid Snail fastens itself to the rocks.

The RIBBED SNAIL is a long sharply pointed snail, with very prominent lengthwise ribs on the light brown shell. This is found only in deep water.

The SAND FLAT SNAIL and the MUD FLAT SNAIL are brothers who cannot live together; the Sand Flat Snail lives north of Cape Cod, and is yellowish white, while the Mud Flat Snail lives south of Cape Cod and is an olive black. Both are very common.

Now let us turn to our other pile, where we have collected all the Bivalve Mollusks together. Here is a great mixture of Clams, Mussels, Scallops and Cockles.

The Scallop shells have a wing-like "ear" which projects on either side of the hinges where the two shells are united. The

GIANT SCALLOP is about five inches in diameter, of a light orange to brown color, fading into white. The COMMON SCALLOP is about two and a half inches long, and has fewer but more prominent ridges radiating out from the hinge.

The COCKLE shells have a wavy scalloped margin, much more distinct than that of the Scallop shells of our coast. The Common Cockle varies in size from one-half an inch to two inches; and there is a Dwarf Cockle less than half an inch in diameter. Both the Cockles have strong ridges radiating out from the hinge.

The Mussels are generally blue or black in color, though there is one uncommon variety with brown shells.

The COMMON MUSSEL, which forms dense beds on the pebbly bottoms of bays and beaches between tide marks, is a deep blue, with a smooth shell some three inches in length when full grown.

The BEARDED MUSSEL is a deep water form which is sometimes washed ashore; it is a huge Mussel, five inches long; and the deep brown shell is covered with tufts of hairy growths.

The RIBBED MUSSEL is a dweller of the tidal mud flats, where its dirty brownish green shell seems quite at home. The shell, three inches long, has strong ribs running lengthwise.

The RAZOR CLAM is the only shell that is very much longer than it is wide; its slender gray-white or bluish shell is more often found broken than complete.

The deep water clams, often cast up on the beach, are the Flat-shelled Clam and the Arctic Clam. The Giant Clam is found all along the Atlantic coast on open sandy beaches. The Hard-shell Clam lives south of Cape Cod, its place being taken north of the Cape by the Soft-shell Clam.

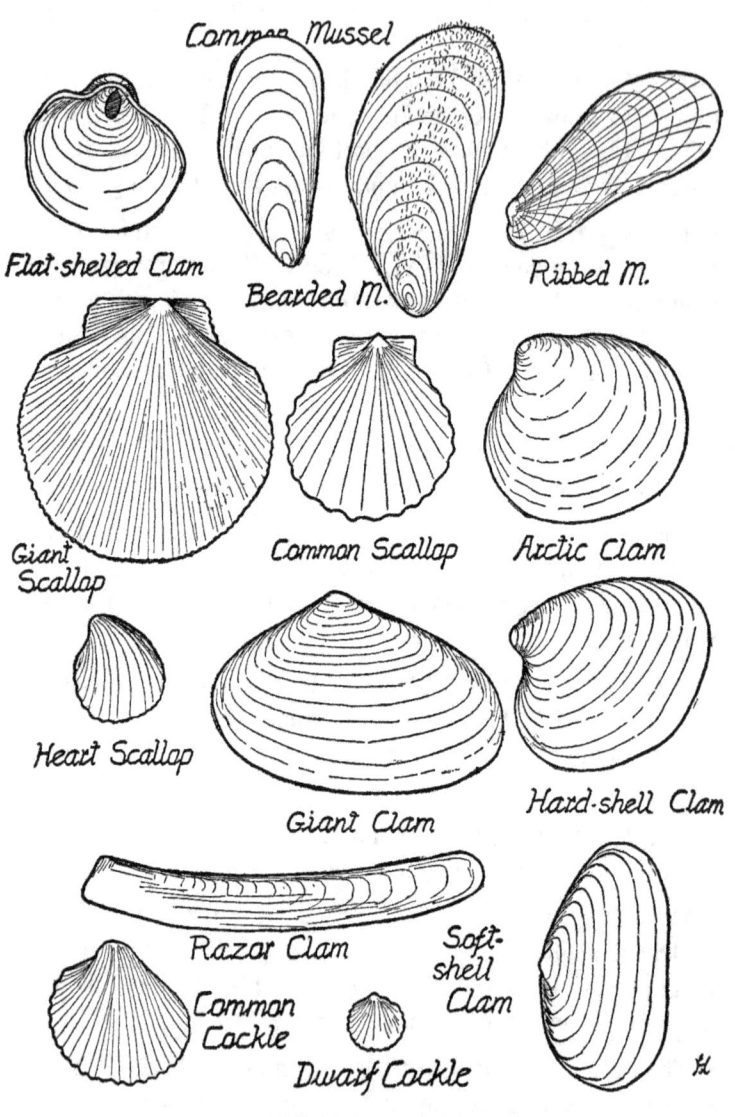

BIVALVE SEA SHELLS

The FLAT-SHELLED CLAM has its two shells of differing shape and size; they are one to three inches long, of a salmon or copper color. A hole through the flattened shell is an unusual characteristic; it serves as a means of muscle attachment to the bottom.

The ARCTIC CLAM is about three inches in diameter and can be recognized by the coarse, wrinkled black shell.

The GIANT CLAM is four to seven inches long, with a shell that is generally straw colored or brown.

The HARD-SHELL CLAM is found on muddy or sandy bottoms south of the Cape, and is the common clam used for eating. The SOFT-SHELL CLAM inhabits similar places north of the Cape.

HOW TO RECOGNIZE THE SEA SHELLS

I. If the shell belongs to a Univalve Mollusk, that is, is a single, snail-like shell,
  1. And if it is 1 inch or less long,
    A. With a shelf inside the shell, it is . . . . . .
          BOAT SNAIL, CUP SNAIL
    B. Without a shelf inside,
      a. Conical in shape, it is . . . . LIMPET
      b. Spiral in shape, it is . . . .
        TROCHID SNAIL, RIBBED SNAIL, OYSTER DRILL, SAND FLAT SNAIL, MUD FLAT SNAIL, PERIWINKLE, PURPLE SNAIL
  2. And if it is 2 inches or more long,
    A. Broader than long, it is . . . . MOON SNAIL
    B. Longer than broad,
      a. Four to nine inches long, it is . . . .
        KNOBBED WHELK, CHANNELED WHELK
      b. Two to four inches long, it is . . . .
        SMOOTH WHELK, COMMON WHELK, TEN-RIBBED WHELK

II. If the shell belongs to a Bivalve Mollusk, that is, is one of a pair of shells, like a Clam,
  1. And if the shell has a wavy margin, it is . . . . .
    GIANT SCALLOP, COMMON SCALLOP, COMMON COCKLE, DWARF COCKLE, HEART SCALLOP
  2. And if the margin is entire, it is any of the variety of . . . . CLAMS, MUSSELS

AUTUMN

CHAPTER 11

THE REAR GUARD OF THE FLOWERS

JUST at the time when we feel that the colorful days of summer are over, we are treated to a rare sight. The faded, and perhaps dusty, green of the fields and roadsides is enlivened by the two most gorgeous tints that Nature can provide: purple and gold.

Asters and goldenrods outnumber all the other autumn flowers. And their appearance is usually taken as a reminder that crisp and cool days are near at hand. Be that as it may, let us take a walk afield and see what these last of the pageant of flowers have to tell us.

THE ASTERS

In the rather dry fields and open thickets which lie on either side of the road there are hundreds and hundreds of Asters: pale lavender ones and rich purple ones, some that are light violet and others that are almost pure white. As we pick a few here and there we are surprised to find out that, after all, an Aster is not "simply an Aster."

Here is one with large heart-shaped leaves and pale blue flowers. Here is another, almost as tall as a man, with long slender leaves and purple flowers. And so on in bewildering fashion. No wonder—for there are over two hundred different kinds of Aster growing in the United States.

One of these Asters which prefers thus to grow in the dry

and sunny roadside places, has white petals surrounding a yellow center. This CALICO ASTER grows to any height from one to five feet, and is the only white Aster with long narrow leaves.

The rest of the Asters we see beside the road are some shade of purple or violet. This one, with only four or five big broad violet flowers at the ends of the stiff stems, is the LATE PURPLE ASTER. It seldom grows more than a few feet high, and can be readily remembered by the oblong leaves which clasp the stem tightly.

Quite different is the erect little STIFF ASTER, a foot or so high and with eight to ten purple flowers in a cluster at the top of the stalk. The leaves are narrow and slender, growing all around the stocky stem.

The branched and spreading plants of the SMOOTH ASTER bear many blue to violet colored flowers on the topmost stems and branches. It seems to be a much less compact and bushy plant than either the Late Purple Aster or the Stiff Aster.

All the Asters, however, are not flowers of dry fields and roadsides. Some of the most beautiful ones retire to the damp shade of the woods or prefer to grow along stream margins and in the swampy parts of fields and woods. Two white Asters—the Mountain Aster and the White-topped Aster—have such habits, as well as many of the purple and blue varieties.

The MOUNTAIN ASTER is a sturdy plant which grows from one to three feet high, bearing at the top of its zigzag stem a group of large flowers with straggly white petals. As we enter into the shade of the moister parts of the woods we see clusters of these Mountain Asters, and we may wonder how we can recognize them from the other white varieties. A look at the

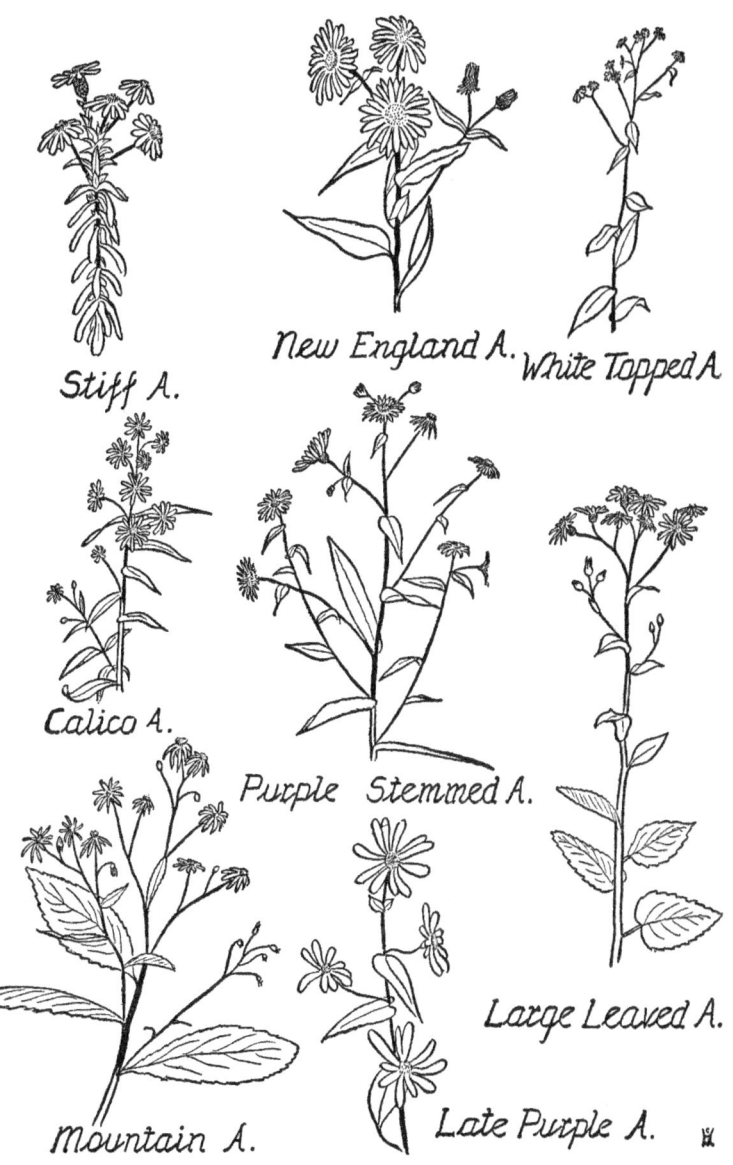

AUTUMN FLOWERS: THE ASTERS

leaves settles all doubt on that point. They are large and long, starting narrow at the point where they are attached to the stem and then widening out to a toothed and pointed blade.

The only other white Aster we see on our walk is the WHITE-TOPPED ASTER, with long narrow leaves clasping the stalk, and small white flowers forming a flat-topped cluster at the tip of the stem.

In these same moist shaded woods there is a pale-blue Aster known as the LARGE LEAVED ASTER. The name explains itself. It is the only purple Aster with such large heart-shaped leaves. Like most of the Asters, it grows anywhere from one to three feet in height. The stem seems unusually stout and rugged, with a reddish tinge to it.

For some time we have been walking down hill, and now we find ourselves in the marshy ground around a poorly drained stream. Here we discover the two most princely of the Asters, growing in all their glory to be six and even eight feet tall.

The more slender and openly branched of the two is the PURPLE-STEMMED ASTER. The slender pointed leaves grow snugly around the stalk; in some cases they are sharply toothed. The flowers appear for the most part to shade into a light lavender or purple.

But we cannot take our eyes from the other giant Aster. The stout stems of the NEW ENGLAND ASTER, almost hidden from view by a mass of long narrow leaves with entire margins, bear at their tops dozens of rich purple flowers. Some of these deeply colored flowers measure two inches across. It is a worthy rival of the much-prized cultivated flowers.

THE GOLDENRODS

Running the Asters a close second with over a hundred different varieties, the Goldenrods do their share to add a touch of color to the autumn fields and hillsides. In spite of the ill fame they have acquired because of their supposedly dangerous "hay-fever" qualities, they are still a popular flower. Much of this disease has been found to be caused by other plants than the goldenrod.

There is only one of these that lacks the golden yellow color. That is the SILVERROD. The stout stems do not branch, and grow to several feet in height. At the junction of the leaves and the stem, near the upper third of the plant, grow the little pale-yellow or white flowers. They increase in size and number towards the tip of the stem. Like most of the Goldenrods this Silverrod prefers to grow in dry and sandy fields.

As in the case of the Asters, let us see what common members of this family grow along the roadside and in the neighboring fields.

At first they all look alike. But having learned to use our eyes just a little from our previous study of the Asters, we surprise ourselves at the very start by recognizing that some of the Goldenrods along the road have flat-topped clusters of flowers while others have the flowers in a spire-like mass with the cluster ending in a gracefully bending shaft of golden yellow.

One of these flat-topped varieties is a dwarf sort of plant, being lucky if it reaches a foot or so in stature. This is the SLENDER FLAT-TOPPED GOLDENROD. Its leaves are so long and narrow that they resemble blades of grass; and each leaf has but one vein running lengthwise through it. The BUSHY FLAT-

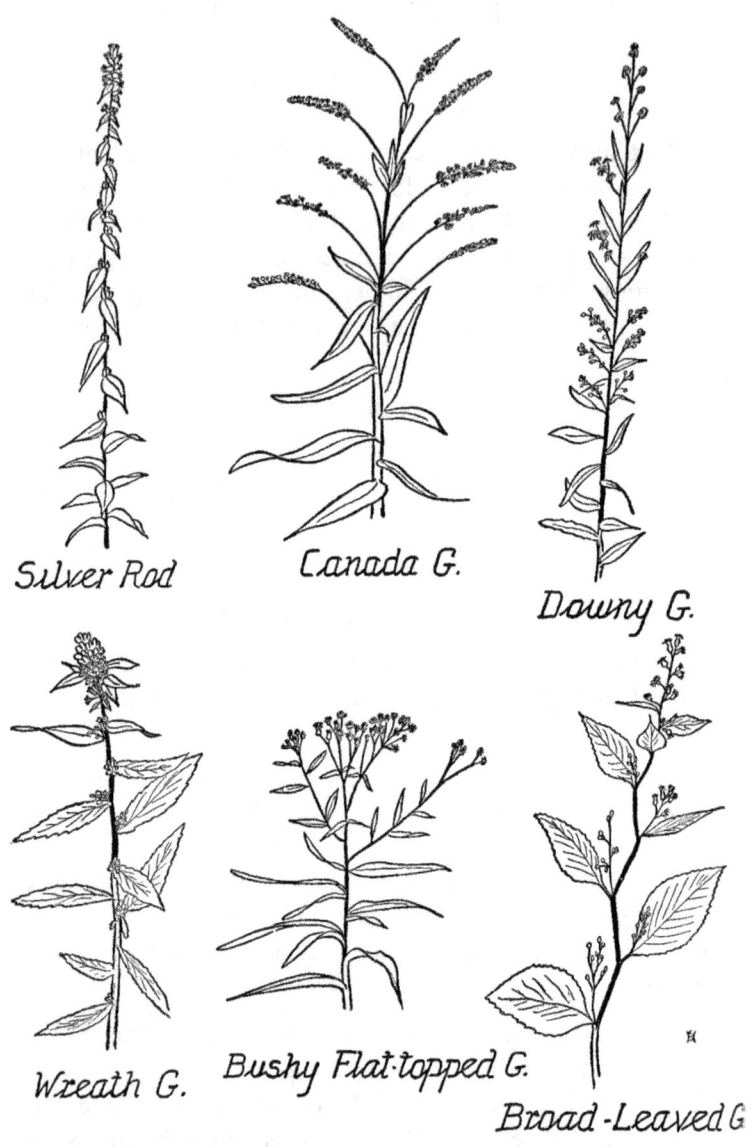

AUTUMN FLOWERS: THE GOLDENRODS

TOPPED GOLDENROD, on the other hand, grows to be two to four feet high. Its leaves are not quite so narrow, and have three veins to a leaf.

Of the pointed varieties, we see what seems to be thousands of a straight-growing little Goldenrod named the DOWNY GOLDENROD. Usually about one to three feet high, this flower forms solid beds of yellow in many a field; the upper quarter of the stalk is nothing but a mass of golden flowers.

Leaving the road, we pass through an open bit of woodland. Here we see, mixed with our old friends the Asters, some other kinds of Goldenrod. Here is a modest and retiring little plant, slender and not too abundantly covered with leaves. Each leaf is pointed at the tip, and toothed along the edge. Most of the flowers are growing out of the stem just above the leaves; though in some cases a few clusters form a solid bit of yellow at the top of the stalk. This is the WREATH GOLDENROD.

Another Goldenrod of the woods is the BROAD-LEAVED GOLDENROD. In addition to the most noticeable big oval-shaped leaves with saw-tooth edges and sharp tips, this Goldenrod has a peculiar zigzag stem. The flowers are not very numerous and as a result the whole plant is easily overlooked.

But there is another Goldenrod which one can certainly not overlook—the big glowing CANADA GOLDENROD. We wee it growing on hillsides, in fairly shaded woods, and along the tiny streams. But wherever we find it, we admire the solid yet spreading cluster of yellow flowers. The abundance of its flowers, as well as the height of the whole plant—up to five feet—makes it an easily recognized Goldenrod.

OTHER AUTUMN FLOWERS

The fields and woods are made colorful in September and October by other flowers, too. There are the Milkweeds, for example.

The COMMON MILKWEED, or SILKWEED as it is sometimes called, grows anywhere. We find it along roadsides, in the ditches, filling the waste places and thriving in the fields. The milky juice of the stout stem needs no introduction, I am sure. It is a big plant, often reaching a height of five feet; with many purplish flowers in umbrella-shaped clusters on individual stalks.

In swamps and other wet places we may come across the SWAMP MILKWEED, with more slender stems and with flowers shading into red and rose rather than dark purple with a tinge of green as in the Common Milkweed.

If we explore drier situations we find another member of this family, though it is not commonly called a Milkweed. This is the BUTTERFLY WEED. It pushes its stout and stock stem a foot or so above the meadow grasses; the end of the stem bears clusters of bright orange flowers.

Of course there are dozens and dozens of other flowers too, which persist through September and into October. There are the Hawkweeds, for instance, which can be found along the roads and in the grassy fields. Two of them are small plants with leaves growing only around the base of the stem. These basal leaves are naturally hidden in the grass. The long stem projects upwards and bears a few flowers, each with strap-shaped petals. The KING DEVIL has a bright yellow flower, while the DEVIL'S PAINTBRUSH (or ORANGE HAWKWEED) has an orange one. The rough hawkweed is a big bush plant growing

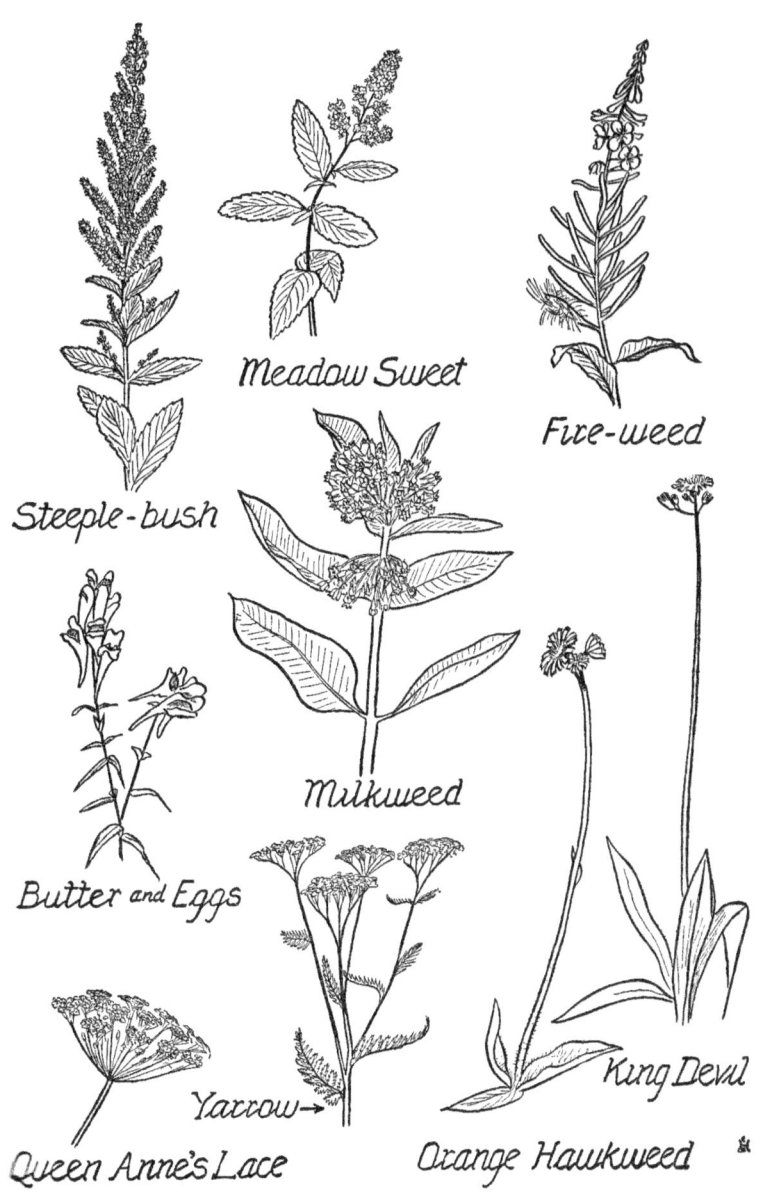

SOME OTHER AUTUMN FLOWERS

up to four feet high, with a stout hairy stem bearing small yellow flowers.

The VELVET MULLEN with its woolly leaves and tall erect stalk has small yellow flowers along the five to six feet of flower stem. This common roadside plant is one of the commonest "weeds" in the eyes of the farmer.

In overgrown pastures, often accompanied by erect little Red Cedar trees, the STEEPLEBUSH comes into its own. The spires and plumes of the pink or red flowers, clustered at the ends of the stems, grow in bushy masses several feet high.

The MEADOWSWEET is a flower at first glance quite like the Steeplebush. But more careful observation shows us that the flowers are generally much lighter pink in color (often white), and that they are not clustered in such pointed spire-like masses. The Meadowsweet plant forms irregular bushy growths along the roadsides, three or four feet high.

YARROW is a very common weed. The two or three foot tall stems bear delicate fern-like leaves; and near the top are several flat-topped clusters of very small white flowers. Yarrow grows everywhere, usually where there is plenty of sunshine.

QUEEN ANNE'S LACE is another common white flower of sunny fields; its lace-like flat-topped cluster of tiny blossoms is supported by a number of gracefully curved stems.

THE REAR GUARD OF THE FLOWERS

HOW TO RECOGNIZE THE FLOWERS

WHICH ARE RED, PINK OR ORANGE IN COLOR

I. If the color is red,
  1. And if the flower parts are in threes, it is
       RED TRILLIUM
  2. And if the flower parts are not in threes, it is
       COLUMBINE
II. If the color is not red,
  1. But if it is pink or purplish-red,
      A. With the flowers in plume-like clusters,
         it is . . . . STEEPLEBUSH, FIREWEED
      B. With the flowers scattered on bushy stems,
         it is . . . . MEADOWSWEET
  2. But if it is orange,
      A. With only one or a few flowers at the end of the
         stem, it is . . . . ORANGE HAWKWEED
      B. With many flowers at the end of the stem,
         it is . . . . BUTTERFLY WEED

HOW TO RECOGNIZE THE FLOWERS

WHICH ARE BLUE OR DARK PURPLE IN COLOR

I. If the plants are small, usually less than six inches tall,
   1. And if the leaves are very small or grass-like,
      A. With light blue flowers, it is . . . . . . BLUET
      B. With dark blue flowers, it is . . . BLUE-EYED GRASS
   2. And If the leaves are not small nor grass-like,
      A. With flowers in clusters on the stalk,
         it is . . . . HEAL ALL
      B. With flowers not clustered, it is BLUE VIOLET
II. If the plants are large, usually more than six inches tall,
   1. And if the leaves are long and grass-like, it is
                                    BLUE FLAG
   2. And if the leaves are broad, not like grass leaves,
      A. And if the leaves are compound, it is   LUPINE
      B. And if the leaves are simple,
         a. With light blue, very small flowers,
            it is . . . . FORGET ME NOT
         b. With lavender or purplish flowers,
            it is . . . . DAISY FLEABANE,
                                    WILD GERANIUM
         c. With deep blue or dark purple flowers,
            it is . . . . MILKWEED, the ASTERS

THE REAR GUARD OF THE FLOWERS

HOW TO RECOGNIZE THE FLOWERS

WHICH ARE YELLOW, YELLOWISH-WHITE OR
BROWNISH-YELLOW IN COLOR

I. If the flowers grow only one or a few on a stem,
   1. And the flowers are very small, less than half an inch long,
      A. With grass-like leaves, it is YELLOWSTAR GRASS
      B. With leaves in fives, it is . . . . FIVE FINGER
   2. And if the flowers are larger, more than half an inch long,
      A. With drooping flowers, it is
         DOG TOOTH VIOLET
      B. Without drooping flowers, it is
         YELLOW VIOLET, BLACK EYED SUSAN, KING DEVIL
II. If there are many flowers clustered on the stem,
   1. And if the leaves are fern-like,
      A. With flowers in erect groups, it is
         WOOD BETONY, TANSY
      B. With flowers in drooping clusters, it is
         DUTCHMAN'S BREECHES
   2. And if the leaves are not fern-like,
      A. With plant low, growing in swamps or streams, it is . . . . .COWSLIP
      B. With plants taller, of dry places, it is
         MULLEN, the GOLDENRODS

For keys to green, brown, and white flowers see Chapter 4.

CHAPTER 12

WHEN PLANTS TRAVEL

EVEN the smallest child knows that the chief difference between animals and plants is that animals can move about while plants cannot. We are so used to seeing the trees and shrubs and flowers anchored in one spot by their roots that we rarely stop to think that plants do need to travel once in a while.

For what if all the baby plants should have to grow up in the same place where their parents and grandparents lived? But how, I hear you asking, can a plant move away to a new place when it is so firmly anchored to the earth? The full-grown plant cannot do it. It is clearly up to the baby plant while yet sleeping contentedly in the seed to do the traveling. It is the seed, and its surrounding fruit, which must find a way to travel to new places in which there will be plenty of room to grow. Otherwise we would find all the dogwood trees in one spot, crowding each other for light and life. And nearby would be a jungle of maples engaged in the same struggle to keep alive.

In order that these young plants might reach new places Nature has thought up some clever tricks by which the seeds and fruits are able to go traveling. The wind goes everywhere; so why not use it to carry the young plants afar? Animals wander about; so why not have the animals carry the plants? That seems perfectly reasonable. And that is exactly what is done.

WHEN PLANTS TRAVEL 187

Let us see what some of these tricks are by which seeds get carried to distant new homes.

The trees, the flowers and all the other kinds of plant life have learned to use four different ways of getting their babies—carefully tucked away in the seeds—to their future homes.

In a way it is like "hitch-hiking," which some young people have tried as a means of getting somewhere without walking there, by begging for a free ride in some passing automobile. The seeds get their free rides most commonly on the speedy wings of the wind, being carried along like balloons and parachutes. Other seeds depend upon animals to carry them, by becoming stuck in their fur or clothing or by being carried off as food. Almost all the seeds we are familiar with travel by either of these two methods.

But there are two more ways. One, is to sail along on the water of a stream. The other, is to be shot into the air by a trigger-like piece of plant machinery.

TRAVELING ON THE WINGS OF THE WIND

In order to be carried along by the wind, seeds must weigh as little as possible. Sometimes the seeds are as small as grains of dust; and like grains of dust are carried along in the air. The larger seeds have flat wing-like surfaces which offer enough resistance to the wind to keep the seeds afloat for some time. Some seeds are attached to a feathery mass of light hairs, which help to keep them aloft.

There are many kinds of such riders on the air, which we can find if we use our eyes. Take Maple trees, for instance. After the tree has blossomed we see the little seeds in pairs, with a curved flattening part growing out of each seed. When the seeds are ripe they lose their hold on the branch and whirl to the ground. But they do not fall directly beneath the mother tree. With the aid of their "planes" they travel a short distance before they land and thus reach less crowded paces in which to make their homes.

The same "plane" idea is found in the Ash and Elm trees, as well as in that stranger to our native woods known as the Ailanthus tree. If you don't know what an Ailanthus tree looks like, you will become more fully acquainted with it in a later chapter.

A more clever trick still is found in the way the Linden tree tries to send its children out into the world. The seeds are joined to a stem above them and this stem ends in a broad parachute-like brown leaf. When these seeds float to earth they look for all the world like three roly-poly little men holding on for dear life beneath a parachute.

Watch this kind of seed fall from the tree, and you will see that it can travel only very short distances; and no distance at all if a wind isn't blowing. To get farther away from their parent trees, the baby plants have to float more like balloons than parachutes. Such plants are light fluffy things which sail on and on in the air even in the gentlest sort of breeze.

It seems almost foolish to take the time to name seeds which travel in this way—they are so familiar to every boy and girl. The Dandelion and the Thistle, for example, have the tiny seeds supported by the downy tuft of hairs. The swamp-dwelling Cat-tail and the roadside Milkweed seeds float along and even upwards when there seems to be no breeze at all. How far such seeds can travel before they settle down to become self-respecting plants is beyond our imagination to

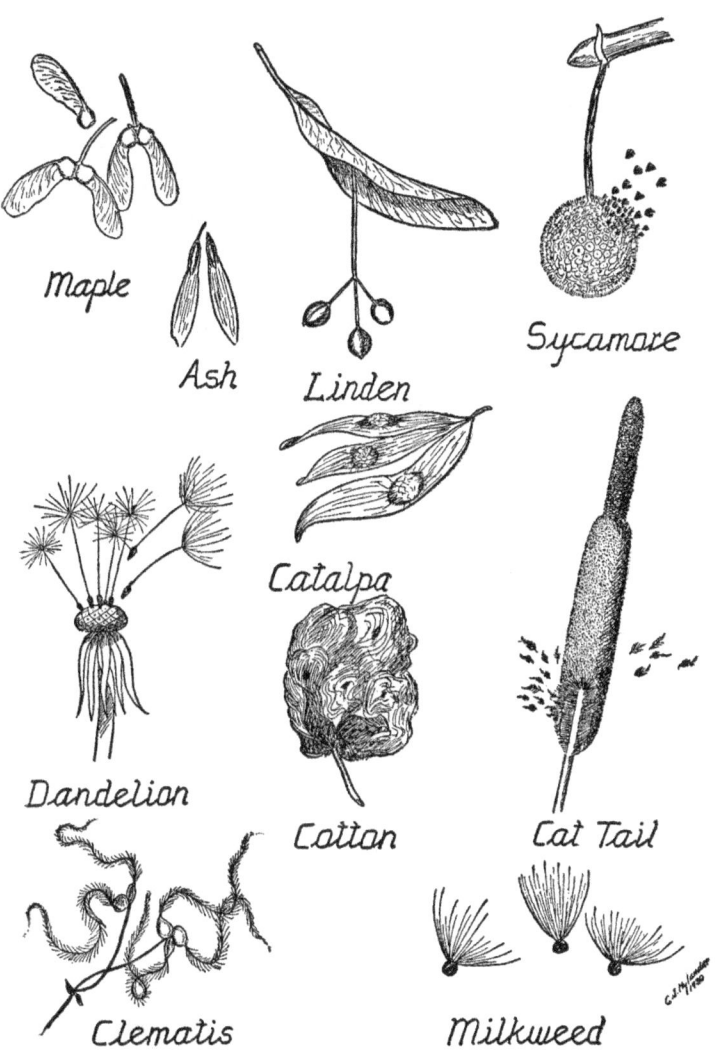

SEED DISPERSAL BY WIND

suggest. Why not try following such a seed sometime and really see how far it can go?

Perhaps some of you have seen the Clematis vine covering a rambling old stone wall with its mass of white fluffy hairs and seeds. Each seed is the fortunate owner of a long feather-like stem by whose aid it can reach new fields and fences.

While we are talking about seeds carried by the wind we must not forget one plant which Man has found very useful. Nature has surrounded the Cotton seed with a mass of light fibers, which we have found to be so useful in making cloth.

TRAVELING WITH THE AID OF ANIMALS

There is one very serious drawback to the method of traveling we have just described. The baby plant and its protective fruit have to be so light that only small amounts of provisions can be carried along. For plants need food in order to live, just as animals do. And the baby plant, like the baby animal, cannot get his own meals as soon as he is born. Our familiar animals are fed by their mothers; but these baby plants have left their mothers far behind them. But the little plant tucked up inside the seed need not worry. His mother has packed the seed full of food; enough food to keep the young plant alive many weeks. It is very seldom that this store of food is used up before the plant grows roots and leaves. Once the plant develops these, it can take care of itself.

While we are talking about seeds and the food they carry for the young plants, we might notice that this has been of great importance to Man. Most of the food we eat is plant food. And we eat only the parts of the plant where the food is stored. Plants do store their food in other parts, such as the roots and stems; but the greatest amount of it in a small space is to be

WHEN PLANTS TRAVEL

found in seeds. So Man, with his usual ability to urge Nature along to do what benefits him, has grown plants merely for the seeds they have. This is true of corn, wheat, oats, rice, barley and all the "grains" or "cereals." The food which the wheat plant stores in its seed, as preparation for the life of a new wheat plant, may eventually find its way to our breakfast table as a piece of bread or toast.

But to get back to our story.

Many plants have developed tricks by which they fool animals into carrying the seeds great distances. Animal-carried seeds can carry much more stored food with them than the light wind-carried ones. Two ways in which plants have tried to do this are: first, by spines or prickles on the outside of the fruit so that they fasten themselves to the fur of animals, and second, by surrounding the seed with such a tempting bit of fruit that the animals want to eat it!

How often, when we take an October walk through the woods, we come out simply covered with bothersome little burrs and prickly seeds stuck tightly to our clothing. And how seldom, as we spend impatient minutes picking them off, do we realize that plants have played a trick on us and used us to give their seeds a free ride out into the world.

All these little fruits with claws and hooks on them go by a great number of different names, such as "beggar-ticks," "stick-tights," "tick trefoils," and "burrs." Such fruits carry their precious seeds long distances while they are fastened to the fur of an animal. When at last they are shaken or picked off, they drop to the earth and are ready to start a new colony of the plants as soon as Spring comes.

Another trick Nature has tried is to make the part of the fruit which surrounds the seed so tasty and attractive that

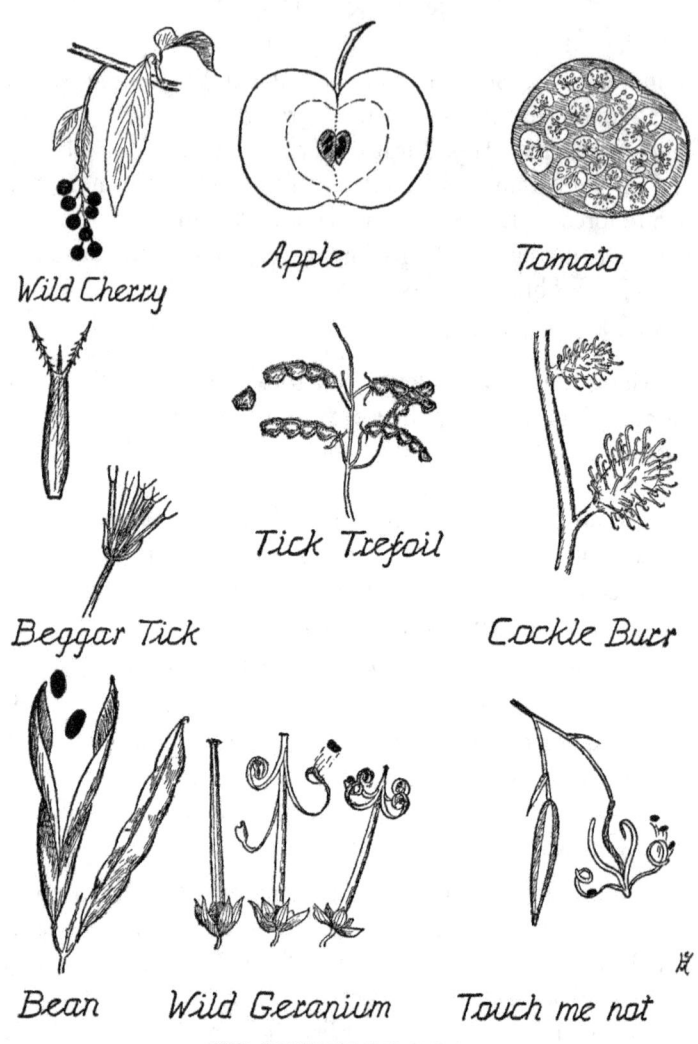

SEED DISPERSAL BY ANIMALS

WHEN PLANTS TRAVEL

animals and man can't resist eating them. In this way the hidden seeds are sometimes carried a long ways before the fruit is entirely eaten and the seeds thrown away. Very few animals like to eat seeds. And so the baby plants in the seeds reach new places in which to grow. It is for this reason that Nature has surrounded the seeds of berries with such tempting flavors; and hidden the seeds of apples, pears and peaches in such nice juicy wrappers.

Often animals like squirrels and chipmunks, in carrying away a winter's supply of nuts (which are seeds too), forget where they stored them. And those left grow into new plants in the very cracks in the stone walls where they have been hidden.

SEEDS THAT SHOOT THEMSELVES AWAY

These are really the most clever of all the devices which Nature has developed in order to give youngsters a fresh start in the world. It is a rather vigorous start at that.

This is what happens.

As the fruit ripens, the tissues around the seeds become very tightly stretched. When the fruit is heated by the warm rays of the sun or is touched by chance, it bursts open and the outer layers of the fruit roll back. Just as a stone is hurled out of a sling when the rubber is released from its stretched position, so the release of the stretched outer wall of the fruit shoots out the seeds. Quite often I have brought home seed pods and later heard the pop-pop of the seeds as they were shot around the room.

The best example of this kind of seed scattering is to be found in the Touch-me-not. And to a less startling degree, the seeds of the common Bean plants are shot outwards as the drying pod curls up. The Wild Geranium also behaves in this way.

The distance covered by this means is naturally very small. Its advantage lies in being independent of wind, water, animals or anything but the plant itself.

SEEDS THAT ARE CARRIED ON THE WATER

I had meant to tell you only of the way plants travel right near home. But the way in which one tree which grows in very hot countries like Africa has learned to send its babies out into the world is too interesting to leave out. Besides, you may see this tree some day; you most certainly have seen its fruit.

It is the Coconut Palm.

As the seeds ripen, they are carefully stowed away in a regular life-boat arrangement. All about the seed is a waterproof boat-like shell. When the time is ready, the coconut drops off the tree, usually into the waters of the stream over which the Coconut Palm is leaning. And so out on its surface floats the little boat bearing its living burden safely to some new distant home.

Now perhaps it is easy to understand why plants have fruits at all. Without the fruit, the unprotected seed would be unable to travel any distance. And plants would soon overcrowd their birthplace.

But with fruits developed to entice animals to carry them along, or constructed so that the wind can carry them great distances, the traveling proposition becomes much easier.

And next time you find your clothes covered with ticks and burrs after a romp in the woods, remember that it is only one of many tricks by which plants get a "free ride" and a chance to see the world.

CHAPTER 13

WHAT'S WHAT AMONG THE BERRIES

The autumn time is a delightful time because of all the good things there are to eat. Grapes and apples, peaches and pears, nuts and pumpkins and everything that goes to make boys and girls feel real good in their insides.

But what interests us just now are the berries. Blackberries, raspberries, blueberries and huckleberries are varieties of fruit which attract the average boy just as much as the bigger farm and orchard products. Many a hike over the scrubby mountains of Mt. Desert Island has been unavoidably slowed up because the trail led through blueberry bushes which were too much of a temptation to my boy companions!

Nature has provided many plants with berries. A great many of these are not considered good eating by us; in fact, some of them are poisonous. To the little fur-bearing animals and birds trying to live through the cold winter, these berries are the chief article of diet.

After the leaves fall off the shrubs and trees, and the woods become more open, we see so many of these berries that it is well worth while taking a walk some October day and seeing how many of them we can collect.

It is in the woods that we will find most of them; though a few manage to appear in more open and sunny places. It does not take us long, as we wander leisurely through the brown and barren thickets, to notice one very interesting fact. Most of the berries are either red or blue! There are a few white and greenish ones; but they are lost in the great numbers of the red and blue ones. Just to be a little scientific about the way we are collecting these, let us pay attention to only the blue ones first.

BLUE BERRIES

As we pass through an open space in the woods we have to force our way through an undergrowth of bushes and shrubs with maple-like leaves. Some of the branches bear clusters of blue berries. This shrub is the VIBURNUM, and is the only tall

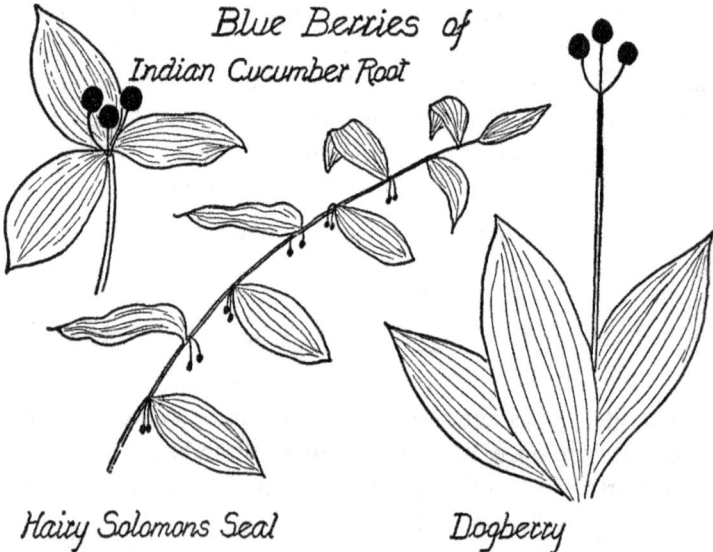

Blue Berries of Indian Cucumber Root

Hairy Solomons Seal

Dogberry

shrubby plant we shall see with blue berries. The rest of them are small and rarely more than a foot high.

That vine climbing along the ruins of a stone wall has a few dried up red leaves still clinging to it. When we see the leaves in finger-shaped clusters of five, we recognize it as the common WOODBINE. But never before had we realized that it bore such nice blue berries.

As we scramble down the side of a little ravine we see an unusual little plant. The stem bears two sets of leaves each in a circular arrangement. Above the upper circle of leaves rises three fairly large blue berries. This is the INDIAN CUCUMBER ROOT. Other similar plants nearby have from two to eight berries on each plant.

Not far from these we see some other blue berries, but these are raised at the end of a long stalk. All the leaves lie flat on the ground at the bottom of the stem. This lily-like plant is CLINTONIA, otherwise known as DOGBERRY.

In climbing up the scattered rocks on the other side of the ravine, we see a little plant clinging for a foothold in a crevice of soil-filled broken-up rock. It is the retiring dweller of the shaded woods known as SOLOMON'S SEAL. The bending stalk has two rows of leaves on either side, and hanging from the junction of leaf and stalk we see pairs of rich blue berries.

RED BERRIES

While we have been collecting the blue berries we have noticed that there are more than twice as many red as blue ones. Perhaps plants have found that red appeals more to the animals than blue; for we remember from the last chapter that plants have colored and juicy fruits mostly to attract animals so that the seeds will be carried to new homes.

Because it usually is more orange than red, let us mention the BITTERSWEET first. This vine climbs over stone walls and around the lower limbs of trees. About several weeks before Thanksgiving its brilliant berries attract many to pick it as a home decoration. As we have already said, this does no harm if only *some* of the plant is taken.

As we walk along we notice a tiny creeping plant with dark evergreen leaves. There seems to be lots of it beneath the big hemlock trees. We notice some now with bright red berries along the almost-hidden stem. This is the common PARTRIDGE BERRY.

In an open bit of woods we discover another little plant with

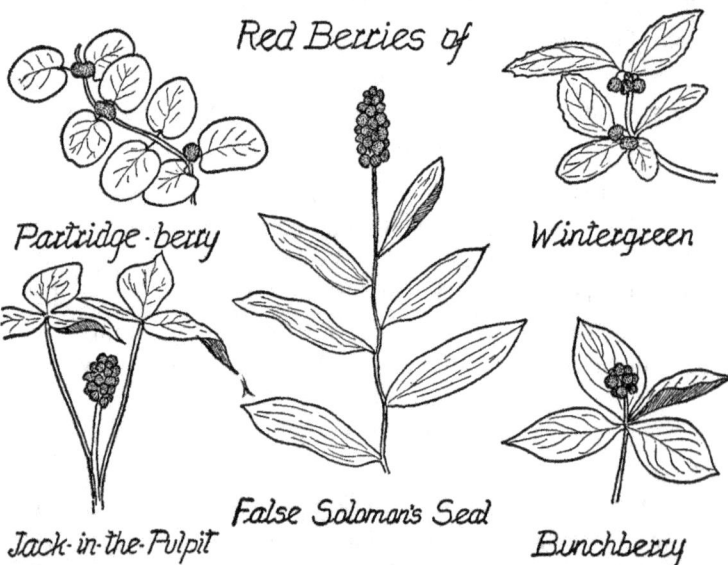

Red Berries of Partridge-berry, Wintergreen, Jack-in-the-Pulpit, False Solomon's Seal, Bunchberry

red berries. This looks like a dwarf Dogwood tree, if we can judge from the few withered leaves about the erect stem. The plants are only three to six inches high; each one bears a cluster of seven or eight bright red little berries. Though called BUNCHBERRY, a more appropriate name is the usual one of DWARF CORNEL. Cornel is another name for Dogwood.

Near some evergreen trees we find another little plant just a few inches high. The leaves are thick and dark green, and must be evergreen. The erect stalks carry red berries which have a spicy taste quite agreeable to some people. This is the WINTERGREEN, or CHECKERBERRY. If not eaten by birds or other animals, the berries last on the plants until the following spring.

Much taller and larger than any of these plants we have seen so far, are those of the RED BANEBERRY. Along a bank we see several of these, each one having an erect stalk about which are clustered over a dozen large red berries.

Very abundant in some partly-cleared woods, the FALSE SOLOMON SEAL pushes up its coarse stem above the surrounding growth. The zigzag stem has at its tip a dense cluster of reddish-speckled berries.

And in the swamps we find our childhood friend—the JACK IN THE PULPIT. The pulpit is gone, and we find the Jack has become an erect cluster of shining red berries.

The little cluster of berries nestling in the top leaf of the CANADA MAYFLOWER (also called Wild Lily of the Valley) are at first a brownish green, then darken and become speckled with brown, and finally turn a russet red.

There is only one common berry that is white. The WHITE BANEBERRY, looking much like its relative the Red Baneberry in general appearance, has an erect cluster of white berries each with a blue spot on it.

CHAPTER 14

HOW THE TREES PREPARE FOR WINTER

Trees are living things, just as much as animals and people are. For this reason they are very sensitive to any changes in their surroundings. Unless the air has a certain amount of warmth in it, with plenty of moisture, and unless there is plenty of sunlight and the right kinds of soil, the trees stop growing and die.

Now it so happens that the amount of sunlight and the kinds of soil have nothing to do with the preparation of the trees for winter. It is the warmth or coldness of the air and the amount of water in the ground that have a lot to do with it. For when the soil water gets too cold, it is not absorbed by the trees. We shall see that it is this change from warmth to coldness upon the approach of winter, that makes the trees prepare for a change of seasons.

When it comes to the end of summer, we notice that there are really two kinds of trees. Some of them decide to stay green all winter and take a chance on battling with the cold winds and the heavy loads of snow. We call these Evergreen Trees. Somehow or other, these Evergreen Trees with their tiny needle-like leaves are able to keep growing and living throughout the winter. Since they do not need to prepare for winter, we will leave them out of this story.

The other kind of tree, about in October, goes through a series of changes which make the autumn landscape very

HOW THE TREES PREPARE FOR WINTER 201

beautiful. The leaves turn all different colors, and then they fall by the hundreds until all the branches of the trees are bare. We call these Deciduous Trees, because they prepare for winter by shedding all their leaves at once. It is these trees that we will talk about.

Why is the temperature of the water supply so important to the trees?

Trees, like all other living things, need food. When animals or people want food, they move around and eat up other animals or plants. Trees, on the other hand, like all plants, *make their own food.* This food, which we call starch and sugar, is manufactured in the leaves in tiny rooms called cells. Each cell is packed full of round little green workmen who labor from sunrise to sunset to make enough food for the whole tree.

One cannot make something out of nothing; these green bodies in the leaves make the starch and sugar food out of two very common substances which are always present all around the trees—air and water. However, when the water is too cold, these Deciduous Trees are unable to make food. So that is why, as soon as we have frosty nights along in October, we notice remarkable changes taking place in the trees as they prepare for winter.

As the water gets too cold, the little green bodies in the cells of the leaf begin to stop working, and soon die. While they were alive they had yellow and orange colors mixed with them, but the green was so much brighter and stronger that no one could see the other colors. Now, however, the green color disappears. So we see the green leaving the leaves, and in its place appear yellow and orange tints.

Sometimes there is a brilliant red coloring, too. This is caused by a substance in the sap of the leaf. The red color is most striking in leaves which get a lot of sunlight; it sometimes appears even in summer when a branch is injured.

The brown color is merely the usual shade found in any dead plant matter. In some trees, such as the Oaks, this is a common change as soon as the cool autumn nights come around.

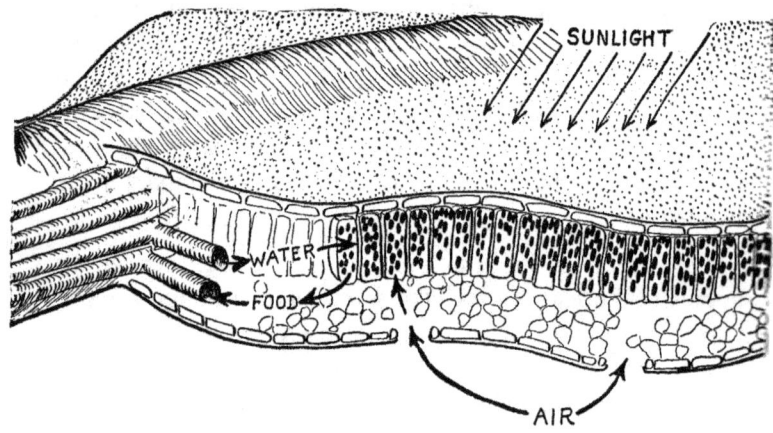

The Workshop inside of a Leaf

I am sure you have noticed that certain trees always turn certain colors every autumn.

There is the Swamp Maple, for instance. And the Staghorn Sumac. Both of these turn a brilliant red which resembles the crimson colors of a sunset sky. With a more sedate shade of red, the Dogwood trees spread their purplish-red leaves as a background for the clusters of crimson berries.

When it comes to the yellow colors we find a great variety. The Tulip tree leaves turn a golden yellow with a hint of red

HOW THE TREES PREPARE FOR WINTER   203

in them. The same is true of the Sassafras leaves. Beech leaves become a very delicate yellow, transparent as sunlight coming through the deep woods. The Sugar and Norway Maples, too, form solid masses of golden yellow foliage.

As we see the yellow color merge into brown, we choose the various kinds of Oaks and Hickories, which show a great number of shades from light yellowish-brown to a dark brownish-black.

The colors do not last very long. For a week or two they are at their best, and then some windy rainy night comes along. The next morning the colorful millions of leaves are whirling along the ground and the limbs of the trees are bare.

The fall of the leaves is really of great value to the trees. For that is the only way the trees can get rid of all the waste products which have been piling up inside the tree all summer. These waste materials are sent to the leaves until the leaves are full of them. And when the leaves fall off, all these waste products fall with them to the ground. The tree is then ready to start afresh the next season.

These new leaves are all formed inside the buds before the winter starts in. So that the next spring, no time need be wasted before the leaves can unfold and become of sufficient size to make food for the tree in another growing season.

During the winter, with its scars where the leaves fell off well sealed up by cork, the tree merely goes into a resting condition, much like the long winter's sleep of the frogs and snakes. Looking like a dead thing, the tree lives through the winter, its bare branches unaffected by the cold and the wind, until finally the warmer days of spring arrive. Then as the frozen layers of the soil become thawed out, the roots send the welcome water up to the buds. In remarkably quick time the leaves burst out and the little green workmen in the fresh new leaves use this water to make food for the tree during another growing season.

CHAPTER 15

HOW THE ANIMALS PREPARE FOR WINTER

ALL animals are not lucky enough to live in countries where it is summer all the time. In fact, most animals live in places where there is a change of seasons. We are familiar with the coming of winter in this part of the United States; but how many of us ever stop to think of what happens to the animals after the warm days have gone by?

There are two conditions in an animal's surrounding which are very important to him. These are sufficient food, and comfortable temperatures. When winter sets in, these two conditions are much changed. The animals are forced to accommodate themselves as best they can to freezing temperatures and a scarcity of food.

In preparing for winter, animals behave differently according to whether they are "warm-blooded" or "cold-blooded." A warm-blooded animal is one that is able to keep his body temperature at a certain fixed point—usually warmer than the outside air—no matter how the weather changes. There are only two kinds of warm-blooded animals—the mammals and the birds. They are much more active than the cold-blooded animals, and keep the warmth from leaving their bodies by a covering of feathers or fur.

A cold-blooded animal varies the temperature of his body as the outside temperature changes: on a cold day, his body becomes so cold that he is unable to move about. And on a warm day, his body sometimes may become heated up to such a point that the animal becomes motionless through laziness. Most of the animals are cold-blooded; such as the reptiles (lizards, turtles, snakes), the amphibians (frogs and toads), the fishes, the insects and all the tiny water-animals.

WHAT THE WARM-BLOODED ANIMALS DO

First let us see how the warm-blooded animals prepare for winter. We will take the mammals, for example. A mammal (as we have already said) is an animal usually covered with fur, which feeds its babies with milk. The lions, tigers, giraffes, camel, bears, wolves, squirrels and rabbits are all mammals. So are monkeys, apes—and people.

If a mammal is very active and needs a continuous supply of food, he comes out of his warm burrow every once in a while in search of something to eat. Anyone who has taken a walk in the woods and fields in the winter time, knows how many tracks of these mammals can be seen. Rabbits and foxes, and sometimes deer, will thus appear at times during the winter. Their thick furry coat keeps them warm and comfortable.

Other mammals store up enough food to tide them over the winter. We have all seen the chipmunks and squirrels busily engaged in collecting acorns and nuts before the first snow falls.

And then some mammals, like the bear, roll up in a cozy warm hollow tree or cave, and go to sleep for several months. Perhaps this makes them forget how hungry they are. Anyway, they use up very little food when they are so inactive. Very few of the mammals try to leave the place where winter has set in, and move to a warmer climate. One reason for this may be that they cannot travel fast enough.

HOW THE ANIMALS PREPARE FOR WINTER

The other warm-blooded animals, the birds, do not all do the same thing. The bravest and hardiest birds decide to stay where they are during the winter. This is especially true around cities where people have put out feeding stations, and where trees and bushes with lots of berries and seeds on them are plentiful. The Nuthatches and Creepers, Blue Jays and even Blue Birds, survive the winter somehow without freezing or starving to death. Other winter birds, like the Junco and Snow Bunting, come down to spend the winter with us because it is warmer here than in their usual home up in Canada and around Hudson Bay.

But most of the birds fly south in winter; we call this migrating. Bird migration starts southward as the leaves commence to fall off the trees. And soon the Robins and Warblers, and most of our songbirds have left us. Covering hundreds of miles a day, some of these birds travel five and six thousand miles in order to avoid winter and the scarcity of food. The most interesting thing about bird migration is that the same birds, by some unknown sense, can find their way back to the same places every year. When this means a round trip of ten thousand miles every twelve months, it seems nothing short of a miracle.

WHAT THE COLD-BLOODED ANIMALS DO

The cold-blooded animals with backbones inside their bodies—that is the Reptiles, Amphibians and Fishes—either go into a resting condition where all activities are for the time suspended, or else they continue living on under the new condition. This last applies to all the fish of lakes and oceans, because the temperature of the water below the surface stays almost the same, winter or summer. So to the fishes there is no change of seasons as there is to the land animals living above them.

The water-dwelling amphibians and reptiles burrow into the mud and ooze at the bottom of ponds, and sleep there until the ice melts above them. This is what happens to the frogs and newts, as well as to any half-formed tadpoles. For company, in the cold dark pond bottom, there are the different kinds of turtles who are doing the same thing. Some of these water-dwellers have lungs, but they are able to breathe after a fashion through their skins, and thus get enough air to keep alive.

Other cold-blooded animals have no bones inside their bodies. Of these lower forms of animal life, the insects are the most common. For them the winter season means a long period of rest, provided the insect can live more than one season.

The ants, butterflies and bees complete their life activities in the short span of a few weeks; so for them winter does not mean sudden death. They would die anyway.

Other insects are able to live through the winter while they are still eggs. The grasshoppers, crickets and walking sticks thus pass the cold months. Some insect relatives like the spiders and millipedes may either survive the winter as eggs or as young babies which hide away in webs and burrows.

The unusual things which happen to an insect's egg before it hatches into a full grown insect have already been suggested in the Story of the Caterpillar. The scientific name of the caterpillar is larva. The dragonfly spends the winter either as a larva under the water or as eggs attached to sticks or stones in the pond. Butterflies and moths, as well as beetles and most two-winged flies, spend the winter in the stage after the larva—

HOW THE ANIMALS PREPARE FOR WINTER

known as the pupa stage. This corresponds to the cocoon stage of the butterfly.

Some of the insects may remain alive during the winter as sleeping (hibernating) adults. The black and yellow hornet and some other wasps abandon their usual nests as the cold weather comes on, and hide in narrow crannies under loose bark and in heaps of rocks.

The bumblebees remain in their warm and protected nests; only a few of them—usually the queen bees—live through to the next spring. Mosquitoes and gnats sometimes live through the winter by hibernating in hollow logs and even inside houses.

Some of the butterflies, like the Mourning Cloak and the Angle Wing, either spend the winter as adults or imitate the birds and migrate to more comfortable climates. Moths may at times be found sleeping away the winter in thick clumps of grass. Any warm winter's day may awaken them in considerable numbers.

WINTER

CHAPTER 16

WHAT THE EARTH IS MADE OF

During the spring, summer and autumn most of the earth is covered with such a thick covering of plant life that we see very little of the earth itself. But in winter there is plenty of opportunity to find out something about the rocks and minerals which make up the earth's surface.

Perhaps you think the earth is nothing but dirt and sand and gravel; or as it is called, soil. However, this covering of soil is really very thin. There are places in Maine where the scattered evergreen trees and berry bushes have to grow on a soil surface only a few inches deep. Even in good farming country the soil may be but a few feet deep, except where rivers or glaciers have piled up big heaps of it. All this soil has come from the breaking up of rock into smaller pieces.

Most of the earth is solid rock with a thin layer of soil covering it in spots. Some places, such as mountain tops, do not even have this thin covering of soil. It is really the rocks from which all soil comes, which represents what the earth is made of.

FIRE-BORN ROCKS

'Way back in the beginning of things, as the earth was being made fit for living things to appear, all the rocks were in a melted and liquid condition. As time went on these very hot and molasses-like rocks cooled off and hardened. Such rocks are called very fittingly "fire-born" rocks—IGNEOUS ROCKS. Some of these cooled masses of rocks have existed until today in the places where they were born. Others are being formed from time to time as lava flows appear from volcanoes and deep cracks in the earth.

It is easy to recognize these fire-born rocks among the stones and boulders about us as we walk in the woods and fields any winter's day. Here is one with characteristics common to all the rocks of this type. The rock is coarse in structure, so that separate grains of the minerals can be seen. This is GRANITE, one of the commonest of rocks throughout the New England states. It is composed chiefly of quartz crystals and bits of mica. Mica is another name for isinglass. In color Granite is usually gray, greenish-gray, red or pink.

If we happen to be exploring the region around the Palisades of the Hudson River, or certain steep-sided hills of Connecticut or New Jersey, we can see another kind of fire-born rock. These rocky ridges are composed of a finer-grained rock known as DIABASE. Trap rock is quarried and broken up for paving roads and making gravel walks.

WATER-BORN ROCKS

For millions of years rain has kept falling over the fire-born rock surface; and rivers have been carrying to the lakes and oceans tons of worn-off bits of rock. These tiny grains of rock began to pile up at the bottoms of the bodies of water. Hundreds of feet deep these deposits became. As time passed the layers of sand and gravel and clay slowly were pressed into a new kind of rock, known as "water-born" rock—SEDIMENTARY ROCK.

WHAT THE EARTH IS MADE OF

Oceans and lakes have had a habit of drying up and exposing their bottoms as new land. When this happens the rocks formed under water by the pressing together of the layers of sand or clay, naturally become a part of the land surface. Such rocks usually show the layers of material from which they were formed.

Some day you may pick up a stone which reminds you of a cake stuffed full of raisins and nuts. Pebbles of all sizes will be stuck together by some sort of finer material. This is a water-born rock known as CONGLOMERATE, or Pudding Stone. We can imagine how it was formed, by the pebbles being carried by a swift stream, to be dropped to the bottom of a big lake. After thousands of years, the sand filtering down between the pebbles cemented everything together as a new kind of stone.

But most of the water-born rocks are made of finer bits of rock than pebbles. SANDSTONE is a rock made up of layers of small quartz grains cemented together by an iron compound. That is why so many of them are various shades of red and reddish-brown. The peaks and hill tops of the Appalachian Mountains furnish plenty of stones of this sort.

Sand is a coarser material than clay, as most of you know. The sand deposits become Sandstone, while the clay deposits form a soft rock known as SHALE. Shale is generally a grayish-blue rock, though red Shales are found in some places. If we pick up a fine-grained gray rock, and find we can easily split it up in layers (due to many small mica particles), we can be fairly sure we have a piece of Shale. Shale rocks, when they have been exposed to great pressure or heat, change into SLATE, which splits even more readily into paper-like layers.

There is another common water-born rock which was

formed in a far different fashion. LIMESTONE is usually a soft and whitish stone which is found here and there throughout New England and the Atlantic Coast states. Lime is an abundant mineral in salt water. From it many animals like the corals build up their skeletons; and when these animals gather in great numbers and die, their lime skeletons fall to the bottom of the water and pile up just as the sand and clay particles do. These lime deposits in time become limestone. If limestone becomes exposed by Nature to tremendous heat or pressure it becomes MARBLE; just as Shale becomes Slate. One can always be sure whether a stone is Limestone or Marble, because it is the only stone that bubbles and fizzes when any acid is dropped on it.

Next time you take a walk, pick up a few stones and see if you can pick out a fire-born or a water-born rock. If it has no layers in it and is composed of both quartz and mica, the chances are that it is a fire-born rock—perhaps granite. If there seem to be layers of cemented particles, then it is a water-born rock, either sandstone, shale or limestone. If you can picture then how they came into existence this part of the out-of-doors will take on a new meaning for you.

Recognizing rocks by name is quite a difficult task, but well worth the trouble. If we go about it scientifically (as we did in our collecting of flowers, leaves and shells) we will have much less trouble. Two things are necessary in rock identification: a small bottle of hydrochloric acid and a magnifying glass.

Suppose that we have taken a nature walk, and have returned with a pocket full of pieces of rocks. We first take each one and allow a drop or two of the acid (be careful and don't let the acid get on your hands or clothing) to fall on it. If the drop bubbles up and fizzes, we put the rock in one pile; if it does not we put it in another pile.

The first pile will contain two kinds of rocks which react in this way to acid—Limestone and Marble. The difference between them is that Marble is crystalline and has a glassy appearance, while Limestone is dull and rough. LIMESTONE may be white, gray, green and even black in color; it is a sedimentary rock formed from shells and corals. MARBLE may be white, gray, pink, black or a mixture of colors; and is the result of Limestone which has undergone great changes during the past millions of years.

The second pile, made up of rocks which do not bubble with hydrochloric acid, is such a big pile that we had better separate it into two smaller piles, which we can do by breathing on each piece of rock and smelling of it right away. If we smell an odor of clay, the rock is either Shale or Slate. In both cases the rock is very fine-grained, made up of particles of sand or mud less that 1/500 of an inch in diameter! SHALE is a sedimentary rock, usually gray or blue-black, which chips into flakes but does not split into thin sheets. SLATE is Shale which has been changed by some natural force into a more brittle rock, thus splitting into papery layers.

There is left in this second pile of rocks all those pieces which do not bubble with acid and do not smell like clay when breathed on. Let us try splitting or crumbling these rocks with our fingers, or perhaps another stone. We find that some sort of the rocks crumble easily while others do not. The ones that crumble and split thus readily are either GNEISS or SCHIST, two rocks formed by natural changes from either igneous or sedimentary rocks. GNEISS is a coarse rock, with the mineral particles visible without a magnifying glass; the coarse particles form straight or wavy bands through the rock. SCHIST is a leafy or scaly rock which splits into crumbling bits; a common Schist is Mica Schist, which contains a lot of mica crystals.

Those rocks which do not split or crumble are: BASALT (not glassy surface) and OBSIDIAN (with a glassy surface), both of which have the individual grains which make up the rock so small and so densely packed together that it gives the rock a smooth even texture. In contrast with these two rocks, we find others where the individual grains are quite large, giving the rock a coarse appearance. Such coarsely grained rocks are: CONGLOMERATE, where the individual particles making up the rock are pebbles the size of a pea or larger, smoothly rounded; BRECCIA, where the particles are the same size as in Conglomerate, but angular instead of rounded; GRANITE (the common igneous rock), a mixture of quartz, feldspar and mica in which some grains are large and some small, but none of them larger than a pea; and SANDSTONE (the common sedimentary rock), where the particles vary in size from 1/500 of an inch to the size of a pea, but are all a uniform size.

MINERALS

But what are rocks made of?

Both the fire-born and the water-born rocks are made of the same things—called minerals. Each kind of rock may have any amount of the mineral in it. For example, the useful mineral, iron, is found in great quantities in the rocks of certain states; and in the same rocks in another state there is no iron at all.

A mineral is a substance which always contains the same

WHAT THE EARTH IS MADE OF

things. The rarer a mineral is, in general, the more expensive and valuable it becomes. Gold and silver are not very common minerals, and for this reason have been used for thousands of years as material out of which to make money and precious ornaments. Some minerals like platinum and radium are much rarer than gold or silver.

But most rocks are not made up of gold, silver and platinum. Yet every rock is nothing but a mixture of minerals—so what can it be made of?

Two of the commonest minerals which make up the rocks are quartz and mica. Perhaps you already are familiar with both of these. Quartz is glassy and crystal-like, and may be white, gray or rose-colored. Mica is gray or black, and is found in thin sheets that split like layers of paper. Mica can be seen in granite, mixed with quartz.

Collecting minerals is not difficult, if you keep in mind all that you have learned about the different kinds of rocks, and if you realize that often one cannot find a mineral all by itself, but must be able to recognize it as part of a rock which also contains other minerals.

Let us try and arrange the common minerals in some sensible order, so that it will be easy for us to identify them. The materials necessary on a mineral hunt are: a good sturdy fingernail, a penny, an old knife and a piece of glass. To these may be added our little bottle of acid. In classifying minerals, we consider it very important to be able to tell the hardness of the mineral; that is why we take along the materials just mentioned, for with them we can tell just how hard or soft the mineral in question is.

Unfortunately minerals have no common names. Se we will have to use the scientific names; but if we separate them into syllables and pronounce them carefully we ought to have little trouble at least in reading them.

Here is a piece of rock, made up of several different minerals. The first thing we do is to see whether we can scratch that part of the rock we are interested in with our fingernail or not. If we can, the mineral must be either BIOTITE or GRAPHITE, if it is dark brown or black. For those are the only black minerals soft enough to be scratched with the fingernail. BIOTITE is Black Mica, commonly found in Granite. And of course GRAPHITE is the soft black mineral which marks on paper and is used in lead pencils.

Suppose that we were able to scratch the mineral with our fingernail, but that it was light in color instead of dark? Then the chances are that it is either Muscovite, Kaolin, Halite, Talc, or Gypsum. MUSCOVITE is White Mica, and differs from the other three in being able to split into thin sheets. KAOLIN is ordinary clay, soft and white or gray in color. HALITE is nothing but rock salt, sodium chloride; much harder than Kaolin and found in various colored crystalline masses. The salty taste is a means of identifying it. TALC and GYPSUM are also much harder than the Kaolin, but do not have the salty taste; Talc has a soapy greasy feeling when one rubs a finger on it, while Gypsum does not.

So that if we can scratch a mineral with our fingernail, it may be: Biotite, Graphite, Muscovite, Kaolin, Halite, Talc or Gypsum.

If we cannot make any impression on the mineral with our fingernail, we try our luck with the penny. If the penny can make a scratch on the rock, we drop a little acid on the mineral; if it bubbles it is CALCITE, the chief mineral in Limestone. This is the same mineral that makes up the shells of marine animals. If the mineral was scratched with the penny, but does not bubble with acid, it is either GALENA or COPPER. The former is silvery gray, while the latter is red.

If the penny was unable to make any impression on the mineral, we have to try next our old jackknife. The jackknife scratches the surface without any trouble, which tells us that the mineral is one of the following: Serpentine, Dolomite, Limonite, Chalco-pyrite and Hematite. The only one of these with a greasy feeling is SERPENTINE; in color it may be olive green or blackish green, or white. It separates into silky threads and fibers and is found only in igneous and metamorphic rocks. Its common name is Asbestos. HEMATITE and CHALCO-PYRITE are crystalline and glassy; the former is an iron rock, thus reddish-brown to black in color, while the latter is a copper rock, and is therefore more yellow in color, sometimes the shade of pure brass. LIMONITE and DOLOMITE are dull and non-crystalline; Limonite, which contains a lot of iron, is reddish-brown to black, while the Dolomite is light colored.

Supposing that the mineral was unable to be scratched with our fingernail, with a penny or with the jackknife? We have left the hardest minerals, some of which are semi-precious stones. We try the piece of glass on the mineral, and if it is able to make any impression, the mineral is either HORNBLENDE, or OPAL. Hornblende is black or green, while Opal is white or transparent. Then finally we have the minerals which cannot be scratched even with glass; such as Magnetite, Pyrite, Feldspar, Quartz, Amethyst, Agate, Jasper, Flint and Garnet. Two of these have a glassy luster, or shine, like a polished metal; these are MAGNETITE and PYRITE, the former being black and the latter golden yellow. Pyrite is often called Fool's Gold; it is really a mixture of iron and sulphur, instead of gold. The hard minerals without a metallic luster are all unable to split into flat flakes, except the Feldspar; which is white or gray in color and commonly found in granite and sandstone. QUARTZ may be colorless, rose or black. AMETHYST is usually purple. AGATE is marked with colored bands and rings. JASPER is dark red, streaked with purple. FLINT is dull, dark gray or black. GARNET is usually dark red or dark brown.

This makes quite an imposing array of minerals. But then, what can one expect when he is attempting to study the materials out of which the earth is made?

HOW TO RECOGNIZE THE ROCKS

I. If the rock bubbles with acid,
   1. And it is glassy, crystalline, it is . . . . . MARBLE
   2. And if it is dull, not crystalline, it is . LIMESTONE
II. If the rock does not bubble with acid,
   1. And if it smells like clay, it is . . . SHALE, SLATE
   2. And if it does not smell like clay
     A. But if it splits or crumbles, it is GNEISS, SCHIST
     B. But if it does not crumble,
        a. And if the individual grains of the
           rock are large, it is SANDSTONE, QUARTZITE, GRANITE, CONGLOMERATE, BRECCIA
        b. And if the individual grains are small,
           densely packed, it is . . OBSIDIAN, BASALT

WHAT THE EARTH IS MADE OF

HOW TO RECOGNIZE THE MINERALS

I. If the mineral can be scratched with the fingernail,
   1. And if it is dark-colored or black, it is
          BIOTITE, GRAPHITE
   2. And if it is light-colored or white, it is
          MUSCOVITE, KAOLIN, HALITE, TALC, GYPSUM

II. And if the mineral cannot be scratched with the fingernail,
   1. And it can be scratched with a penny, it is
          CALCITE, GALENA, COPPER
   2. And if it cannot be scratched with a penny,
      A. But can be scratched with a knife, it is
          SERPENTINE, DOLOMITE, LIMONITE, CHALCO-PYRITE, HEMATITE
      B. But cannot be scratched with a knife,
        a. Yet can be scratched with glass, it is
          HORNBLENDE, OPAL
        b. And cannot be scratched with glass, it is
          MAGNETITE, PYRITE, FELDSPAR, QUARTZ, AMETHYST, AGATE, JASPER, FLINT, GARNET

CHAPTER 17

CHRISTMAS TREES

THERE are two kinds of trees.

One kind has fitted itself for living through a cold and snowy season without losing its leaves. The leaves of this kind of tree are very small and covered with an armor of shiny green. If these leaves are long and narrow they are called needles; if they are flat and closely pressed together they are called scales.

Such trees as these are known to most people merely as "Christmas trees"; older persons may call them Evergreen trees, but their real name is Cone-bearing Trees because their fruits are in the form of brown cones.

It is easy to recognize these trees in winter, because they have their green leaves covering the branches while the other kind of tree is leafless. In summer, the Evergreen trees can be recognized by the small needle-like or scale-like leaves.

The other kind of tree, about which we will talk in the following chapter, has broad thin leaves which drop off the twigs as soon as autumn appears. The leafless branches and bare trunks make us think that the trees are dead. But of course they are not; they are only sleeping. All those tiny buds along the twig will burst into life as soon as the warm days of spring arrive. These trees which lose all their leaves in winter are called Deciduous Trees.

So the first thing for one to do if he wishes to find out what

CHRISTMAS TREES

kind of a tree he is looking at is to decide whether it is an Evergreen or a Deciduous Tree. In winter this is particularly easy as we have now found out.

If we are walking in the woods of southern New England and New York, and in the Atlantic coast states more to the south, we find ourselves in woods made up mostly of Deciduous trees. As we go northward the Evergreens increase in numbers until we reach the summits of the mountains in northern Maine and Canada. Here there is almost nothing but Evergreen trees. Pines and Hemlocks, with a few Cedars, grow more to the south of New York than the other Evergreens. Northward we find Spruces and Fir Balsams in dense forests. The biggest and oldest trees in the world are Evergreens—the Redwoods of the California mountains.

Even though there are not many Evergreen trees in the woods where most of us live, still there are some. And so many of them are "imported" to be planted as ornamental trees about our homes and in our parks, that we ought to have a speaking acquaintance with some of the more common varieties.

Looking closely at the twigs of the Evergreens, we notice that some of the tiny leaves are long and sharp, like needles, as we have already mentioned; while others have very small scale-like leaves which overlap each other like shingles on a roof. First let us become familiar with a few of the former.

EVERGREENS WITH NEEDLE-LIKE LEAVES

We will imagine that we have been out walking in the woods in northern Maine, Massachusetts, New York and Pennsylvania—all at once. We have brought back with us a collection of twigs, taken from all kinds of Evergreen trees.

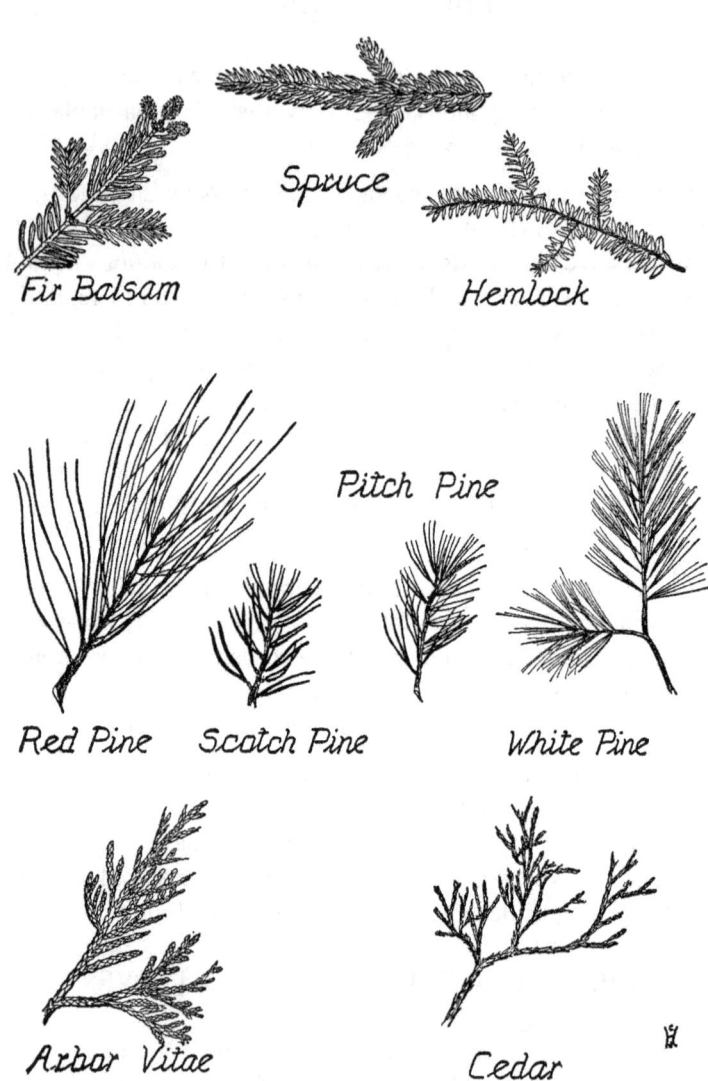

SOME COMMON EVERGREEN TREES

CHRISTMAS TREES

If we can tell these apart, it will be easy next time we see an Evergreen to take a look at the needles or scales and tell at once the name of the tree.

Let's see what we can do with our collection.

We make two piles of our twigs, putting in one pile all those with needle-like leaves—this becomes a big pile—and into another, smaller pile, those with scale-like leaves. We set aside the scale-leaved pile for a while.

In the pile of needle-leaved Evergreens before us is a bewildering mixture of Pines, Spruces, Firs and Hemlocks.

The PINES.

These are the twigs which have the needles much longer than any of the others, and the needles are grouped in clusters along the stem. Sometimes there are two needles in a cluster; in another twig there may be three to a cluster; and here are several twigs with five needles in each bunch.

The WHITE PINE has five needles in a cluster. These needles are soft, bending easily; and their bluish-green color gives the whole twig a rich dark color. Each needle is three to five inches long. We remember that we picked this twig from a high tree—it must have been over eighty feet tall—with a clean-cut and regularly branched trunk. The foliage on the branches, which came out at right angles from the main trunk, formed parallel layers of dark blue-green.

The PITCH PINE has three needles in each cluster. Each needle is about three inches long, perhaps a little shorter, and unusually stiff. The needles are a yellowish-green color. This came from a grove of trees on a sandy dry plain; and we saw the same trees on some rocky ledges in Maine. It was a stumpy little tree of a ragged and unkempt appearance; no where near as attractive as the White Pine, which grows in the richer soil of more favored locations.

But here are several different-looking twigs, and yet all with two needles in a cluster. As a matter of fact, we find that there are three kinds, all with the same number of needles in a group.

The RED PINE has two needles in a cluster, with each needle being very long (three to six inches) and bending easily. In color they are a brownish green. This tree we found in the more northern forests; around southern New York it is located only in parks and around homes.

The AUSTRIAN PINE has two needles in a cluster, but the needles (even though as long as those of the Red Pine) are stiffer and more yellow in color. This tree is a stranger to our country; it was brought over from Europe, and we find it growing along the edges of large estates and private homes.

The SCOTCH PINE, also with two needles in a cluster, is all that is left of our Pine group. These needles are blue-green, like those of the White Pine, and are very short; their average length seems to be a little less than three inches. This is another immigrant from Europe, and was found also only in cultivated places.

The SPRUCES.

From our pile of Evergreen twigs with needle-like leaves we now separate all those with needles not in clusters, but scattered all around the stem. The arrangement of the stiff, square needles in this fashion gives the twig a bottle-brush appearance and feeling.

We remember picking these twigs from trees which tapered gracefully upwards into a cone-shaped mass of dense foliage.

CHRISTMAS TREES

These trees were not common in the woods south of New York and Massachusetts; northward into Maine and the mountains of New Hampshire and New York they formed most of the forests.

Here are some Spruce twigs with bluish-gray needles.

One is the WHITE SPRUCE with needles shading into a blue-white sort of green. The thick and bushy twigs came from a swamp and pond-margin tree.

The other is the COLORADO BLUE SPRUCE, which has needles much grayer and bluer. This tree is a cultivated one, having been brought east for decorative purposes.

The other Spruces have yellowish-green needles.

It is hard to tell these apart. One, the RED SPRUCE, has slightly shorter needles. This twig came from a tree which was one of an endless forest in the northern Evergreen areas of New England and New York.

The other is the NORWAY SPRUCE, a tree brought over from Europe and found only under cultivation. It can be more easily recognized by the habit of the tree; the ends of all the branches droop earthwards as though too weary to hold themselves upright.

But what about these twigs with needle-like leaves arranged more or less along two sides of the stem, so that the whole twig has a flattened appearance? We see that the needles themselves are flattened, too, instead of being square like those of the Spruces.

These belong either to the Fir Balsam or the Hemlock.

The FIR BALSAM has fragrant twigs which make the balsam pillows so familiar to anyone who has toured through the Adirondacks or the White Mountains. The flattened needles are a lighter green on their undersides; each needle is half an inch or more in length. It is the Fir Balsam, as well as the Spruce, which is most likely to be your Christmas tree. Rarely is it found in the woods south of the Adirondacks and the White Mountains.

The other twig with flattened needles is a HEMLOCK. The needles are a lighter blue-green on their underside than was the case with the Fir Balsam. And each needle is very much smaller and more delicate looking, usually being less than half an inch in length. These tiny needles give to the whole tree a delicate and fern-like appearance. It is the one Evergreen that we find in great numbers in New York and southwards. It seems to prefer growing in shaded ravines and moist valley slopes.

Even though it is not a true Evergreen, the TAMARACK, or LARCH, should be mentioned. It has long needles arranged in star-shaped clusters, and thus seems as though it could be confused with the Pines. But the needles are shorter, and occur at least six or ten in a cluster. And strangely enough these needles are shed every autumn, like all the Deciduous trees. Thus we find a cone-bearing tree leafless and bare during the winter months.

EVERGREEN TREES WITH SCALE-LIKE LEAVES

Now for our other little pile of Evergreen twigs. We are relieved to find that there are only two kinds of these scale-leaved twigs!

One, the CEDAR, has an irregular and ragged sort of twig. It came from a small pillar-like tree of an open field. Like its relative, the Juniper, its fruit is a blue berry instead of a cone. The Juniper is a prickly Evergreen shrub which some of you may unpleasantly remember—if you have ever attempted to push your way through a dense tangle of Juniper bushes in getting from one huckleberry patch to another.

The other scale-leaved twigs form regular fan-shaped "sprays" which look as though they have been pressed flat. These fan-shaped twigs make the ARBOR VITAE an easy tree to remember. It is a common Evergreen about homes; to the north it becomes more common. In parts of Maine it forms solid woods along both sides of the highways.

The shrubby evergreens, even though they are not trees, might well be mentioned here. The common variety is the JUNIPER, an evergreen forming dense low thickets in old pastures and the edges of woods. The small pointed needles, light blue-green on their undersides, are very sharp. Pushing one's way through a Juniper bush is about as pleasant as attempting to travel through cactus undergrowth.

In the northern woods another shrubby evergreen is sometimes met with. The YEW is a low, spreading evergreen with flattened leaves like a Fir Balsam. But the leaves are broader and longer, generally of a yellow-green color. The fruit, instead of the cone usually thought of in connection with an evergreen, is a bright red berry.

HOW TO RECOGNIZE THE EVERGREEN TREES

I. If the leaves are small scales, overlapping,
   1. Forming fan-shaped flattened sprays, it is
                                    ARBOR VITAE
   2. Forming irregular sprays, it is . . . . . CEDAR
II. If the leaves are needle-like, long and pointed,
   1. In clusters,
      A. Of two needles in a group, it is
                           SCOTCH PINE, AUSTRIAN PINE, RED PINE
      B. Of three needles in a group, it is . PITCH PINE
      C. Of five needles in a group, it is . .WHITE PINE
   2. But not in clusters, with
      A. Needles flattened, it is HEMLOCK, FIR BALSAM
      B. Needles square, it is . . . . . .BLUE SPRUCE, NORWAY SPRUCE, WHITE SPRUCE, BLACK SPRUCE, RED SPRUCE

CHAPTER 18

THE LEAFLESS TREES

BUT why are not all the trees Evergreen?

This is not an easy question to answer so that you can readily understand it. The leaves of trees are the work-rooms where the food for the tree is manufactured. In order to make as much food as possible, the leaf has to spread out as broad a layer of green substance as it can, to absorb as much sunlight as possible. The broader and thinner the leaf is, the more food can therefore be produced.

The disadvantage of the broad thin leaf is found in winter. For it cannot stand the wintry storms and snows. The only way is for the tree to drop all the leaves, and make a new set every spring. It goes to all this trouble, just to have efficient food-making leaves every growing season.

In the Evergreens, the smaller leaf cannot make as much food as the Deciduous ones in summer; but such leaves are able to keep on making the year 'round. So you see that there are advantages to both.

There are many more Deciduous trees than Evergreen trees. So at first sight, it seems perhaps that it will be more difficult to learn to know them. But even if it is—just a little—I think you will find the Deciduous trees more interesting because one has to be a more clever detective to tell them apart.

Being leafless at this time of the year, the Deciduous trees must be studied in a different way from the Evergreens. We must look at the twigs carefully and see what there is that can help us on them. We notice the buds, of course; and under each bud we see a peculiar mark left where the stem of last summer's leaf was attached. This little mark is called a leaf-scar. And it is just as different for every kind of tree as a finger print is for each boy and girl.

It will be easy to notice differences in the twigs if we look for the buds and leaf-scars. No two buds have the same shape, size, color, or amount of hairy covering. And the leaf-scars of no two trees have the same curve, length, width and number of dots in them.

Other things will help us in identifying Deciduous trees in winter; for example, whether there are thorns on the twigs or not; the color of the bark on the trunk; the kind of fruit; and sometimes even just the kind of place where the tree grows.

Here are several twigs we have collected. The first thing we notice about them is that some of them have two buds (and therefore two leaf-scars) at the same level on the twig, on opposite sides. Other twigs have only one bud at one place on the twig, with another bud farther up along the twig or below it. We can separate all our twigs into two piles, putting in one pile all those with "opposite" buds and into another pile all those with "alternate" buds.

So the first thing to notice about a Deciduous tree, if we can get a twig from it, is whether the buds are arranged singly and alternately along the stem, or in pairs and opposite each other.

The Deciduous trees with opposite buds and leaf-scars are the Horse Chestnut, the Dogwood, the Catalpa, the Ashes and the Maples.

The Deciduous trees with the alternate buds and leaf-scars

are the Locust, the Hawthorn, the Oaks, the Birches, the Nut trees, the Beech, the Elm, the Sycamore, the Ironwood, the Ailanthus, the Tulip, the Sassafras, the Cherries and the Poplars.

But don't get discouraged. Each of these is as different from each other as a spruce is different from a pine.

First let us take a look at some opposite-budded Deciduous trees.

DECIDUOUS TREES WITH OPPOSITE BUDS AND LEAF-SCARS

Look at the bud at the very top of the twig. Is it big and fat—many times larger than the little buds along the sides of the twig? And is it perhaps covered with a sticky gummy coating? If so, then the twig belongs to the—

HORSE CHESTNUT. Beneath each of the buds is a large leaf-scar shaped like a triangle upside down. The tree itself is a sturdy thirty-to forty-foot mass of coarse and stout branches. All the lower branches tend to curve upwards like the antlers of deer. The bark is grayish-black, broken up into many plate-like scales. Perhaps you have seen Horse Chestnut trees in blossom in spring, truly a very unusual sight, with the big clusters of erect pinkish-white blossoms. This tree is found around cities only and never wild in the woods; it was brought to this country from its home in Asia.

But suppose the twig we are looking at has no bud at the end of the twig at all; and the remaining buds are in threes instead of twos opposite each other on the stem. In this case the twig has come off a—

CATALPA. Like the Horse Chestnut, the leaf-scar is very large, but round instead of triangle-shaped. Above each leaf-

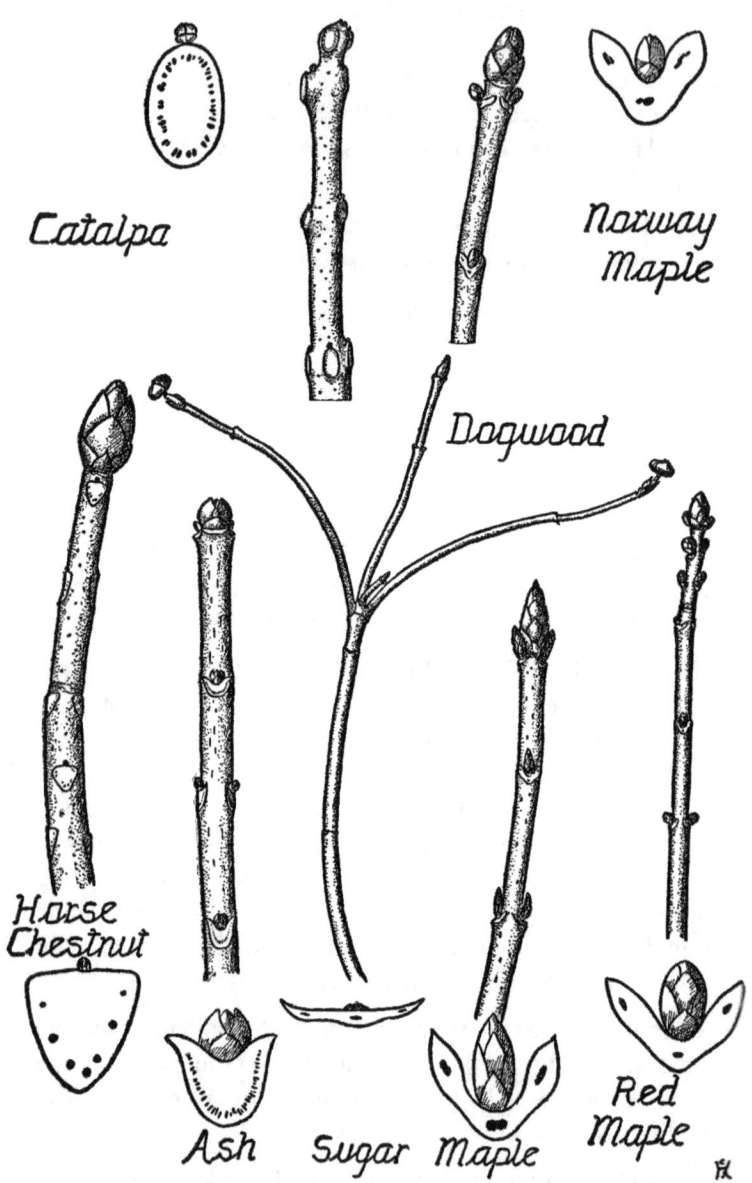

DECIDUOUS TREES WITH OPPOSITE LEAF-SCARS

236

scar is perched a very small bud. Also like the Horse Chestnut, the Catalpa is not a native tree of this region. Its home is in southern United States; from there it has been introduced to more northern homes as an ornamental tree. So we can't expect to find the Catalpa out in the woods. In autumn and early winter this small tree can be recognized by the long bean-like pods that hang gracefully from all the branches.

Here, however, we have some twigs in which the end buds are neither unusually large and sticky, nor absent. Now we have to look closely at the leaf-scars. Are they very, very small? So small that they look like crescent-shaped streaks beneath the opposite buds? And are the buds small and pointed, of a purplish-brown color and raised on a sort of shelf? If so, the tree is a—

DOGWOOD. No other tree is so beautiful at all seasons of the year as this small tree so common in our woods. The white blossoms in spring, the clusters of red berries in autumn; the dense mass of foliage about the twisted limbs in summer; and the slender graceful branches which curve upwards at the tips like the horns of so many deer—evident in winter. The bark is easily recognized, being a regularly-cracked design reminding us of the skin of an alligator.

We feel quite sure that we can recognize the Horse Chestnut, the Catalpa the Dogwood now. So we sort out all the twigs in our pile which belong to these trees. We find we have still several left—which must be Maple and Ash twigs.

As we look carefully at them, we discover that some of the buds are rough and covered with a coating of down hairs, while others are smooth and even shiny. The smooth and shiny buds belong to the Maples; and the rough hairy ones to the Ash.

The ASH trees, besides having rough and downy buds, have U-shaped leaf-scars with a row of dots in each one. The Ash trees are usually tall straight trees, with grayish bark. This bark usually has firm and regular flat-topped ridges.

There are several different kinds of Ashes found in our woods. The WHITE ASH likes to grow near swamps and streams; its leaf-scar is like a shield with a little nick in its upper margin. The RED ASH has a leaf-scar that is more nearly semi-circular, while the BLACK ASH has an almost circular scar. Both of these Ash trees like to grow in ordinary woods. Many Ash trees reach a height of 75 and 100 feet.

The MAPLES are perhaps our best known Deciduous trees with opposite buds. The leaf-scars are usually V-shaped; but whatever the shape there are always just three groups of little dots in each leaf-scar. Besides being very common in the woods, the Maples grow in great numbers along our streets, in our parks and around our homes.

The NORWAY MAPLE has reddish-green or yellowish-green buds. It is the only Maple in which the edges of two opposite leaf-scars meet in the sides of the twig to form an upward-projecting tooth between the two buds. It is not a native American tree, and hence is found only under cultivation. Like the other Maples, the fruit is the winged structure we have already discovered in our first chapter.

The SUGAR MAPLE has small, sharply-pointed brown buds. The leaf-scar is in the form of a very narrow V. This large tree (75 to 100 feet high) is common in rich woods everywhere. Unlike the smooth black bark of the Norway Maple, the bark of full-grown Sugar Maples is grayish and furrowed into loose chunks as if a plow had gone up and down the trunk of the tree. The sap of this tree gives us a delicious sugar known as Maple Sugar.

The other very common Maple is the RED MAPLE. This tree likes to grow in swamps and along pond margins. The bright red buds, together with the reddish parts of the young twigs, readily identify it. The leaf-scars are broad and U-shaped. Young Red Maples have a smooth gray bark like that of Beech trees. But when full-grown (its height is usually about 50 feet) the older portions of the trunk are dark grayish-black and furrowed.

The SILVER MAPLE has bud and leaf-scars like the Red Maple. If one has only the twigs of the two, they are hard to tell apart. But the trees themselves are very different. The bark of the Silver Maple is shredded so that long stringy pieces hang down from the trunk. All the branches droop downwards, with upcurved tips.

DECIDUOUS TREES WITH ALTERNATE BUDS AND LEAF-SCARS

The first thing we notice about these trees is that some of them have twigs with sharp thorns. There are three such trees with alternate buds and thorns: the Black Locust, the Honey Locust and the Hawthorn.

The BLACK LOCUST is a very common tree in this part of the United States. It can be recognized by the stout and scraggly branches which give the whole tree a rough and coarse appearance. The bark is very rough, having deep furrows running lengthwise of the trunk. The twigs have small thorns *in pairs* on either side of each leaf-scar.

The HONEY LOCUST is not as common as the Black Locust. The thorns of this tree look like spines; they are so long, and grow singly above each leaf-scar. These spines are usually branched. Both of the Locust trees have bean-like pods for fruit.

The HAWTHORN is a small and spreading tree with long sharp thorns which also occur singly above each leaf-scar. Unlike the Honey Locust, these thorns are found branched only infrequently.

Now for the trees with alternate leaf-scars and no thorns. We find a great variety of twigs before us—with all shapes and sizes of buds and leaf-scars. Perhaps the best way of starting out is to separate into one pile all the twigs which have clusters of buds at the tip of the twig. If there are three, four or even more buds grouped together at the end of the twig, we can be fairly sure that the twig came from an OAK tree.

But this is only a beginning. For there are dozens of kinds of Oak trees. Of course we all know that Oaks are the trees which bear acorns. And if we are interested in collecting acorns, we soon see that every Oak tree has a very different kind of acorn. These acorns are more easily described in pictures than in words, so I will let the illustrations speak for themselves.

Looking at the buds very carefully we see that some of the Oak twigs have long and sharply-pointed buds, while others have short, blunt ones. The long pointed buds tell us that the tree is either a PIN OAK, a RED OAK or a CHESTNUT OAK. The short plump buds tell us the tree is either a WHITE OAK, a SCARLET OAK, or a BLACK OAK.

The PIN OAK is a medium sized tree with a straight main trunk from which grow many side branches covered with short stubby twigs. The bark is quite smooth and dark brownish-black. The Pin Oak has the smallest buds of any of the Oaks.

 Red Oak
 Bur Oak
 Black Oak

 Pin Oak
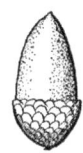 White Oak
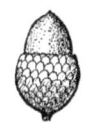 Scarlet Oak

 Chestnut O.
 Swamp White O.
 Scrub O.

 Bear Oak
 Post Oak

HOW TO RECOGNIZE THE OAKS BY THEIR ACORNS

The RED OAK is our tallest Oak, sometimes growing 100 feet high. The trunk has a grayish-brown bark that splits into flat topped ridges. The buds are at least twice as big as those of the Pin Oak; they are quite fat, each but being a trifle swollen at the bottom.

The CHESTNUT OAK looks a lot like the Red Oak, as far as the twigs are concerned. The buds are perhaps a little more sharp and cone-shaped. The full grown trees can be told apart by their bark. That of the Chestnut Oak is black with deep broad lengthwise furrows which are lighter colored. Both the Chestnut Oak and the Red Oak grow in drier and more wooded locations than the Pin Oak, which prefers low swampy lands.

The WHITE OAK is a very common tree. The old trees can be recognized by their light gray, flaky bark. The tree sometimes grows to be 50 and 75 feet high; but it does not look so tall because the main trunk soon branches out and some of the limbs grow even downwards. This gives the tree a gnarled and twisted appearance. The buds are broad and blunt, and very small when compared with all the other Oaks except the Pin Oak.

The SCARLET OAK is another medium sized tree, about 30 to 50 feet high. The bark is dark brown and covered with ridges. The easiest way to recognize the twigs is by the big broad buds covered with woolly hairs near the tip.

Then there is the BLACK OAK with very large buds, all covered with woolly hairs. It grows to be a very large tree.

All the twigs with alternate buds which we have talked about so far either had thorns or had clusters of buds at the tips of the twigs. But here are some twigs with alternate buds that have neither thorns nor clustered buds. And there are so many of them!

Let us separate all these twigs into two piles after we have

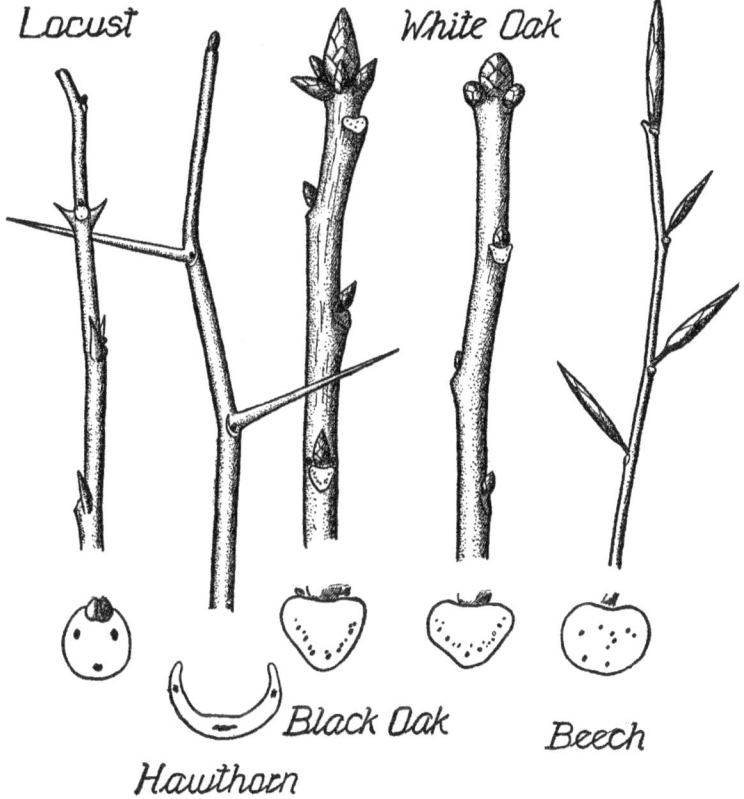

DECIDUOUS TREES WITH ALTERNATE LEAF-SCARS

looked at the leaf-scars to see whether they are larger or smaller than the buds above them. If the leaf-scars are smaller than the buds, the tree is either an ELM, BEECH, IRONWOOD, SYCAMORE, CHERRY, BIRCH, or POPLAR. If the leaf-scar is as large as the bud or larger, the tree is either a SASSAFRAS, TULIP, AILANTHUS or NUT tree.

First let us get acquainted with those twigs on which the leaf-scars are smaller than the buds. And at once we see two that we know we will remember very easily. One of these has such long sharply-pointed buds that they look almost like thorns! This is the—

BEECH, a tree very conspicuous by its smooth gray bark. It is a very attractive tree, and tempts many people to cut their initials in the bark—which of course should never be done. Beech trees love to grow in moist shaded woods; often they inhabit the deep ravines and glades where Hemlocks are found. Below the long brown buds are small oval or semi-circular leaf-scars.

The SYCAMORE is the other tree with unusual twigs. The leaf-scars are thin and narrow, and grow almost entirely around the bud. The bud itself is different from anything we have so far seen, because it consists of a single bud-scale and is sharply cone-shaped. The full grown tree is also unusual in that the outer dark greenish-brown bark peels off in big pieces, exposing the yellowish-white under bark. On some branches the outer bark may have entirely fallen off, leaving the whitened limbs. The fruit is a hanging ball; some people call this tree therefore the Buttonball Tree. It likes to grow along streams and swampy places.

Then there are two trees in this group, with very small buds on the twigs. One of them is the—

IRONWOOD, which has small egg-shaped leaf-scars with little hairy buds above them. In spring the twigs have catkins on them, like the Birches. The Ironwood is a small tree with a

THE LEAFLESS TREES 245

trunk covered by smooth grayish-black bark. This bark is raised into lengthwise rounded swellings which look like the muscles in the human arm. This tree is commonly mixed with Dogwoods and Birches in the eastern woods.

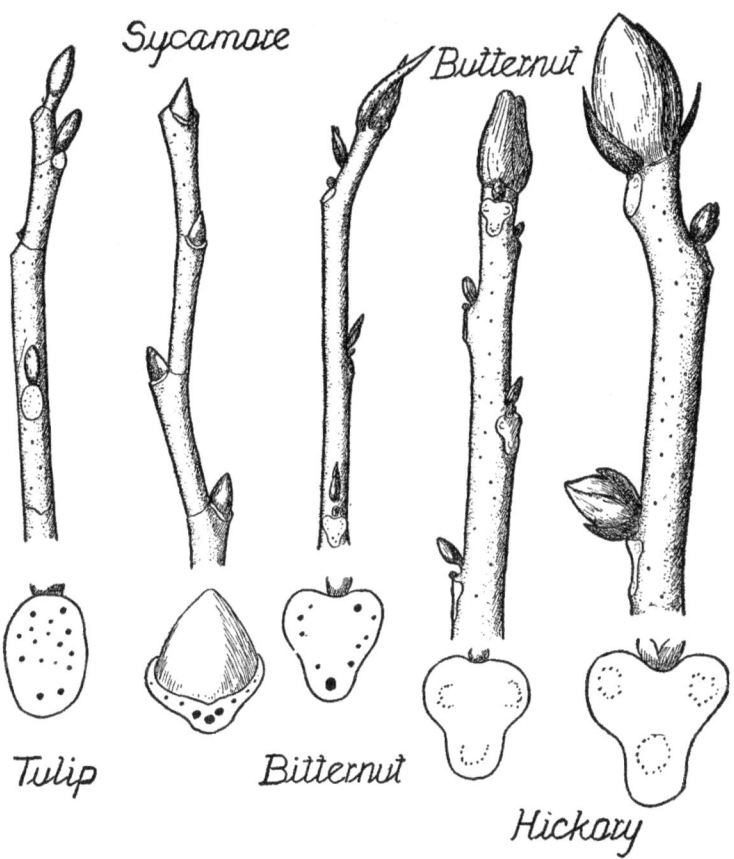

MORE DECIDUOUS TREES WITH ALTERNATE LEAF-SCARS

The very common ELM has small and pointed buds which lie close to the twig. The small leaf-scar is raised above the rest of the twig. The tree itself can always be recognized by the vase-shaped mass of limbs which branch gracefully outwards so high up from the ground.

The Cherry and Birch trees both have unusual marks circling the trunk crosswise which makes it easy to recognize them. These horizontal lines are coarse and few on the bark of a Cherry, and more delicate and numerous on the bark of a Birch.

The BLACK CHERRY is a coarse-looking tree with black bark that peels off in big patches. The buds are small and red. The CHOKECHERRY is nothing but an overgrown shrub; much smaller than the Black Cherry. Its buds are larger and brown.

The common Birches are the Gray Birch, Black Birch and Silver Birch. All of these have smooth bark except when very old; and in some cases this bark peels off in thin paper layers. The leaf-scars are small and either oval or semicircular. The seeds are formed in drooping catkins.

The GRAY BIRCH is wrongly called White Birch by many people. The real White Birch is a European tree, and its nearest relative in this country is the Paper Birch so common in the Evergreen forests of northern New York and New England. Our Gray Birch is a short-lived tree, not more than 20 or 30 feet high, always leaning over due to a weak root system. The bark is reddish-brown on young trees, and dirty white on full-grown ones. It prefers to grow in clearings in the woods, and in fields and pastures.

The BLACK BIRCH is also common in these woods. This grows to be 75 feet high. The buds are twice the size of those of the Gray Birch. Young trees look very much like Cherry trees; but if in doubt, taste the bark of the twigs and you will never forget the difference. Black Birch tastes like Wintergreen, and Cherry tastes sour and bitter.

The SILVER BIRCH likes to grow in wetter places than any of the other birches. It is further different by having the silvery yellow bark peel off in silky paper shreds. The buds are much like those of the Black Birch.

The only trees now left in this group with alternate buds and leaf-scars smaller than the buds are the Poplars. The young twigs are usually a yellowish-brown, with reddish buds or buds covered with dusty gray hairs.

The ASPEN POPLAR is a common small tree with greenish-gray smooth bark. The leaf-scars are like triangles upside down, while the buds are cone-shaped and pointed.

The COTTONWOOD tree is the largest Poplar. It has light yellow twigs, with long sharp buds which point outwards from the twig.

Now we have come to the last group of the Deciduous trees—those with alternate buds and leaf-scars whose buds are no larger than the leaf-scar and usually smaller than it.

The SASSAFRAS is different from the rest of these trees in the greenish-brown color of the twigs as well as their spicy taste and smell. Both buds and leaf-scars are small. The Sassafras is ordinarily a small tree, though south of New York it reaches heights of 50 and 60 feet. The bark of full-grown trees is deeply ridged and furrowed like that of the Locust.

The TULIP tree has unusual shaped buds; they are flattened and spoon-shaped, being made up of two bud-scales pressing against each other. The twigs are shiny yellowish-brown in color with large circular leaf-scars, reminding us of those on the Catalpa. The Tulip tree is a splendid straight, tall tree with gray bark regularly marked lengthwise by clear-cut ridges.

The AILANTHUS, unlike the other trees in this group, is a

stranger to this country. But it seems to have liked the change, for it has spread rapidly from the cities into the surrounding woods. It is a common tree of ash-heaps and waste places. The twigs are stout and yellowish-brown with huge heart-shaped leaf-scars.

And now for the Nut trees.

The SHAG-BARK HICKORY, as well as the other Nut trees, has twigs very readily recognized by the very large end buds. The leaf-scars under the side buds on the twigs are large and more or less heart-shaped. The outer dark scales of the big rounded end bud sometimes separate to show us the inner light-colored downy bud-scales. The tree lives up to its name. Its bark peels off in long ragged strips which hang to the trunk attached at one end or the middle. This gives the bark a shaggy appearance.

The PIGNUT is a smaller tree than the Shag-bark. Its bark is firm and gray with narrow flattened ridges. The leaf-scar is like that of the Shag-bark, but the buds are smaller and more yellowish-gray.

The BUTTERNUT has very distinctive bark when full-grown. The trunk has broad flat ridges that are light gray, while the hollows between the ridges are black. The buds on the sides of the twigs usually grow in pairs, one above the other. The leaf-scars are like those on the other Nut trees.

The BITTERNUT is the easiest to recognize, because the buds are yellow and hairy and dotted with bright yellow spots.

THE LEAFLESS TREES

HOW TO RECOGNIZE THE DECIDUOUS TREES IN WINTER

THAT HAVE BUDS AND LEAF-SCARS OPPOSITE EACH OTHER ON THE STEM

I. If there is no end bud, and the leaf-scar is round, it is . . . . CATALPA

II. If there is an end bud, and the leaf-scar is not round,

   1. If the end bud is large and sticky, and the leaf-scar triangular, it is . . . HORSE CHESTNUT

   2. If the end bud is not large and sticky, and the leaf-scars are V-shaped, crescent-shaped or shield-shaped,

      A. With a small crescent-shaped leaf-scar, it is . . . . DOGWOOD

      B. With a large V-shaped or triangular leaf-scar,

         1. With a row of dots in the leaf-scar; hairy buds; it is . . . . ASH

         2. With three groups of dots in the leaf-scar; smooth buds, it is

            a. With red buds, it is
               RED MAPLE, SILVER MAPLE

            b. With brown buds . . . . SUGAR MAPLE

            c. With greenish buds,   NORWAY MAPLE

HOW TO RECOGNIZE THE DECIDUOUS TREES IN WINTER

THAT HAVE BUDS AND LEAF SCARS ALTERNATE WITH EACH OTHER

I. If the twig bears thorns, it is. .LOCUST, HAWTHORN
II. If there are no thorns, but
   1. If the buds are clustered at the ends of the twigs, and if
      A. The buds are long and pointed, it is
         PIN OAK, RED OAK, CHESTNUT OAK
      B. The buds are short, plump, it is
         WHITE OAK, SCARLET OAK, BLACK OAK
   2. If the buds are not clustered at the ends of the twigs, and if
      A. Leaf-scar is larger than the bud above, it is
         SASSAFRAS, TULIP, AILANTHUS, HICKORY, BUTTERNUT
      B. Leaf-scar is smaller than the bud above it, it is   BEECH, SYCAMORE, CHERRY, BIRCH, IRONWOOD, ELM, POPLAR

CHAPTER 19

OUR WINTER BIRDS

BIRDS are the form of animal life which we are most likely to find in the woods and fields during the winter months. Naturally, there will be squirrels and chipmunks and an occasional larger mammal. But birds are far more frequently seen.

With their cheery notes and lively habits, it is pleasant to have them about us in the winter. They are well prepared by Nature to withstand the cold; but often their natural food supplies are buried under snow and ice, or by some chance destroyed. So if we want them to stay with us, it is wise to provide food for them.

In feeding, they may be considered to belong to two classes: the insect-eating birds and the seed-eating birds. For the former the best food is suet. It should be securely tied to limbs so that Crows and Jays may not carry it away whole. Then the Woodpeckers, Nuthatches, Chickadees, and other insect-eating birds will find it. Many a seed-eater, also, will be glad of it especially in winter when all food is scarce. But most birds even normally enjoy a varied diet. The Chickadees like raw pork rind fully as well as suet, and delight to peck at old beef bones. But Chickadees will also eat seeds, especially in winter, preferring those of the sunflower. Many wintering birds, such as Robins and Bluebirds as well as tree Sparrows and Juncos, eagerly eat scattered crumbs. To the seed-eaters almost all seeds are desirable. Chaff from the barn floor contains, besides the common grass seeds, those of various weeds, and is inexpensive and well liked. Seeds of sunflower, hemp, and Japanese millet are eagerly eaten by most winter birds.

A feeding shelf or bird shelter will soon make many feathered friends for you; and it is surprising how tame some of the winter birds become. The food of each of these birds is later noted in detail.

Some of the winter birds are with us the year 'round. They are summer birds who have accustomed themselves to staying here in the winter instead of migrating southward. These are called permanent residents, in contrast to the migrating birds from the north (Canada and Hudson Bay) who spend their winters in our comparatively warm regions.

First let us see who the permanent residents are.

PERMANENT RESIDENTS

All the larger birds come under this heading, such as the "game birds" and the "birds of prey." By "game birds" we mean the big ground-nesting birds, who fly poorly because of their weight, and who are prized by the hunter as food. These include the BOB WHITE, the RUFFED GROUSE and the PHEASANT. The BOB WHITE is a brown stout bird about 10 inches long, who likes to run about in the grass of meadows and fields. The RUFFED GROUSE, on the other hand, prefers to hide in the underbrush of the woods. When walking in the woods one is often quite startled by the sudden whirr of wings as this heavy bird rises from the ground. About 17 inches in length, brown and white in color, the RUFFED GROUSE is a splendid looking bird. The PHEASANT has come a long way from its native home—China. It has spread from civilization into the woods, and

BIRDS OF PREY

is often found near towns and homes. The male is golden brown with a long black tail, black head and white ring around his neck.

The "birds of prey" are those which catch and eat meat—preferably in the form of other birds and small mammals. To be able to do this well they have long sharp claws and hooked beaks. The EAGLE, the HAWKS and the OWLS belong to this group. Like the "game birds" they are with us at all times of the year.

The eastern BALD EAGLE is now becoming rare except in the mountainous regions of New York and northern New England. Civilization does not agree with it; with the coming of Man into any region, the EAGLE disappears. This powerful and majestic bird is, as you know, the emblem of our country. It is usually found near water, for fish is its favorite food. The bird is not really bald-headed, although the white feathers of the head in contrast to the black of the body make it appear so.

While the Eagle will reach a length of 30 inches, the HAWK is usually only 10 to 15; although occasionally one will be as long as 20 inches. The CHICKEN HAWK, or RED-TAILED HAWK, has a white breast edged with brown, and grayish-black wings and back. In spite of its name, it rarely eats chicken. Most of its food is mice, frogs, reptiles and insects. The brownish-red tail distinguishes it from its slightly smaller relative, the RED SHOULDERED HAWK. Both of these hawks live in woods near small ponds and streams. Another hawk of about the same size (15 inches) is COOPERS HAWK, which has a grayish-black back and wings and a brown and white barred breast. Unlike the other hawks, this one is really destructive and will raid a farm yard in search of food. The SPARROW HAWK (length 10 inches) is the smallest member of the family. It prefers the open spaces, often perching on fences and telegraph poles from which it sweeps down to capture mice or other small mammals and insects.

The OSPREY HAWK is more like an Eagle than a Hawk, both in habits and appearance. It is a large bird, with a length of two feet and a wing spread of four feet or more. Its dark brown and black wings and back, white head with a dark streak running back on each side past the eyes, powerful hooked beak are familiar to anyone who has explored the northern Atlantic coast. It lives on fish, and thus is found only near water. The nest is a huge ungainly affair of twigs and branches, perched on some rock or ledge; often these nests are large enough for a person to sit in comfortably.

The OWLS are peculiar birds in that their eyes face frontwards, instead of being on the sides of the head as is true of all other birds. This gives them an appearance of wisdom which is not carried into practice in their behavior. They are either entirely or partly night-hunting birds, and seldom fly about in the daytime. The SCREECH OWL is the most sociable member of the family, and often nests near human dwellings. It may be gray or reddish-brown, and is about 9 inches long. It lives on mice, insects, spiders, reptiles, fish and earthworms. The Screech Owl has shorter tufts of feathers (ears) than the LONG EARED OWL, whose size is much larger too (14 inches). This is the most beautiful owl, with is gray and white lengthwise striped plumage and browns discs around the eyes. The BARRED OWL (more commonly known as the Hoot Owl) has no ear-tufts; it is a big bird, sometimes reaching a length of 20 inches.

These large birds, which some of us may see in the winter, are not as common around cities and suburban homes as the smaller of our permanent residents. There are about fifteen of these with which we ought to be familiar. Taking New York City as the average, the following are the birds we might see any winter's day.

Those with red somewhere on their bodies are the Woodpeckers. The HAIRY WOODPECKER and the DOWNY WOODPECKER are small birds, 6 to 9 inches long, and very much alike. White breast, black and white wings and back, black and white head with a red patch near the top. They both eat insects and grubs, but only the DOWNY WOODPECKER becomes sociable enough to be a steady visitor at a feeding shelf. The FLICKER and the RED-HEADED WOODPECKER are 9 to 12 inches long. The Flicker is often found on the ground, chasing ants, his favorite food; while the Red-headed Woodpecker is on tree trunks catching flies on the wing or nibbling fruits and nuts. The FLICKER is golden-brown with a black "bib" under its throat, and a red patch on its head. The Red-headed Woodpecker is black and white with an entirely red head.

If the season is not too severe, the BLUE JAYS and BLUEBIRDS will decide to weather the cold winds and take a chance among the Juncos and Chickadees. It seems almost unnecessary to describe these two common birds. The reddish-brown breast of the otherwise all blue BLUEBIRD, and the beautiful crest of the blue and white BLUE JAY are familiar to every observing child. Though a thief and a murderer during the nesting season, the Blue Jay is a sprightly and handsome bird.

If the birds are not noticeably red or blue, they belong in that large group of birds of inconspicuous color which includes most of our winter birds. The purplish-black and brownish-black of the STARLING and the CROW set them apart

SOME WINTER BIRDS

and generally travels in noisy flocks of several hundred, even a thousand, birds. The CROW is undoubtedly the most clever of birds; he would have to be to keep in existence with so many farmers and fruit-growers on the war path to destroy him. As a matter of fact, the Crow does about as much good as harm; at certain seasons he eats bushels of harmful insects, such as grasshoppers and beetles. In the winter Crows gather in flocks in woods near lakes or rivers, where they may be seen roosting in the bare limbs of deciduous trees.

The brilliant yellow and black of the GOLDFINCH change in winter to a grayish-brown olive-tinted coat. He eats seeds of any kind. And wherever these seeds are above the snow drifts, Goldfinches will be found.

Industriously running up and down the tree trunks, and investigating every nook and cranny in the branches, the little NUTHATCH seems absolutely unafraid of man. With his black-capped white head, white breast and grayish-black back, this bird can be easily recognized as he restlessly explores the bark of trees for worms and grubs.

The CHICKADEE is the best known and loved of the winter birds. When Warblers and Swallows and Thrushes have left us, and frost and snow possess the land, the Chickadee comes into his own. His cheery notes ring out in the bleak winter woods. He comes about our homes performing his acrobatic feats in the trees of the lawn, and is among the first to find the feeding shelf. At such times his friendly social qualities are the delight of all. Always on the go, half the time head downwards, he clings to the tips of branches in search of insects and their eggs. This black-capped gray and white bird is very easily recognized.

A bird which is as quiet as the Chickadee is noisy is the

OUR WINTER BIRDS

little BROWN CREEPER. Like the Nuthatch, he spends his life climbing tree trunks and prying under the bark for bugs and worms. The brown back and white breast set him apart from the grayish-black Nuthatch of similar habits.

WINTER MIGRANTS FROM THE NORTH

In winter we find with us certain birds from the far North where there is absolutely no hope of food supply in the winter. These winter visitors appear in November and December and stay with us until March or April. The most common of these birds are the Junco, Snow Bunting, White-throated Sparrow, Shrike, and the Pine Grosbeak.

The JUNCO is a slaty-black bird about 6 inches in length, with a white breast. It comes in great flocks, often noisy but cheery, to one's feeding shelf. It prefers to feed in groups along fence-rows in weedy fields and along the borders of the woods. He is of great value to the farmer, for he eats any and all the weed seeds he can find.

The SNOW BUNTING is a member of the Sparrow family, but is unusual for its size of 7 inches as well as for its white breast and head, tinged with brown. It feeds entirely on seeds. Like the Junco, it travels in flocks which are readily noticed by their cheery and animated behavior. The Snow Bunting is very hardy and seems to be able to stand any sort of weather.

The WHITE-THROATED SPARROW is quite often a companion of the Juncos. Like them, he searches for weed seeds in the places bare of snow. Berries and small fruits will often attract him. This sparrow is a summer resident of Northern New York and New England, where his delightful call is often heard in the evening and early morning.

The PINE GROSBEAK is a very fearless bird which comes to

us from the evergreen forests of the north. He is a slaty-gray bird, marked with red or olive yellow. The large clumsy beak distinguishes him from other birds; with it he feeds on the berries of Mountain Ash, Sumac and Cedar.

There remains only the strange hawk-like bird of the north known as the SHRIKE. Due to its habit of catching mice and birds smaller than itself and spiking them on thorns to keep them for a future meal, this bird is often called the Butcher Bird. It is ten inches long, grayish white with black wings and black stripes across the eyes.

If you are not familiar with these winter birds now is the time to make friends with them. Now is your chance, putting out suet or seeds—well protected from raids by the greedy squirrels—and then watching for the birds to arrive. A great many of the smaller ones which we have just described will soon discover your hospitality; and you will be well repaid for your trouble by these interesting visitors.

APPENDIX

APPENDIX

THESE chapters have introduced you to the most common forms of mineral, plant and animal nature. That does not mean that the kinds of minerals, plants and animals described in this book will be the only forms you meet with on your nature ramblings; nor does it mean that you will be certain of finding all these. In case you are curious about something you have discovered, which is not described in this book, I hope you will not rest satisfied until you have found out what it is. To do so means reference to the special guides and field books which go much more into detail that was possible in such an elementary book as this. For the benefit of those who wish to go on further, the following list of reference books is suggested; they will help greatly in identifying strange new specimens.

MINERALS

A good introduction to the field of rocks and minerals is found in a publication of the New York State College of Agriculture at Cornell. It is called simply "Rocks and Minerals"; and is Vol. 21, No. 3, published in 1928. It is distributed free.

Then there is the excellent "Field Book of Rocks and Minerals," by Frederick B. Loomis, published in 1923 by Putnams. This is written for the old and experienced mineral-collector, and will answer all questions on the subject.

PLANT LIFE

It is hardly necessary to advise anyone about a good Flower Guide; there are dozens of books on the market, written both for children and adults. But the most beautiful color illustrations are found in the two volumes of "Wild Flowers of New York." published by the University of the State of New York as Memoir 15, in 1923. It is just as useful for a resident of New England or states south of New York as for an inhabitant of New York.

The "Field Book of American Wildflowers," by Ferdinand S. Mathews, published by Putnams in 1912; as well as his "Book of Wild Flowers for Young People," also published by Putnams, will be found very useful.

The study of trees in winter is completely and interestingly told by Blakeslee and Jarvis in their book "Trees in Winter," published by Macmillan in 1926.

For the study of trees in summer, the "Field Book of American Trees and Shrubs," by Ferdinand Mathews and published by Putnams in 1915, is very useful.

In addition, as in the case of the flowers, there are a great many Tree Books available, any one of which will undoubtedly be of some help in answering your questions.

There are three books on Ferns, any one of which will be found very helpful. The "Field Book of Common Ferns," by Herbert Durand and published by Putnams in 1928, is the most complete and accurate. It is perhaps not as interestingly filled with side comments and descriptions as the other two: "How to Know the Ferns," by Frances Parsons, published in 1920 by Scribners, and "Our Ferns in Their Haunts," by Willard N. Clute, published by Frederick A. Stokes in 1901.

APPENDIX

Mosses are adequately described in either of two books: "Mosses and Lichens," by Nina L. Marshall, published by Doubleday, Page in 1907. And "How to Know the Mosses," by Elizabeth M. Dunham, published by Houghton Mifflin in 1916.

Mushrooms are not only described but beautifully illustrated in "The Mushroom Book," by Nina L. Marshall, published by Doubleday, Page in 1902." A smaller but just as efficient book is "Mushrooms; a Handbook of Edible and Inedible Species," by W. B. McDougall, published by Houghton Mifflin in 1925.

There remains only the simplest green plants, known as the Algae. These are popularly described in the first part of Augusta F. Arnold's "The Sea Beach at Ebb Tide," published by Century in 1901. A more scientific treatment of the subject is found in "The Algae of Connecticut," by Clarence J. Hylander, published by the Connecticut Geological and Natural History Survey as Bulletin No. 42 (Hartford, 1928).

ANIMAL LIFE

When it comes to a consideration of reference books on animal life, we find such a bewildering number of bird books that we wonder whether after all there are any other animals! From this great number, we might choose, for purposes of answering questions on identification, the following: the two huge volumes on "Birds of New York," by E. H. Eaton, published by the University of the State of New York at Albany in 1910; "Field Book of Wild Birds and their Music," by Ferdinand S. Mathews, published by Putnams in 1921; "Book of Birds for Young People," by the same author and publisher. The "Bird Book," by Chester A. Reed, published by Doubleday,

Page in 1915, has excellent photographs of the eggs of various birds; and "The Book of Bird Life," by Prof. Arthur A. Allen, published by D. Van Nostrand in 1930, tells interestingly and accurately the life story of birds.

Mammals are well described in Volume IV of the Nature Lovers Library, published by the University Society in 1917 under the title "Mammals of North America," by H. E. Anthony. The "Field Book of North American Mammals," by the same author, published by Putnams, is an excellent handy guide to our furry friends.

The snakes and turtles, and any other reptiles one might find, are more than adequately described by Raymond L. Ditmars in his "Reptile Book," published by Doubleday Doran in 1930. Snakes alone are the subject of Ditmar's "Snakes of the World," published by Macmillan in 1931.

Frogs and toads and other amphibians are completely covered by "The Frog Book" of Mary C. Dickerson, published by Doubleday, Page in 1906.

Insects in general are treated in the "Field Book of Insects," by Frank E. Lutz, published by Putnams in 1921. In addition there is the "Insect Book," by Leland O. Howard, published by Doubleday, Page in 1902. Not to mention all the butterfly guides, we can assure you than any moth or butterfly you will find will most likely be illustrated in color in either of W. J. Holland's two beautiful books "The Moth Book" and "The Butterfly Book," the former published by Doubleday, Page in 1905 and the latter by Doubleday, McClure in 1898.

Marine life of the invertebrate orders in completely described in "The Sea Beach at Ebb Tide," by Augusta F. Arnold, published by Century in 1901.

INDEX

A

Agate, 222
Ailanthus, 188, 247
Alder, 139, 140
ALGAE, 147 to 153
Amethyst, 222
AMPHIBIANS, 3 to 16
   in winter, 208
Anemone, Rue, 59, 60
Anemone, Wood, 59, 60
ANIMALS, warm-blooded vs. cold-blooded, 205 to 209.
Apple, fruit, 192
Arbor Vitae, 226, 231
Ash, fruit, 188, 189
  leaves, 144, 145
  twigs, 236, 238
ASTERS, Calico, 174, 175
  Large Leaved, 175, 176
  Late Purple, 174, 175
  Mountain, 174, 175
  New England, 175, 176
  Purple-Stemmed, 175, 176
  Stiff, 174, 175
  Smooth, 174
  White-Topped, 175, 176

B

Baneberry, Red, 199
Baneberry, White, 199
Barnacles, 158, 158
Bat, 129
Beach Flea, 161, 163
Beech, coloration, 203
  leaves, 139
  twigs, buds, 243, 244

Beggar Ticks, 191, 192
Bellwort, 57, 63
BERRIES, 195 TO 199
Biotite, 220
Birch, flowers of, 25, 26
  twigs of, 246-247
  leaves of Black, Yellow, Paper, White, Gray Birch, 139, 140
BIRDS, of spring, 28 to 46
  of winter, 251 to 260
  in winter, 207
  keys to, 46 to 50
  Bitternut, 245, 248
  Bittersweet, berries, 197
  Blood Root, 59, 60
  Blue Jay, 256, 257
  Bluebird, 34, 35, 37, 256
  Blue-eyed Grass, 66, 67
  Blue Flag, 53, 55, 56
  Bluet, 66, 67
  Bobolink, 36, 37
  Bob White, 36, 252
  Bracket Fungi, 105
  Brittle Star, 154
  Brown Creeper, 257, 259
  Bunchberry, 57, 198, 198
  Burrs, 191, 192
  Butter and Eggs, 181
  Buttercup, 54, 55
BUTTERFLY, eggs, 71
  life history, 71 to 75
  adults, 75 to 79
  key to, 83
BUTTERFLIES, Angle Wing, 77, 78
  Banded Purple, 77, 78
  Fritillary, 77, 78 267

INDEX

Butterflies (Continued)
  Monarch, 76, 77
  Mourning Cloak, 77, 78
  Painted Lady, 77
  Red Admiral, 77, 79
  Silver Spot, 77, 78
  Sulphurs, 77, 78
  Swallowtails, 76, 77
  Vice-Roy, 76, 77
  Wood Nymph, 77, 78
Butterfly Weed, 180
Butternut, leaves, 141, 142
  twigs, 245, 248

C

Calcite, 220
Canada Mayflower, 57, 61, 199
Cardinal, 40
Catalpa, flower, 21
  leaves, 143, 144
  fruit, 189
  twigs, 235, 236
Catbird, 40, 41
Caterpillars, 71, 72
Cat-tail, 188, 189
Cedar, 226, 230
Cedar Waxwing, 41
Chalco-pyrite, 221
Cherry, flower, 22
  leaf, 139, 141
  fruit, 192
  twigs, 246
Chestnut, 139
Chickadee, 34, 257, 258
Chimney Swift, 32
Chipmunk, 132
Chrysalis, 72, 73, 73
CLAMS, Arctic, 168, 169
  Flat-shelled, 168, 169
  Giant, 168, 169
  Hard-shell, 168, 169
  Razor, 167, 168
  Soft-shell, 168, 169

Clematis, 189, 190
Club Moss, 99, 100
Cockle Shell, Common, 167, 168
  Dwarf, 167, 168
Coconut, 194
Cocoon, 73
Columbine, 59, 62
Comb Jellies, 155
Conglomerate, 215
Copper, 221
Cotton, 189, 190
Cottonwood, see POPLAR
Cowslip, 54, 55
CRABS, Blue, 161, 162
  Fiddler, 161, 162
  Green, 161, 162
  Hermit, 161, 162
  Jonah, 163
  Rock, 161, 162
  Sand, 161, 162
Crow, 256
CRUSTACEANS, 160 to 162

D

Daisy Fleabane, 66, 67
Dandelion, 188, 189
DECIDUOUS TREES, 233 to 250
Deer, 130
Diabase, 214
Dogberry, flower, 64
  berry, 196, 197
Dog-tooth Violet, 63, 64
Dogwood, flower, 20, 21
  coloration, 202
  leaves, 143, 144
  twig, 236, 237
Dolomite, 221
Dutchman's Breeches, 63, 65

E

Eagle, 253, 254
Earth Star, 103, 145

INDEX 269

Elder, 144, 145
Elm, flower, 23, 25
  leaf, 139, 140
  fruit, 188
  twigs, 245
EVERGREEN TREES, 224 to 233

F

FERNS, life history of, 92 to 94
  key to, 109
FERNS, Beech, 93, 98
  Brake, 97, 96
  Christmas, 93, 96
  Cinnamon, 95, 97
  Hay Scented, 95, 97
  Interrupted, 95, 97
  Lady, 94, 97
  Maidenhair, 98
  New York, 97
  Oak, 93, 98
  Polypody, 93, 96
  Royal, 93, 95
  Sensitive, 93, 94
  Wood, 96
Fir Balsam, 226, 229
Fireweed, 181
Fish, in winter, 207
Five Finger, 65, 67
Flicker, 30, 31, 256
Flint, 222
Flowers, of spring, 51 to 68
  of autumn, 173 to 182
  societies, 51 to 52
  of trees, 17 to 27
  parts of, 18 to 20
  keys to, 68, 69, 183 to 185
Forget-me-not, 54, 55
Foxes, 131
FROG, eggs, of, 4 to 6
  tadpoles, 6 to 9
  adults, 12, 13
FROGS, Bullfrog, 13, 15
  Green, 13, 15
  Leopard, 13, 14

Pickerel, 13, 15
Spring Peeper, 13, 14
Tree, 13, 12
Wood, 13, 12
Fruits, wind carried, 187 to 190
  animal carried, 190 to 193

G

Galena, 221
Garnet, 222
Geranium, Wild, 63, 192, 194
GOLDENRODS, Broad Leaved, 178, 179
  Bushy Flat Topped, 177, 178
  Canada, 178, 179
  Downy, 178, 179
  Slender Flat Topped, 177
  Wreath, 178, 179
Goldfinch, 35, 37, 258
Granite, 214
Graphite, 220
Ground Cedar, 100, 101
Ground Pine, 99, 100
Grouse, Ruffed, 252
Gypsum, 220

H

Halite, 220
HAWKS, Cooper's, 254
  Red Shouldered, 253, 254
  Red Tailed, 253, 254
  Sparrow, 253, 254
Hawkweed, Orange, 180, 181
Hawkweed, Rough, 180
Hawthorn, 240, 243
Hazel Nut, 138
Heal All, 67, 68
Hematite, 221
Hemlock, 226, 230
Hepatica, 59, 61
Hickory, flower of, 26
  leaf of, 142, 143
  twigs of, 245, 248

Hornblende, 221
Horse Chestnut, flower of, 22
  leaves of, 142, 143
  twigs of, 235, 236
Horseshoe Crab, 160, 161
Horse-tail, 99, 100
Hummingbird, 30

I

Indian Cucumber Root, 196, 197
Indigo Bunting, 35, 37
Insects in winter, 208, 209
Ironwood, 244

J

Jack in the Pulpit, flower, 54, 55
  fruit, 198, 199
Jasper, 222
Jellyfish, 154

Junco, 257, 259
Juniper, 231

K

Kaolin, 220
Kelp; see SEAWEEDS
Kingbird, 36
King Devil, 180, 181
Kingfisher, 37, 39

L

Leaves, of trees, 134 to 146
LICHENS, Cup, 108, 108
  Lungwort, 106
  Old Man's Beard, 107, 107
  Parmelia, 106
  Reindeer, 107, 108
  Rock Tripe, 106
  Scarlet-Fruited, 108, 108
Limestone, 216
Limonite, 221
Limpet, 157, 164
Linden, 188, 189

Locust, leaves, 141, 142
  twigs, 239, 243
Lupine, 57, 62

M

Magnetite, 221
MAMMALS, in winter, 206
  in general, 128 to 133
Maple, flowers, 24, 25, 25
  coloration, 202
  fruits, 187, 189
MAPLES, Mountain, 143, 144
  Norway, 144, 145, 203, 236, 238
  Red, 144, 145, 236, 239
  Silver, 144, 145, 239
  Striped, 143, 144
  Sugar, 144, 145, 203, 236, 238
Marble, 216
MARINE INVERTEBRATES,
  153 to 170
Maryland Yellowthroat, 40, 41
Meadowlark, 36, 37
Meadow Rue, 58, 59
Meadowsweet, 181, 182
Milkweed, 180, 181, 188, 189
MINERALS, 218 to 223
MOLLUSKS, 156 to 158, 163 to
  169
Moss, life history of, 88, 89
MOSSES, Catharine, 91
  Cedar, 91
  Feather, 91
  Fork, 91
  Hairy Cap, 91, 92
  Mnium, 90
  Peat, 90
  Pincushion, 91
  Tree, 91
Moth, eggs of, 71
MOTHS, Cynthia, 80, 81
  Cecropia, 79, 81
  Hawk, 81, 82
  Io, 80, 81
  Leopard, 81
  Luna, 79, 81

INDEX

Moths, (Continued)
  Polyphemus, 79, 81
  Rosy Maple, 80, 81
  Sphinx, 80, 81
  Tiger, 80, 81
  Underwing, 80, 81
Mouse, 132
Mountain Ash, 21, 141, 142
Mullen, Velvet, 182
Muscovite, 220
Mushrooms, 101, 102
MUSHROOMS, Amanita (Fly) 103, 104
  Boletus, 102, 103
  Coral, 103, 105
  Club, 103
  Destroying Angel, 103, 104
  Field, 103, 104
  Galera, 103, 104
  Inky Cap, 103, 104
  Russula, 103
  Shaggy Mane, 103, 104
Mussel, Common, 167, 168
  Bearded, 167, 168
  Ribbed, 167, 168

N

Newt, 11
Nuthatches, 34, 257, 258

O

Oak, flowers of, 26, 26
  coloration, 203
  acorns of, 241
OAKS, Black, 136, 137, 243, 242
  Chestnut, 136, 137, 242
  Pin, 136, 137, 240
  Post, 136, 137
  Red, 136, 137, 242
  Scarlet, 136, 137, 242
  Swamp White, 136, 137
  White, 136, 137, 242, 243
Opal, 221
Oriole, Baltimore, 31, 34
  Orchard, 34

Osprey Hawk, 253, 255
Ovenbird, 43, 44
Owl, Screech, 255
  Long Eared, 255
  Barred, 255

P

Partridge Berry, 198, 198
Pewee, 43, 44
Pheasant, 252
Phoebe, 31, 33
Pignut, 248
Pine Grosbeak, 259
PINES, Austrian, 228
  Pitch, 226, 227
  Red, 226, 228
  Scotch, 226, 228
  White, 226, 227
Poplar, flowers of, 23
POPLARS, Aspen, 138, 139, 247
  Cottonwood, 139, 140, 247
  Large-toothed, 139, 140
  White, 139
Porcupine, 132, 133
Puffball, 103, 105
Purple Martin, 32
Pyrite, 221

Q

Quartz, 222
Queen Anne's Lace, 181, 182

R

Raccoon, 130
Redstart, 39, 41
Red-winged Blackbird, 37, 38
REPTILES, 110 to 127
Robin, 30, 31
ROCKS, 213 to 222
Running Pine, 99, 100

S

Salamander, 11
Sand Dollar, 160

Sandpiper, 39
Sand Shrimp, 163
Sandstone, 215
Sassafras, 137, 138, 203, 247
Saxifrage, 60, 63
Scallop, Common, 167, 168
  Giant, 167, 168
  Heart, 168
Scarlet Tanager, 43, 45
Scouring Rush, 99, 100
Sea Anemone, 154
Sea Cucumber, 156, 157
Seal, 129
Sea Shells, 156 to 170
Sea Urchin, 154, 155
SEAWEEDS, Bladderwrack, 150, 151
  Brown Silkweed, 150
  Delesseria, 152
  Devil's Shoe Lace, 151, 152
  Green Mermaids Tresses, 149, 149
  Green Silkweed, 149
  Henware Kelp, 150, 151
  Irish Moss, 152
  Common Kelp, 150, 151
  Nigger Hair, 152
  Red Thread Weed, 152
  Ribbon Weed, 149, 149
  Rockweed, 150, 151
  Sea Colander, 151, 152
  Sea Lettuce, 148, 149
Serpentine, 221
Shad Bush, 22
Shale, 215
Shrike, 257, 260
Silverrod, 177, 178
Skunk, 130
Skunk Cabbage, 53, 55
Slate, 216
SNAILS, MARINE, Boat, 164, 166
  Cup, 164, 166
  Moon, 163, 164
  Mud Flat, 164, 166
  Oyster Drill, 157, 164
  Periwinkle, 157, 164
  Purple, 158, 164
  Ribbed, 164, 166
  Sand Flat, 164, 166
  Trochid 164, 166
  Worm, 164
Snakes, 116 to 127
SNAKES, Black, 118, 119
  Copperhead, 119, 124
  Garter, 119, 121
  Grass, 120, 123
  Ground, 120, 123
  Hog-nosed, 124
  Milk, 119, 122
  Rattlesnake, 119, 124
  Red-bellied, 120, 123
  Ribbon, 121, 123
  Ring-necked, 120, 123
  Water, 121, 122
Snow Bunting, 259
Solomon's Seal, 58, 59, 196, 197
  False, 59, 61, 198, 199
SPARROWS, Chipping, 38
  Field, 37, 38
  Song, 37, 38
  White-throated, 257, 259
Spring Beauty, 58, 59
Spruces, 226, 229
Squirrels, 131 to 132
Starfish, 153
Starling, 256
Steeplebush, 181, 182
Strawberry, 65, 67
Sumac, 141, 142, 202
Swallow, Bank, 38
  Barn, 31, 32
  Tree, 41
Sycamore, leaves of, 139, 141
  fruit of, 189
  twigs of, 244, 245

T

Talc, 220
Tamarack, 230

Tansy, 66, 67
Thistle, 188
Thrasher, 40, 41
Thrush, Hermit, 42
  Veery, 42, 43
  Wood, 43, 44
Tick Trefoil, 191, 192
Toad, eggs, 4
  tadpoles, 10
  adult, 11, 13
Tomato, 192
Touch-me-not, 192, 193
Towhee, 43, 45
TREES, in winter, 200 to 204
  make food, 201, 202
Trillium, Red, 62, 63
Tulip Tree, flower of, 22
  leaves of, 137, 138
  coloration, 202
  twigs, 245, 247
Tupelo, 137, 138
Turtles, 111 to 116, 126
TURTLES, Box, 115, 116
  Mud, 113, 114
  Musk, 113, 114
  Painted, 113, 114
  Snapping, 112, 115
  Spotted, 113, 114
  Wood, 115, 116

V

Viburnum, 196
Violet, Blue 54, 55, 61
  Yellow, 63, 64
  White, 61, 63

Vireo, Red-eyed, 31, 33
  Warbling, 33

W

Walnut, 141, 142
Warbler, Black and White, 43, 45
  Chestnut-sided, 41
  Pine, 43
Weasel, 130
Whelk, Smooth, 164, 165
  Ten Ribbed, 164, 165
  Common, 164, 165
  Knobbed, 164, 165
  Channeled, 164, 165
Wild Cat, 131
Willows, 23, 138, 139
Wintergreen, 198, 199
Wood Betony, 63, 65
Woodbine, 197
WOODPECKERS, Downy, 30, 31, 256
  Hairy, 256
  Red-headed, 30, 31, 256
WORMS, MARINE, Bristle, 160
  Clam, 159, 160
  Paddle, 159
  Scale, 159
Wren, 31, 34

Y

Yarrow, 181, 182
Yellow Star Grass, 66, 67
Yew, 231